Education and Society in Germany

Education and Society in Germany

H.-J. Hahn

BERG

Oxford • New York

First published in 1998 by
Berg
Editorial offices:
150 Cowley Road, Oxford, OX4 1JJ, UK
70 Washington Square South, New York, NY 10012, USA

Berg is the imprint of Oxford International Publishers Ltd.

Library of Congress Cataloging-in-Publication Data

A catalogue record for this book is available from the Library of Congress

British Library Cataloguing-in-Publication Date

A catalogue record for this book is available from the British Library

ISBN 1 85973 912 1 (Cloth)
         1 85973 917 2 (Paper)

Typeset by JS Typesetting, Wellingborough, Northants.
Printed in the United Kingdom by Biddles Ltd, Guildford and King's Lynn.

Contents

List of Figures

Preface

A discussion of education in relation to social change may inevitably evoke reminiscences of the 1960s and the height of German modernism and give rise to accusations of anachronism and an outdated methodology of Education Studies. However, both pedagogics and modernism are deeply indebted to the Enlightenment, an age which discovered the childhood psyche, the process of growing up, of self-reflection and self-awareness.

The experience of the Enlightenment and the tradition of education in Germany are different from those of its Western neighbours: the German concept of *Bildung* concentrated on character perfection within an artistic and secularized Christian environment, but at the expense of social, economic and political considerations. The German *Bildungsroman* (novel of education) is unique in European literature, portraying adolescence and the organic, psychic, artistic and intellectual maturation of the artist hero, with little reference to the social and economic themes contained in the *roman social* or its British equivalent. As a result of this elevated and aesthetic approach to education, German scholarship tended to be lacking in positivist and empirical research. Despite its often abstract and theoretical nature, however, its more metaphysical and epistemological outlook has made an invaluable contribution to the furthering of empirical knowledge.

An entertaining introduction to the tradition of German education – as seen through British eyes – is Thomas Carlyle's *Sartor Resartus* (1834).[1] This biography of Professor Diogenes Teufelsdröckh from Weissnichtwo describes an apparently aimless, badly organized and rather inert education system, a *Gymnasium* where 'hide bound Pedants, without knowledge of man's nature' cram their pupils with 'innumerable dead Vocables' (R. 99). At university, young Teufelsdröckh encounters 'controversial Metaphysics, Etymology, and mechanical Manipulation falsely named Science' (R. 99). And yet, such an atmosphere, free of the serious constraints of more disciplined studies, allows him to read and expand his mind at leisure, so that he matures into a supreme product of that 'learned, indefatigable and deep thinking Germany [. . .] where abstract Thought can still take shelter' (R. 3). Teufelsdröckh's life-work becomes the 'Philosophy of Clothes', 'a masterpiece of boldness, lynx-eyed acuteness, and rugged independent Germanism and Philanthropy' (R. 5f). In spite of Carlyle's benignly satirical description, one has the feeling that Teufelsdröckh's research would pass today for a major sociological study, introducing scholars to empirical fieldwork.

Mark Twain, a satirical American commentator, often prepared to cast a critical eye on matters German, is moved to describe German university life, however, in terms of benevolent admiration, praising an academic freedom which produces industrious and scholarly academics. He notes the efficient and organized manner in which lectures are delivered and expresses high regard for the *Gymnasium* with its comprehensive scholarly curriculum, producing students highly proficient in classics and endowed with broad academic knowledge.[2] Early nineteenth-century German philologists had a compelling influence on American university life and many American students spent time in Germany, where they endeavoured to assimilate German scholarship in the humanities, particularly classical philology, even if their own puritanical tradition prevented their complete immersion in these studies, and confined them to the more practical aspects of scholarship with an emphasis on strict empirical research.[3]

This book is not written solely for the education specialist; its interdisciplinary approach is geared also towards German Studies, as developed in recent years: a study of institutions, their history and philosophy, all contributing to a 'German tradition'. Though it takes a chronological line, there are certain recurring themes. The evolving German university culture and the phenomenon of the German mandarin, whose influence on scholarship and learning was often reactionary, are treated as major themes. Discussed in relation to these are industrial training and vocational education, interpreted as correctives or additions to the more theoretical approach to learning. Humboldt's pioneering work and its tradition, as well as the concept of *Reformpädagogik*, are regarded as generally positive contributions to the development of a peculiarly German education programme; institutions such as the *Gymnasium* and the churches, as well as the rise of nationalism, are forces usually seen as distorting or slowing down reform programmes.

While the main part of the book concentrates on twentieth-century develop-ments, it would have been a serious omission to ignore the Humboldtian tradition and its partial success in surviving the effects of Germany's industrial revolution. Education during the Third Reich, though intrinsically less important than is often assumed, proved decisive in bringing to the fore deficiencies in the German system, with antecedents in the Weimar Republic and the Second Empire, thereby enforcing a wholesale post-war cleansing of anti-democratic elements. Chapter 8 discusses education since unification and covers other related aspects, since education in Germany today can only be understood against a background of the social and economic developments which have been generated by the coming together of the two Germanies.

Each chapter consists of a main section, examining educational and social developments within a specific period. It is supplemented by a number of short authentic texts in German which serve to illustrate the more salient points under consideration. Texts are complemented by a brief commentary, with a translation of the less common vocabulary.

Finally, I wish to thank my teachers and students for all the support and guidance which I have received over the years. I have taught 'Education and Society', a favourite topic of mine, for many years, both within German Studies and also as a component in Comparative Education. I owe particular gratitude to my wife who helped me put the subject-matter into recognizable English and who employed her British pragmatism to discourage my inclination to wander off into speculative theorizing, often at the expense of clarity and logical progression.

Oxford, January 1997

Notes

1. T. Carlyle (1903), *Sartor Resartus*, London. Subsequently quoted in text with R. plus page number in parenthesis.
2. Mark Twain (1982), *A Tramp Abroad*, Hippocrene Books, US, Chapter 4.
3. Cf. C. Diehl (1978), *Americans and German Scholarship 1770–1870*, New Haven and London.

The German Concept of *Bildung*

Introduction (Setting the Scene)

It has become customary to associate the name of Wilhelm von Humboldt (1767–1835) with the emergence of a national German concept of education (figure 1). Humboldt is regarded as the founder of the German *Gymnasium* and, in addition, as one of the major contributors to the concept of the modern German university. This is all somewhat surprising if we consider that Humboldt's reforms were largely confined to a short period between April 1809 and June 1810, and were restricted to Prussia, where he served as Director of the section for *Kultus und Unterricht* (Culture and Education) and where, as an Imperial Knight, he suffered the disadvantage of being seen as a 'foreigner'. It is obviously a gross generalization to attribute an inordinate influence to one particular person and it can be demonstrated that Humboldt served to represent the reform movement as a whole, taking the opportunity to initiate reforms whenever the time appeared auspicious.

This study does not attempt to summarize, even briefly, the biographical and historical factors which transformed Humboldt into the symbol of Germany's educational renaissance, but certain factors are significant. As a nobleman, Humboldt had early access to the literary salons of the Berlin Enlightenment and was later to cultivate the friendship of Schiller and Goethe and enter the literary and philosophical circles of Weimar culture. He also enjoyed the company of Romantic philologist August Wilhelm Schlegel and of Friedrich Heinrich Jacobi, the prominent advocate of Spinoza's enlightened religious philosophy and an eminent precursor of religious individualism, particularly in its pietistic form. During his diplomatic service Humboldt met the great reformer Freiherr von und zum Stein, who incorporated the educational reforms into the grand liberal reform plan instituted by Stein in an attempt to modernize Prussia in the aftermath of her defeat by Napoleon (1806). Indeed, reforms in general and educational reforms in particular, fostering intellectual and cultural achievements, were to be Prussia's means of compensating for her territorial losses in the war with Napoleon[1] and of setting her on the road to becoming Germany's premier power.

In a wider sense, this reform movement was a response to the French Revolution. Supported by the majority of German men of letters,[2] it seemed, at least in its

Figure 1 Wilhelm von Humboldt, commemorative coin from 1796

earlier stages, to promote the ideals of freedom, emancipation and patriotism, all attributes of the Enlightenment, itself the progenitor of modernism in general and the democratic nation state in particular. Kant's famous essay on the Enlightenment defined the movement as 'Ausgang des Menschen aus seiner selbstverschuldeten Unmündigkeit. Unmündigkeit ist das Unvermögen, sich seines Verstandes ohne Leitung eines anderen zu bedienen'.[3] (Man's escape from his voluntary immaturity. Immaturity is the inability to make use of one's intellect without the guidance of another.) Such a definition emphasizes learning and intellectual development. Indeed, all modern Western concepts of education take the Enlightenment as their starting point, as it provided the intellectual foundation for the development of public awareness and the growth of democracy. As a result, education was not merely an instrument for meeting the economic and administrative needs of the state; it also promoted personal development, whereby education was a means of overcoming social and economic class restrictions, allowing individuals to 'escape from their voluntary immaturity'.

It is within this context that Humboldt's predecessors should be considered. The new climate had been profoundly influenced by three factors: G. W. Leibniz's philosophy of monads which promoted the perfectibility of man;[4] the Earl of

Shaftesbury's concepts of 'common sense' and 'self-formation' and his general interest in anthropology; and J.-J. Rousseau's philosophy of education in particular. Goethe sees in Rousseau, especially in *Emile*, 'ein Muster wie man unterrichten soll'[5] (an example on how to teach) and German educators of the Enlightenment such as Basedow and Campe were profoundly influenced by Rousseau. Both Shaftesbury and Rousseau emphasized the importance of self-awareness and with it the subjective aspect of education as a process of socialization. Of particular interest is a comparison between Rousseau's philosophy and the development of certain aspects of German education. Rousseau's concept of a union between the public domain of education which produced the *citoyen* and the private, domestic domain, nurturing the *homme naturel*, was not adopted in Germany where the two aspects remained separate. The philanthropists J. B. Basedow, C. G. Salzmann and Humboldt's teacher, J. H. Campe, who pleaded for a middle-class, utilitarian, vocationally orientated form of education, were criticized by Humboldt and his humanist circle for their functionalist approach.

While the development of a middle-class society in Germany was still in its infancy, practical education tended to be devoid of any emancipatory political element. This type of functional education appeared to exclude the nobility, notwithstanding their enviable privileges and elegant life-style. In their *Ritterakademien* they were instructed in riding, dancing and fencing, and Christian Garve, a popular philosopher of the time, recognized that 'durchgängige Ausbildung der ganzen Person' (comprehensive development of the whole person) was the privilege of the nobleman. He demanded a similar form of education for the bourgeois: 'Vom Unadlichen verlangte man vorzüglich Brauchbarkeit zu irgendeinem Geschäfte: und der Unadliche war [. . .] seine übrige Ausbildung zu vernachläßigen, beynah genöthigt.'[6] (Of the common man one demanded chiefly usefulness in some business and the common man was [. . .] almost required to neglect the rest of his education.)

Rousseau, however, had recognized that work and the opportunity to learn a trade distinguished the citizen from the nobleman, for, just as any person living within society at the expense of others, 'celui qui mange dans oisiveté ce qu'il n'a pas gagné lui-même le vole' (an idle man who has done nothing to earn what he eats, is a thief). Rousseau concludes therefore: 'dans la société, où il vit nécessairement aux dépens des autres, il leur doit en travail le prix de son entretien; cela est sans exception'[7] (within the bounds of society, where man is necessarily dependent on others, he owes it to others to work to earn his keep; that is the rule). Only Fichte, Hegel and, a generation later, Marx recognized the significance of work and work-related education as important factors in man's self-realization within his own society. The contemporaries of Humboldt and Goethe were more concerned with man's perfectibility within an ideal sphere and with the need to overcome the social division between the bourgeoisie and the nobility.[8]

Another interesting difference between the German concept of *Bildung* and the French concept of education involves the role of the state. Rousseau's notion of *citoyen* integrates man into society and fosters a recognition of the *volonté générale* (general will), of responsible, democratic citizenship. At almost the same time as Rousseau's *Emile* appeared, Frederick the Great of Prussia was expressing his thoughts on education. Denouncing ignorance as indecent, obscene and a blight on the modern state, he saw education, nevertheless, as a means of producing *Untertanen* (subjects), not liberally minded citizens.[9] As a result of such crude functionalism, Humboldt's generation of German educators developed a healthy suspicion of state control and advocated that education should be free from state influence. Humboldt's essay 'Ideen zu einem Versuch, die Grenzen der Wirksamkeit des Staates zu bestimmen' (1792) (Suggestions for defining the limits of state effectiveness) sees the state as guardian, delivering material support for education and guaranteeing competent teachers and optimum teaching conditions, but not interfering in educational matters such as the syllabus and avoiding the role of 'Zuchtmeister der Gesellschaft'[10] (society's prefect). The concept of academic freedom was accepted within a state-funded education system and ensured that the function of the state was limited to matters of finance and the supervision of university and civil service entrance examinations for students and teachers.

The Neo-Classical Concept of *Bildung* and the Humboldtian Reform Programme in Prussia

Humboldt's reforms can best be understood if viewed as part of the movement of German idealism. These humanist ideals, conceived by Goethe and Schiller, developed further through the Romanticism of Schleiermacher and Fichte, were to survive, albeit in a diminished form, until well into the twentieth century.

Established to counteract a negative perception of the Enlightenment and influenced by a number of its pedagogical and philosophical concepts, this reform programme was, nevertheless, part of the wider rejection of French hegemony. However, on closer inspection, it becomes obvious that such a programme emerged in the form of a discourse, assimilating many aspects of its precursor. The following three overarching ideals constituted the new German philosophy of education:

1 Individualism: The ideal of personal development consisted of attaining 'Selbstbewußtsein' (self-assurance), a typically German form of emancipation, not in the sense of freedom from the bonds of society, religion or state, but – as indicated in Kant's essay – freedom from ignorance in the widest possible sense. A memorable example of this form of emancipation is found in Goethe's *Faust*, where 'Selbsterkenntnis' (self-knowledge) is seen as the highest form of knowledge, allowing man a subtler understanding of the world:

daß ich erkenne, was die Welt
Im Innersten zusammenhält[11]
(That I may recognize what binds together
The innermost secrets of the universe).

Humboldt concluded that such a comprehensive form of knowledge was best seen in ancient Greece [Text 1]. There 'knowledge' was not the primacy of the intellect, but a form of universal empathy, allowing man to be in tune with the universe. His much-quoted formula of 'Einsamkeit und Freiheit' (solitude and freedom) must be understood in this sense: the pursuit of knowledge, independent of any social or vocational consideration, bestows the confidence to render ourselves open to the secrets of the world. The interaction of Self and Other will ensure that our *Welterkenntnis* will translate into a higher form of *Selbsterkenntnis* and vice versa.

2 Totality: It follows that such knowledge cannot be limited to, or even directed by, the intellect. Influenced by Kant's distinction between *Vernunft* (reason) and *Verstand* (intellect), the humanists saw learning as the flowering of all the human faculties and the previous generation of philanthropists came under attack for their philistine vocationalism[12] which substituted opinion for truth, convention for virtue and usefulness for beauty. In order to realize the harmony of truth and beauty, man's animality must be reconciled with his spirituality; all human faculties must unfold harmoniously. Of particular importance for the new concept of inclusive education was Johann Heinrich Pestalozzi (1746–1827). This Swiss pioneer saw that the simultaneous understanding of number, form and word, his formula of 'head, heart and hand', of the harmonious unfolding of our intellectual, emotional and practical abilities, would lead our 'Erkenntnis von Verwirrung zur Bestimmtheit, von Bestimmtheit zur Klarheit und von Klarheit zur Deutlichkeit hinüber'[13] (understanding from confusion towards certainty, from certainty towards clarity and from clarity towards distinctiveness).

3 Universality: The final element of this neo-classical triad emphasizes the anthropocentric aspect of *Bildung*, initially envisaged as physical development but soon to include the intellectual, emotional and spiritual perfection of the individual, culminating in man's most comprehensive appropriation of 'world'. Unlike animals, men naturally seek to achieve perfection, aspiring ever higher, and, in a never-ending process of education, they are continuously experiencing 'world'. This experience is achieved through language, no longer seen as a mere convention and a means of acquiring knowledge, as it was during the Enlightenment, but language understood as an organic, historically grown medium, through which we experience 'otherness', engage in an animated exchange with past, present and future worlds, and ultimately are empowered to participate in a lively interchange between subject and object, thus creating a new individuality [Text 2].

Such an understanding of language owes much to Herder's philosophy of history as well as to his conception of language as the essence of a nation's character. In Herder's *Briefe zur Beförderung der Humanität* we read:

> Humanität ist der Schatz und die Ausbeute aller menschlichen Bemühungen . . . .. Die Bildung zu ihr ist ein Werk, das unabläßig fortgesetzt werden muß, oder wir sinken, höhere und niedere Stände, zur rohen Tierheit, zur Brutalität zurück.[14]

> (Humanity is the treasure and the reward for all human endeavour . . . .. Its formation has to be constantly reproduced if we are not to be reduced, high and low alike, to a state of base animality, to bestiality.)

However, while Herder formulated his studies on the mother tongue and the development of the *Volk*, Humboldt and his circle, more cosmopolitan in outlook, used language as a means to gain knowledge of many different worlds and cultures. Humboldt was a veritable polyglot and felt that learning a foreign language was a process of mediation whereby we appropriate another world, the 'otherness' of which, being man-made, is not unbridgeably alien but can become part of our own, enriched individuality. Humboldt perceived the study of languages as a form of comparative anthropology or, in contemporary jargon, 'culture studies'. Indeed, the relationship between education and culture became vitally important, as will be demonstrated later, and serves to explain why Humboldt advocated the learning of Greek in preference to the study of any other language, since ancient Greece was seen as the cradle of humanity.

The art historian, Johann Joachim Winckelmann, in his influential study *Gedanken über die Nachahmung der griechischen Werke in der Malerei und Bildhauerkunst* (1755), had anticipated a general shift from the more dogmatic and conceptualized Latin to the more aesthetically conceived Greek. Greek language and culture became the predominant influence and, together with a general preoccupation with aesthetics, promoted beauty as a central objective for the education of man; beauty primarily understood as harmony, as the continuous unfolding of man's intellectual, physical and emotional faculties. In the same vein, the shift towards ancient Greece meant a rejection of French hegemony and, in particular, the misconception, brought about by the slavish imitation of French administration in German courts, that French civilization stood for utilitarian, functionalist vocationalism. Instead, the creative cultural aspect of ancient Greece was emphasized, the pursuit of beauty instead of usefulness, the emancipation of the individual from civic and professional considerations [Text 3]. French philanthropy and the pedagogical ideals of the Enlightenment were rejected in favour of pure self-development. To this day, the German concepts of knowledge and *Wissenschaft* are diametrically opposed to an encyclopaedic, purely factual approach to knowledge and promote a holistic attitude rather than the empiricism of factual accumulative learning, searching instead for the epistemological order, for cosmological coherence:

> Der wissenschaftliche Fortschritt besteht in dem immer weiteren systematischen Vordringen [. . .] in die Breite und Tiefe der Wirklichkeit, zu den Elementen des Seins und Geschehens und zur Erkenntnis ihrer Zusammenhänge, des großen Zusammenhangs der Wirklichkeit überhaupt, die wir Welt nennen.[15]

> (Scholarly progress consists of a continuous systematic advance [. . .] towards the breadth and depth of reality, towards the elements of being and of action and towards an understanding of their context, the comprehensive context of reality as such, that which we call world.)

The curriculum of the Prussian *Gymnasium*, which allocated more than half of its syllabus to languages,[16] indicates the strong emphasis placed on this subject, which was to direct students increasingly towards civilization and comparative anthropology rather than to the acquisition of factual knowledge. A new generation of teachers was introduced: the theology student who taught in the *Lateinschule* whilst waiting for his appointment to a parish was replaced by the philologist who, as the name suggests, was a devotee of language and reason. From 1810 he played an important role in the dissemination of classical and German culture at the *Gymnasium*. The acquisition of culture gained unprecedented prominence, still evident today in official titles such as *Kultusministerium* (Ministry for Education) or *Kulturhoheit*, the virtual sovereignty of individual *Länder* in the administration of their education systems. Even the idea of a *Kulturnation* can be traced back to Humboldt's humanism, awarding education and culture its central cohesive function in the development of a united Germany.

The Continuation of the Reform Movement by Schleiermacher and Fichte

Whilst Humboldt can be seen as the initiator of a new philosophy of education and culture and as the founder of the modern *Gymnasium*, his successors Fichte and Schleiermacher came to prominence by giving the new University of Berlin its particular direction. They continued Humboldt's drive towards academic self-government and freedom of teaching, and in particular his endeavour to replace the vocationally orientated narrow pursuit of specialisms at the country's many academies by *Lernfreiheit* (the freedom of students to choose their own subjects, their own teachers and to migrate from one university to another). Berlin University, founded in the year of Humboldt's removal from office (1810), dispensed with a rigid curriculum and course structure in favour of a wider acquisition of *Wissenschaft*. Research and learning were to be combined, stimulating each other and producing 'men of character'[17] who took immense pride in their *Bildung* and understood academic study to be a life-long process.

Friedrich Schleiermacher (1768–1834), nominated by Humboldt to the University's foundation committee, declared the Faculty of Philosophy to be the central body for the propagation of knowledge, whereas the Faculties of Law, Theology and Medicine were seen as steeped in a narrowly defined vocationalism:

> Offenbar nämlich ist die eigentliche Universität [. . .] lediglich in der philosophischen Fakultät enthalten, und die drei anderen sind die Spezialschulen, welche der Staat entweder gestiftet oder [. . .] in seinen Schutz genommen hat.[18]

> (It seems that the true university [. . .] is only contained within the Philosophy Faculty, and the other three faculties are special schools, either founded by the state or protected by it.)

Though himself a theologian, Schleiermacher constantly strove to relate his discipline to the philosophical mainstream, thereby contributing to a general body of knowledge. He also lectured on pedagogics in general and ensured that the discipline was closely related to both ethics and politics. In common with other representatives of the Romantic movement, he was a committed patriot, actively involved in the liberation movement against Napoleon. The political aspects of the new education system will be considered when we discuss Fichte's role in the Prussian reform movement.

Schleiermacher's most important contribution to the German concept of university education lies in hermeneutics. Influenced by his Bible studies and his translation of Plato's works, Schleiermacher attempted to relate all specific disciplines to general ideas, to the totality of human understanding. 'Understanding' thus becomes a process of eliminating misunderstanding, a continuous and gradual process of coming closer to perfection and to the secret of life: 'Alles Wissen und all unsere Gedanken sind unvollkommen, bis die absolute Totalität ihres Zusammenhanges hergestellt ist.'[19] (All knowledge and all our thoughts are imperfect until they are seen in their full context.) His 'universalist' approach to knowledge became the distinguishing aspect of German university studies, at least as far as the arts were concerned, an influence which continues undiminished up to our own time, though in a more methodical form. Hermeneutics is still the dominant discipline in all arts subjects and Schleiermacher's ideas were revitalized at the end of the nineteenth and again in the middle of the twentieth century.[20]

Johann Gottlieb Fichte (1762–1814) introduced an important corrective element to Humboldt's neo-classical concept of education by relating it to the contemporary political situation. As a result, education policy moved towards a greater awareness of social and public issues, distancing itself somewhat from Humboldt's ideal of freedom from the state. Humboldt's scepticism towards state interference was based on the notion that the state was illiberal, defending the corporate society and, above all, the personal interests of the sovereign. The French Revolution, Napoleon's defeat of Prussia and Austria and the consequent dissolution of the Holy Roman Empire (1806) engendered a new interest in politics and fostered a new patriotism, similar to that which inspired the French troops with a sense of purpose and commitment, based on a new understanding of citizenship. During the cannonade of Valmy (1792), when the French revolutionary troops demonstrated their superiority over the Prussian army, Goethe recognized that a new epoch in world history had begun.[21] Against this background, the social, military and political reforms, initiated by Stein, were intended to 'revolutionize' Prussia from the top down. A new political consciousness was to bring about a revised attitude towards the state and citizenship, with Prussia emerging as the standard-bearer of patriotic liberalism.

Fichte's philosophy was based on freedom, achieved through action, which would liberate the individual from the constraints of nature and provide genuine independence (*Selbständigkeit*), Fichte's own interpretation of emancipation. He also saw his new ideal of *Selbständigkeit* as freedom from the eighteenth-century age of egoism and advocated a *Nationalerziehungsplan* (national concept of education), expressed in his *Reden an die deutsche Nation* (1807–8). The promotion of national consciousness would need to overcome divisions of class and social background, achieved by involving all pupils in physical work, removing them from the seclusion of family life and bringing them together in one common school [Text 4]. Like Rousseau and Pestalozzi, Fichte advocated the establishment of *Erziehungskolonien* (educational colonies) which, not unlike contemporary officer cadet schools, would emphasize intellectual and physical abilities and encourage the new national consciousness.

At a higher level, universities should also be sufficiently independent to escape what was seen as the degenerate and corrupt influence of society. Students should be educated in a new spirit of responsibility towards the community and should, in return, benefit from its financial support. When Fichte became Berlin University's first *Rektor* in 1810, he attempted to establish it as a centre for German national education. Attracting the best minds, both as faculty and students, it became a focus for patriotism (figure 2). The subsequent subversion of patriotism into chauvinism and national arrogance, sinking to its nadir under Hitler's National Socialism, should not detract from Fichte's original concept of patriotic education. Developments in the first half of the nineteenth century served to illustrate his success and would also justify his desire to combine the modern forces of patriotism and liberalism in an effort to forge a new national consciousness. Students from

Figure 2 Student March to the Wartburg (1817). This march became an important landmark in national liberal student protest, commemorating the third anniversary of the battle of Leipzig where Napoleon was decisively defeated by a Prussian army, many of whose officers had been educated in the spirit of Humboldt and Fichte. It also marked the 300th anniversary of Luther's translation of the Bible at the Wartburg, emphasizing a strong national identification with Luther and the German language. The protesting students used the occasion to burn many reactionary, anti-liberal books. (Reproduced with the kind permission of *Freie Universität Berlin.*)

most German-speaking countries were drawn to Berlin University. They formed *Landsmannschaften*, student houses, accommodating students from specific regions, later combining to form the *Deutsche Burschenschaft* (1815). This movement was inspired by the fraternity and patriotism experienced during the Wars of Liberation (1812–15) and was supported by *Turnvater* Friedrich Ludwig Jahn and by Fichte. Its motto 'Freiheit, Ehre, Vaterland' (freedom, honour, fatherland) became a watchword for democratic patriotism, based on the French Revolutionary ideal of 'la République une et indivisible'.[22] After the defeat of Napoleon, the *Burschenschaften* directed their energies towards the establishment of a sovereign, democratic German nation state and found themselves on a collision course with their reactionary, regional rulers (figure 3). Criticized for its over-idealistic spirit, the contribution of this reform movement to the failed German Revolution of 1848 was, nevertheless, considerable and deserves to be recognized.

The Contribution of *Gymnasium* and *Universität* to a German Concept of *Bildung*

On a general level, both institutions can be discussed together as both were committed to the neo-classical concept of general education. The *Gymnasium* was to prepare students for higher education and in order to concentrate on this function, it had to shed the elitist status of the *Lateinschule*, often also referred to as *Gelehrtenschule*. Such liberalization was never really successful. True, the new institution did not discriminate according to family background in its entry requirements, but as it sought to replace social distinction by intellectual merit, it inevitably retained, at least in part, a vestige of social bias. Since the assessment of intelligence is a difficult and complex process, the lower classes were at a particular disadvantage. The syllabus was originally based on three general areas: education in gymnastics, not so much in the Roman sense of keeping body and mind alert, but more as a challenge to the old *Ritterakademie* which hitherto had been the only school concentrating on physical education. The second area was aesthetics, particularly music and the fine arts, both disciplines paying special attention to harmony, influenced by neo-classical art historians such as Winckelmann and Humboldt. The final element was didactics, conceived in an epistemological mould: it distinguished between a philosophical and a mathematical discipline, the former including languages and history, the latter mathematics and sciences. These various features of didactics, demonstrating symmetry and harmony, action and reaction, themselves reinforced the ethos of gymnastics and aesthetics, illustrating the neo-classical preoccupation with form and proportion. Didactics soon developed into the strongest of the three areas, as a university education, in its pursuit of pure knowledge, required a fundamental understanding of scholarship.

I/21 Kotzebue's murder, 23rd March 1819.

Figure 3 The murder of the spy August von Kotzebue (1819). A dramatist out of sympathy with the new literary and political trends, Kotzebue was recruited as a spy for the reactionary Russian Tsar, who supported the illiberal monarchs of Prussia and Austria. He was stabbed to death by the student Karl Ludwig Sand, a member of the newly established *Burschenschaften*. The murder prompted the authorities to introduce the Carlsbad Decrees (1819), leading to widespread censorship, political persecution and the banning of the *Burschenschaften*. (Reproduced with the kind permission of *Reiss Museum*, Mannheim.)

The *Abitur*[23] reinforced the role of didactics. First introduced in Prussia in 1788 to free education from church influence, it was reformed under Schleiermacher (1812) and by the 1830s had become the prerequisite for university entrance throughout Germany (figure 4). It was considered a guarantee of the maturity of character and intellect necessary to maintain 'die Würde des auf den Universitäten herrschenden Tons'[24] (the dignity of tone prevailing in universities). It soon posed a challenge to the nobility's privileged position, as the term *Berechtigungswesen*, in use until 1918, ensured that the *Abiturient* was entitled to special privileges, including a shorter term of military service and a commission.[25] The *Gymnasium*'s position was further enhanced by the introduction of a special examination for its

Auf diesem Netze zweifellos
Ist die Gefahr schon riesig gross.
Doch keiner ist hier durchgefallen·
Es grüsst die Oberprima Aalen·
I· Maturum ·1914·

Figure 4 The *Abitur* is symbolized here by a net through which weaker pupils might fall. Failing the *Abitur* is referred to as 'durchfallen' and the students are celebrating the fact that nobody failed this important examination. 'Oberprima' refers to the final school year, usually leading to the award of *Abitur*. (Reproduced with the kind permission of *Schubartgymnasium*, Aalen.)

teachers, the *examen pro facultate docendi*, a forerunner of today's *Staatsexamen*. A Royal Edict of 1810 decreed philological, historical and mathematical studies to be core disciplines and made the passing of this scholarly examination – to which a practical teaching test was added – the mandatory teaching qualification at all Prussian *Gymnasien*, exemption being granted only to graduates with a doctorate or a master's degree.[26]

A sound base for young scholars in secondary education having been established, the scene was set for university reforms. Humboldt's aim, in uniting several academies in Berlin to form a university, was

> die Wissenschaften im tiefsten [. . .] Sinne des Wortes zu bearbeiten. [. . .] Ihr Wesen besteht daher darin, innerlich die objektive Wissenschaft mit der subjektiven Bildung, äußerlich den vollendeten Schulunterricht mit dem beginnenden Studium unter eigener Leitung zu verknüpfen.[27]

> (to cultivate scholarship in the fullest sense of the word. [. . .] It consists essentially of the internal merger of objective scholarship with subjective education; achieved externally by taking up university studies under one's own initiative, after completing secondary education.)

It is easy to recognize in this quotation the comprehensive neo-classical ideal of combining self-perfection with the acquisition of universal knowledge. The university was to replace the specialized vocational and utilitarian teaching of the academies. It was also to break the mould of the traditional undergraduate curriculum, a model which still dominates Anglo-American patterns of higher education. Instead, the Humboldtian concept sought to combine learning with research, uniting both elements in an almost Grail-like quest for the source of all knowledge. Scholarship was no longer subject to any social, civic or professional considerations, nor was it restricted by a time factor. For Humboldt, and in his tradition, German scholarship became a life-long pursuit which had to be sought 'aus der Tiefe des Geistes heraus'[28] (from the depth of the spirit); it became a personal obligation which would bestow on the academic a special aura and considerable responsibility. The new university community was no longer based on social bonds. A community of interest between teacher and student, based on a mutual experience of scholarship, was to emerge which was to give the university its unparalleled position in German life but which would also distance it from social and political concerns, placing it increasingly within the confines of the ivory tower.

The *Gymnasium* and *Universität*, as the cornerstones of Germany's new cultural initiative, defined a new dominant role for the middle classes, based not on material wealth or political power, but on educational ideals and a peculiarly German emphasis on *Kultur*. Both from Germany's own viewpoint and from that of other countries, this strong association between education and *Bildung*, and in particular the affiliation with *Kultur*, is often held to be one of Germany's outstanding features, not only in the positive sense of scholarship and learning, but also in the negative connotation of an unpolitical and unworldly attitude. These more negative aspects may have produced a too close and unquestioning relationship with the state and officialdom, at the expense of mature political emancipation. Seen from this perspective, the educational ideals of neo-classicism may have sustained Germany's special development, her *Sonderweg*, which during the second half of the nineteenth century caused her to deviate from Western liberal concepts, supported by an educational elite which formed a one-sided, undemocratic alliance with state power and authority.[29] We have seen earlier, especially during the first half of the nineteenth century, how it can be argued, with similar justification, that it was essentially at educational establishments that enlightened ideas took root, from whence a liberal, democratic spirit began to emerge.[30] Paradoxically enough, while both arguments hold true, the retreat of the middle classes from politics may have been rather more affected by the Lutheran tradition of political abstention and individual trans-cendentalism, forces which were deeply involved in the German concept of *Bildung*. In particular the German Protestant tradition seems to have strengthened the interrelationship between *Bildung* and *Kultur*, leading to an almost Romantic 'untimeliness' and to a rejection of materialism in any form.[31]

The peculiarly German embrace of the neo-classical ideal of fostering the comprehensive development of all human qualities, as evident in the new education system, was also seen in the contemporary development of the German *Bildungs-roman*. It, too, demonstrated how the French concepts of equality and freedom were sublimated into a general form of non-political culture. Goethe's *Wilhelm Meister* is just one example. The young hero is initiated into the arts and love, experiences subsequently reflected at an intellectual level in conversation with an older, noble friend. In the tradition of Rousseau, education, in the narrower sense, is undertaken in the provinces, away from society, and is directed towards an appreciation of harmony, the interaction between singing and hearing, drawing and mathematics. In this 'pedagogical province' a nice balance is maintained between instruction and the unfettered development of personality: 'Weise Männer lassen den Knaben unter der Hand dasjenige finden, was ihm gemäß ist'[32] (The wise allow a boy to make his discoveries in his own way). Central to Goethe's concept is his view of the 'drei Ehrfurchten' (three reverences), a very broad and symbolically expressed feeling of awe towards heaven, earth and man's fellow creatures, which we cannot examine here in detail.[33] This symbolic expression, a gesture of reverence towards everything above, below and around us, culminates in a reverence for oneself, not in an arrogant, self-congratulory sense, but in an attitude of gratitude and obligation, a realization that human life reflects the Divine creation.

It will have become clear from these observations that Goethe's 'pedagogical province' offers 'eine Art von Utopie'[34] (a kind of utopia) and is profoundly affected by religion, not in an exclusively Christian form, but as *Weltfrömmigkeit*, adapted from all world religions and anchored in enlightened rationalism. The utopian nature of Goethe's human education found its initial expression in art, but his later social and anthroposophic interests led him to reject art in favour of an ethical concern to serve mankind. Goethe's Wilhelm Meister eventually rejects art for medicine, rejects a career in the theatre for a life of service to the wider community. The Romantics saw this as a betrayal of art, demonstrating a tendency to restrict education to the *Bildungsbürgertum* (educated middle class), to promote education and culture for a narrowly defined ethical purpose. Goethe himself ridiculed this sentiment in one of his satirical *Xenien*:

> Wo kam die schönste Bildung her,
> Und wenn sie nicht vom Bürger wär?[35]
> (From where would the best education come,
> if not from the *Bürger*?)

The increasing indifference towards socio-political concerns was satirized by the political activist Herwegh: 'Du hast ja den Schiller und Goethe, schlafe, was willst du mehr?'[36] (But you have got Schiller and Goethe, sleep, what more do you want?)

The elitism which academic education fostered among the professional classes also surfaced in the derogatory use of the term *Spießbürger* (narrow-minded bourgeois). By the end of the century there was a manifest and arrogant *Bildungsdünkel* (educational conceit) militating against trade and industry, and in particular against the education provided by the new vocationally orientated schools. Even *Volksschulen* (elementary schools) and working-class associations felt impelled to participate in the general cultural movement, at least partly in an attempt at social improvement.[37] However, this general desire to participate in *Bildung* must also be interpreted in the light of Germany's late development.[38] Education and culture were seen to be important; they even found a place within the framework of modern industrialization. The economist Friedrich List argued for the speedy extension of the railway network in order to disseminate more effectively literary publications, arts and scholarship in general![39] However, liberal and industrial forces were eventually to attempt to break down the barrier between the neo-classical *Bildungsbürger* and the rest of society, but it was the advent of modernism at the end of the century that finally caused cracks to appear in the alliance between *Bildung* and

Bürger. This ideological struggle drew in the more reactionary, nationalist forces and significantly contributed towards the inevitability of war.

The Rise of the *Volksschule* as a Complementary Aspect of the Humboldtian Concept of Education

The *Volksschule* (elementary school), discussed in detail in Chapter 2, will receive only a brief mention here. Humboldt had originally included elementary education as part of a comprehensive educational system, free from any taint of class prejudice. However, his own interest in language and the acknowledged need for a new form of higher education directed his attention away from the *Volksschule* issue. Humboldt relied on the methodology of Pestalozzi who, though more pragmatic, shared his belief in general education as the interdependent development of 'head, heart and hand'.[40] At the same time, Humboldt's own universalist approach may have hindered his full appreciation of the significance of *Volk*, a term which had come into prominence with Herder, but which only attained its more specific political importance with the Romantics. From the early nineteenth century, *Volk* was virtually synonymous with 'nation' and, in its specifically German context, with the concept of a future nation state. It thereby lost the stigma of its social overtones and gained in prominence as the basis for a national culture and for the future German *Kulturstaat*. The social status of the elementary school teacher was consequently raised and special teaching seminaries were established, based largely on Pestalozzi's own school at Ifferten. Having themselves emerged in many cases from the lower ranks of society, these teachers approached the process of education with enormous idealism: eager to emancipate their pupils and their local, mainly rural communities, they demonstrated missionary zeal not only in eradicating illiteracy, but also in advancing the cause of popular culture, taking on the task of choirmaster or beekeeper or introducing new agricultural methods. Adolf Diesterweg, director of several important Prussian teaching seminaries (1820–47), promoted the concept of *Volksbildung*. His own liberal democratic leanings influenced the foundation of teachers' associations, culminating in the creation of the *Allgemeiner Deutscher Lehrerverein* which was to play an important role during the 1848 Revolution [Text 5]. In the post-1848 reactionary climate, especially under the stewardship of the Prussian co-ordinator of elementary schools, Ferdinand Stiehl (1850–72), the clock was turned back and the training of elementary school teachers was considerably constrained by an ecclesiastic, monarchic and authoritarian atmosphere.[41] By 1870 the term *Volksbildung* had completely changed its ethos; it had lost its national, liberal and democratic spirit and had become institutionalized as a force for inculcating in the common people an attitude of submission to authority and to the state.

Conclusion

The aim of this chapter was to focus on the tremendous cultural and social achievements of the neo-classical concept of *Bildung*, which must be appreciated as a major element in the development of modern German culture. It is a concept which even influenced the distinctive ethos of German science and engineering, to be discussed in Chapter 2. At the same time, it failed to maintain its emancipatory momentum in the wake of reactionary and nationalist developments during the second part of the nineteenth century. Three aspects in particular were to become significant, thereby contributing to a peculiarly German form of political culture:

(a) The preponderance of private at the expense of public virtues.[42] The individualistic, often quasi-religious basis of the 'German' concept of education tended to play down the social aspects: the individual's responsibility towards society, the need to defend the political principles derived from the Enlightenment and an emphasis on playing a public role in the service of the community rather than of the state, in the pursuit of fairness and social justice rather than truth and beauty. As a result, the education system, as it developed, was unable to produce genuine socialization, allowed for little social transparency and neglected the establishment of democratic structures.

(b) The dominance of the arts and philosophy at the expense of natural and moral sciences. In particular, the importance placed on the classics and their implicit social exclusivity and the close links between education and culture led to the establishment of a mandarin class of civil servant, who quite simply failed to understand the new forces at work at the dawn of a modern industrial age. The interdependence between education and work was overlooked, along with the establishment of vocational and professional studies.

(c) The overemphasis on *Bildung* at the expense of *Erziehung*. This favoured an education policy which paid insufficient heed to the patriotic concept of education, advocated by Fichte and his liberal-nationalist circle. In particular it failed to support *Volksbildung* as the comprehensive and public education of the whole nation, confining it instead to 'elementary' education, to a purely functional vocationalism, producing loyal and obedient subjects, but not citizens.

Notes

1. M. Behnen (1987), 'Deutschland unter Napoleon. Restauration und Vormärz', M. Vogt (ed.), *Rassow, Deutsche Geschichte*, Stuttgart, p. 362.

2. Humboldt was not one of the Revolution's admirers. He hoped for a renaissance of German thought and culture under the Prussian dynasty. Cf. Humboldt, 'Antrag auf Errichtung der Universität Berlin', Humboldt (1964), *Schriften zur Anthropologie und Geschichte, Werke in 5 Bänden*, A. Flitner and K. Giel (eds), Stuttgart, vol. 4, pp. 113f.

3. I. Kant (1960–4), *Werke in 12 Bänden*, Wiesbaden, vol. 11, p. 53.

4. G. W. Leibniz (1960), *Monadologie*, H. Glockner (ed.), 2nd edn, Stuttgart, paragraphs 49–65.

5. Goethe (1968), *Briefe* (Hamburger Ausgabe), 2nd edn, Hamburg, vol. 1, p. 398.

6. Chr. Garve (1880), *Über Gesellschaft und Einsamkeit*, reprint Hildesheim 1985, vol. 2, pp. 51f.

7. J. J. Rousseau (1762), *Emile ou de l'éducation*, F. and P. Richard (eds), Paris 1964, p. 226.

8. Cf. in this respect Schiller's view of the importance of *Spiel* in relation to man's self-perfection, far exceeding the importance given it by Rousseau and — conversely — the rigid definition of *Arbeit* within German pietist circles where it had become an alternative to prayer and preparation for life in the hereafter. L. von Zinzendorf, a leading pietist, wrote: 'Man arbeitet nicht allein, daß man lebt, sondern man lebt um der Arbeit willen, und wenn man nichts mehr zu arbeiten hat, so leidet man oder entschläft.' (One does not only work in order to live, but one lives for the sake of work and when one can no longer work, one will suffer or die.) (Quoted from H. Hammer (1925), *Abraham Dünninger – Ein Herrenhuter Wirtschaftsmensch des 18. Jahrhunderts*, Berlin, pp. 32f.)

9. U. Aumüller (1974), 'Industrieschule und ursprüngliche Akkumulation in Deutschland. Die Qualifizierung der Arbeitskraft im Übergang von der feudalen in die kapitalistische Produktionsweise', in K. Hartmann, F. Nyssen, H. Waldeyer (eds), *Schule und Staat im 18. und 19. Jahrhundert*, Frankfurt/ M., esp. pp. 54–8.

10. W. Humboldt (1792), 'Ideen zu einem Versuch, die Grenzen der Wirksamkeit des Staates zu bestimmen', W. von Humboldt (1960), *Schriften zur Anthropologie*, vol. 1, p. 135.

11. Goethe's *Faust*, verses 382f.

12. Cf. F. I. Niethammer (1808), *Der Streit des Philanthropismus und Humanismus in der Theorie des Erziehungsunterrichts unserer Zeit*, W. Hillebrecht (ed.), Weinheim 1968.

13. J. H. Pestalozzi (1932), *Wie Gertrud ihre Kinder lehrt, Sämtliche Werke*, A. Buchenau, E. Spranger, H. Stettbacher (eds), Berlin, vol. 13, p. 254.

14. J. G. Herder (1881), *Briefe zur Beförderung der Humanität, Sämtliche Werke*, B. Suphan (ed.), Berlin 1877–1913, vol. 17, p. 138.

15. G. Schischkoff (ed.) (1991), *Philosophisches Wörterbuch*, 22nd edn, Stuttgart, p. 786.
16. Of the 321 hours taught in the final year, 76 hours were devoted to Latin, 45 hours to Greek, 45 hours to German and 4 hours to Hebrew. [Lehrplan des preußischen Gymnasiums von 1816], quoted from E. Spranger (1965), *W. von Humboldt und die Reform des Bildungswesens*, 3rd edn, Tübingen, pp. 254f.
17. W. von Humboldt (1810), 'Über die innere und äußere Organisation der höheren wissenschaftlichen Anstalten in Berlin', in A. Flitner (ed.) (1984), *Wilhelm von Humboldt. Schriften zur Anthropologie und Bildungslehre*, Frankfurt/M., p. 84.
18. F. D. E. Schleiermacher (1957), *Pädagogische Schriften*, E. Weniger (ed.), Düsseldorf, vol. 2, p. 111.
19. Quoted from R. Odebrecht (ed.) (1976), *Friedrich Schleiermachers Dialektik*, Darmstadt, p. 63.
20. For a fuller study of Schleiermacher's hermeneutics cf. H.-G. Gadamer (1990), *Wahrheit und Methode. Grundzüge einer philosophischen Hermeneutik*, 6th edn, Tübingen, pp. 188–201.
21. J. W. von Goethe (1966), *Werke* (Hamburger Ausgabe), 4th edn, Hamburg, vol. 10, p. 235.
22. Cf. U. Schlicht (1980), *Vom Burschenschaftler bis zum Sponti. Studentische Opposition gestern und heute*, Berlin, pp. 15–23.
23. From Latin *abire* (to leave), a school-leaving certificate, sometimes also referred to as *Maturum* or *Reifezeugnis*.
24. 'Edikt wegen Prüfung der zu den Universitäten übergehenden Schüler; vom 25. Juni 1812', quoted from A. Reble (1992), *Geschichte der Pädagogik, Dokumentationsband*, 2nd edn, Stuttgart, p. 411.
25. Many of these privileges were introduced later.
26. 'Edikt v. 12. Juli 1810 wegen Prüfung der Kandidaten des höheren Schulamts', Reble, *Geschichte, Dokumentationsband*, pp. 408f.
27. Humboldt, 'Über die innere und äußere Organisation der höheren wissenschaftlichen Anstalten in Berlin', *Humboldt. Schriften zur Anthropologie*, p. 82.
28. Ibid., p. 84.
29. Cf. W. H. Bruford (1975), *The German Tradition of Self-Cultivation. 'Bildung' from Humboldt to Thomas Mann*, Cambridge; cf. also J. Kocka (1987), 'Bürgertum und Bürgerlichkeit als Probleme der deutschen Geschichte vom späten 18. zum frühen 20. Jahrhundert', Kocka (ed.), *Bürger und Bürgerlichkeit im 19. Jahrhundert*, Göttingen, pp. 48–63.
30. Cf. G. Bollenbeck (1994), *Bildung und Kultur. Glanz und Elend eines deutschen Deutungsmusters*, 2nd edn, Frankfurt/M., p. 165.
31. Cf. F. Nietzsche, '[Die Deutschen] sind von vorgestern und übermorgen, sie haben noch kein heute', *Jenseits von Gut und Böse*, *Werke in drei Bänden*, K.

Schlechta (ed.) (1962), 2nd edn, Munich, vol. 2, p. 706. Cf. also M. Weber (1974), *The Protestant Ethic and the Spirit of Capitalism* (trans. R. H. Tawney), London.

32. Goethe (1967), *Werke* (Hamburger Ausgabe), 7th edn, Hamburg, vol. 8, p. 148.
33. Ibid., editor's notes, pp. 650–64.
34. Ibid., p. 141.
35. Goethe (1988), *Sämtliche Werke, Gedichte 1800–1832*, K. Eibl (ed.), Frankfurt/ M., 1. Abteilung, vol. 2, p. 744.
36. *Herweghs Werke in einem Band*, Nationale Forschungs- und Gedenkstätten der klassischen deutschen Literatur (ed.) (1977), Berlin and Weimar, p. 123.
37. Bollenbeck, *Bildung*, p. 199.
38. Cf. H. Plessner (1959), *Die verspätete Nation, über die politische Verführbarkeit bürgerlichen Geistes*, Stuttgart.
39. Quoted from Bollenbeck, *Bildung*, p. 211.
40. Cf. note 13.
41. Stiehl introduced the *Preußische Regulative*, also known as *Stiehlsche Regulative* (1854), which restricted the education of elementary teachers in accordance with narrowly Christian, reactionary and monarchic principles.
42. For this important concept in political culture cf. R. Dahrendorf (1969), *Society and Democracy in Germany*, New York, chap. 20.

TEXTUAL STUDIES

1. Wilhelm von Humboldt, 'Über das Studium des Altertums und des Griechischen insbesondere'

[. . .] Wenn nun irgend eine Vorstellung menschlicher Vollkommenheit Vielseitigkeit und Einheit hervorzubringen im Stande ist, so muß dies diejenige sein, die von dem Begriff der Schönheit und der Vorstellung der sinnlichen ausgeht. Dieser Vorstellungsart zufolge darf es dem moralischen Menschen ebensowenig am richtigen Ebenmaße der
5 einzelnen Charakterseiten mangeln, als einem schönen Gemälde oder einer schönen Statue an dem Ebenmaße ihrer Glieder; und wer, wie der Grieche, mit Schönheit der Formen genährt, und so enthusiastisch wie er für Schönheit und vorzüglich auch für sinnliche gestimmt ist, der muß endlich gegen die moralische Disproportion ein gleich feines Gefühl besitzen, als gegen die physische. Aus allem Gesagten ist also *eine große*
10 *Tendenz der Griechen, den Menschen in der möglichsten Vielseitigkeit und Einheit auszubilden, unleugbar.*
(A. Flitner (ed.) (1984), *Wilhelm von Humboldt. Schriften zur Anthropologie und Bildungslehre*, Frankfurt/M., p. 21)

Commentary

(numbers in parenthesis refer to line numbers in text)

The essay, written in 1793, was published posthumously and would have been accessible to Schiller and his circle. Humboldt wrote in the spirit of neo-classicism, starting from the fashionable concept of beauty and sensuousness (3). By analogy he relates this aesthetic concept to ethical considerations (4–6), suggesting that in order to attain full moral maturity, a person must develop harmoniously and comprehensively. Humboldt ultimately returns to ancient Greece where harmony between versatility and homogeneity was best seen.

Vocabulary

im Stande sein = to be capable of; Vorstellungsart (f) = idea, conception; zufolge = according to; Ebenmaß (n) = symmetry, harmony; Glied (n) = part; gestimmt sein = to be attuned to; unleugbar = undeniable.

2. Wilhelm von Humboldt, 'Die Sprache als Ausdruck eigentümlicher Geistesform'

Das Wort ist freilich insofern ein Zeichen, als es für eine Sache oder einen Begriff gebraucht wird, aber nach der Art seiner Bildung und seiner Wirkung ist es ein eigenes und selbständiges Wesen, ein Individuum; die Summe aller Wörter, die Sprache, ist eine Welt, die zwischen der erscheinenden außer und der wirkenden in uns in der
5   Mitte liegt; sie beruht freilich auf Konvention, insofern sich alle Glieder eines Stammes verstehen, aber die einzelnen Wörter sind zuerst aus dem natürlichen Gefühl des Sprechenden gebildet und durch das ähnliche natürliche Gefühl des Hörenden verstanden worden; das Sprachstudium lehrt daher außer dem Gebrauch der Sprache selbst noch die Analogie zwischen dem Menschen und der Welt im allgemeinen und
10 jeder Nation insbesondere, die sich in der Sprache ausdrückt. [. . .]
   Die Sprache ist nichts anderes als das Kompliment des Denkens, das Bestreben, die äußeren Eindrücke und die noch dunkeln inneren Empfindungen zu deutlichen Begriffen zu erheben und diese zu Erzeugung neuer Begriffe mit einander zu verbinden. (A. Flitner (ed.) (1984), *Wilhelm von Humboldt. Schriften zur Anthropologie und Bildungslehre*, Frankfurt/M., p. 117)

Commentary

(numbers in parenthesis refer to line numbers in text)

Written in 1806 as part of *Latium und Hellas*, this is the first of his contributions towards a philosophy of language. His understanding of language is strongly influenced by Kant and Schelling, but also by Herder. Like Kant, he considers the word as form rather than matter (5), as a living entity. Anticipating the Romantic concept of mediation between subject and object, he understands language as reconciling the outer world and our inmost sensations (7f), thereby enabling communication between individuals, the nation and the universe as a whole (9f). The study of languages is therefore the essence of all *Bildung*, it helps clarify and conceptualize our world-view (11–13).

Vocabulary

erscheinend = appearing; wirkend = acting; Glied (n) = part; Stamm (m) = tribe; Sprachstudium (n) = study of languages; Bestreben (n) = endeavour; Empfindung (f) = sensation; Begriff (m) = concept.

3. Friedrich August Wolf [1807], *Darstellung der Alterthums- Wissenschaft nach Begriff, Umfang Zweck und Werth*, Weinheim, 1986, p. 21f

Den Griechen [. . .] verdanken die Neuern vorzüglich, daß bei ihnen, die das Schöne immer nach dem Nützlichen suchten, nicht alles Wissen wiederum kastenmässig, dass die bessere Cultur nicht gänzlich in den Dienst der Civilisation zurückgewiesen worden, dass sogar verschiedene Studien, die als eine Art von Luxus unbelohnt bleiben müssen,
5   wenigstens niemanden, der auf des Staates Hülfe verzichtet, untersagt werden.

Commentary

Beauty is given priority over utility; knowledge therefore does not 'degenerate' into civilization and is not restricted to a specific social class, but remains available to all those who can afford its luxury.

Vocabulary

Neuern = later generations; kastenmässig = according to a caste system; zurück- gewiesen = returned to; unbelohnt = unrewarded; untersagt = denied.

4. Johann Gottlieb Fichte, *Reden an die deutsche Nation*

Ein Haupterfordernis dieser neuen Nationalerziehung ist es, daß in ihr Lernen und Arbeiten vereinigt sei, daß die Anstalt durch sich selbst sich zu erhalten den Zöglingen wenigstens scheine und daß jeder in dem Bewußtsein erhalten werde, zu diesem Zwecke nach aller seiner Kraft beizutragen. [Dies wird vor allem darum gefordert] [. . .], weil

5 das gegründete Vertrauen, daß man sich stets durch eigene Kraft werde durch die Welt
   bringen können und für seinen Unterhalt keiner fremden Wohltätigkeit bedürfe, zur
   persönlichen Selbständigkeit des Menschen gehört und die sittliche, weit mehr als
   man bis jetzt zu glauben scheint, bedingt. [. . .] Auch in den neuesten Zeiten und bis
   auf diesen Tag ist die Bildung der vermögenden Stände betrachtet worden als eine
10 Privatangelegenheit der Eltern, die sich nach eignem Gefallen einrichten möchten,
   und die Kinder dieser wurden in der Regel nur dazu angeführt, daß sie sich selbst
   einst nützlich würden; die einzige öffentliche Erziehung aber, die des Volkes, war
   lediglich Erziehung zur Seligkeit im Himmel; die Hauptsache war ein wenig
   Christentum und Lesen und, falls es zu erschwingen war, Schreiben, alles um des
15 Christentums willen. Alle andere Entwicklung der Menschen wurde dem ohngefähren
   und blind wirkenden Einflusse der Gesellschaft, in welcher sie aufwuchsen, und dem
   wirklichen Leben selbst überlassen.
   (*Reden*, 10. Rede, Leipzig, 1909, pp. 182, 188f)

Commentary

(numbers in parenthesis refer to line numbers in text)

Fichte recognizes the need to combine teaching with practical work as part of his
national education plan, insisting on a combination of learning and manual work
to give the student the kind of self-fulfilment through work that Rousseau and –
later – Pestalozzi advocated. He endeavours to free education from domination
by social class and the church. (3) read: 'wenigstens [möglich] erscheine', acknowledging the relationship between material and moral independence (5–8), hence
his revolutionary demand for emancipation from capital and church (13–17) and
freedom from parental influence, demands made repeatedly until the 1960s.

Vocabulary

Haupterfordernis (n) = main demand; Anstalt (f) = institution; Zögling (m) = pupil;
Unterhalt (m) = subsistence; nach eigenem Gefallen = as it pleases them; anführen
= to instruct; Seligkeit (f) = salvation; erschwingen = to afford; ohngefähr obs. for
ungefähr = rough.

5. 'Wanders Aufruf zur Gründung des Allgemeinen Deutschen Lehrervereins' [1848]

[. . .] Und darum ergeht an euch, deutsche Lehrer und Jugenderzieher, nun von uns
aus der Aufruf zur Gründung eines Allgemeinen Deutschen Lehrervereins; an euch
alle, die ihr an der Bildung der deutschen Jugend arbeitet; ob ihr dem Kindlein in der
Bewahranstalt die ersten Laute seiner Muttersprache lehrt oder ob ihr mit eurem
5 Zöglinge den Homer und Cicero lest; ob ihr dem Knaben das ABC aufschließt oder

ob ihr den Jüngling in die heiligen Hallen der Wissenschaft einführt. [. . .] Wir treiben Ein Werk, laßt es uns in Einheit treiben, damit es gedeihe! Lasset uns zusammentreten zu dem Allgemeinen Deutschen Lehrerverein! Sein Zweck ist: die Verwirklichung der einigen deutschen Volksschule in ihrem Gesamtorganismus.

(C. L. A. Pretzel (1921), *Geschichte des Deutschen Lehrervereins in den ersten 50 Jahren seines Bestehens*, Leipzig, p. 44)

Commentary

(numbers in parenthesis refer to line numbers in text)

Friedrich Wilhelm Wander (1803–79), a leading promoter of elementary education and disciple of Friedrich Fröbel (1782–1852), founder of nursery education. Primarily an attempt to unite teachers from every sort of school, but – in the spirit of the new German patriotism – also the desire to create one comprehensive education system, from nursery school to university (3–7). As a consequence, the term *Volksschule* (9) refers to a national school for all the people, not – as later – to the school of the ordinary folk.

Vocabulary

ergeht = is passed on to; Aufruf (m) = declaration; Bewahranstalt (f) = nursery school; Zögling (m) = pupil; treiben = to carry out; Zweck (m) = purpose.

2

A Period of Transition: From the Formation of the Empire to the First World War

Introduction

The Humboldtian system with its idealized concept of *Bildung* had suffered its first setbacks in the post-Napoleonic period of political restoration and, again, in the aftermath of the unsuccessful Revolution of 1848; it experienced a crisis after the Franco-Prussian War and Germany's unification (1871). This crisis, from which the system never wholly recovered, had a number of causes:

(a) The establishment of the long-awaited nation state led to new priorities and a new set of values, already foreshadowed in Bismarck's *Realpolitik* and a general shift in ideology, away from Western concepts of liberalism and democracy, towards the more 'tangible' values of political and military success. Whilst the icons of German idealism, Goethe, Schiller, Kant and Humboldt, remained pre-eminent, humanist idealism was rejected on the grounds that it obscured the real needs of the new German nation state.[1] The industrialist Werner von Siemens recounted with some satisfaction that, after the defeat of Denmark (1864) by Prussia and the German Confederation, British and French journals no longer wrote in praise of German scholarship and music or felt indulgent towards unpractical and romantic Germans, but now voiced their hostility towards a militaristic, imperialist and bloodthirsty Germany.[2] Such a change in perception is well illustrated by a comparison between Mme de Staël's admiration of German cultural achievements (1813) and the despair of Ernest Renan (1879) at the loss of German idealism and the rise of a new illiberal regime, poised for war and a demonstration of its national superiority.[3] In similar vein Friedrich Nietzsche also deplored the fact that victory over France had extinguished Germany's humanist spirit, and many German writers on the political right, such as Paul de Lagarde and Fritz Langbehn, agreed that a cultural crisis had caused the degeneration of the educational system, undermining its elitist function and producing an educated barbarism which weakened individual strength through overloading the *Gymnasium*'s curriculum.[4]

(b) The educated classes themselves felt threatened by the impact of British economic liberalism (*Manchestertum*) and by French-inspired socialism. British advances in the natural sciences and the introduction of free trade were viewed as threats; German *Bildung* and philosophy took up a defensive position. The German scientist was induced to practise his skills with the 'trowel of metaphysics' in his hand and it was seen to be essential that the German pharmacist should make up his prescriptions, fully aware of the effect of his actions on the future of the universe.[5] Such an attitude not only led to a rift between the educated German mandarin and the industrial and social elites, it also changed the positive, idealistic outlook of German *Bildung* to a defensive one, safeguarding its own traditions as essentially German and guarding them jealously against attacks from abroad.[6]

As a result, the advocates of *Bildung* found themselves in a reactionary, conservative position, opposing all innovation in industry and society, including the 'democratic principle'. Thomas Mann in his infamous *Betrachtungen eines Unpolitischen* (1918) formulated the issue memorably, even though his own definition, equating political consciousness with 'Halbbildung' (pseudo-education), was outrageous: 'die deutsche Humanität widerstrebt der Politisierung von Grund aus, es fehlt tatsächlich dem deutschen Bildungsbegriff das politische Element'[7] (German humanity is fundamentally opposed to any politicization, the German concept of education has no political element).

Another threat directed against the classical German concept of *Bildung* emerged from within the recently established *Lebensphilosophie*, promoted by Schopenhauer, Bergson and Nietzsche. Rejecting the supremacy of the intellect and its privileged focus on intellectual reflection, it anticipated the demise of the *Bildungsbürgertum* and its claim to uphold the nation's cultural tradition. The newly emerging youth culture in particular challenged the predominance of the intellect over the physical and emotional aspects of human development. In the face of such criticism, the mandarin class attempted to bolster its position. The pedagogue Friedrich Paulsen endorsed the desirability of creating an intellectual aristocracy, consisting of university and *Gymnasium* teachers, theologians, doctors, judges and higher civil servants:

> Im ganzen bilden die Inhaber dieser Berufe eine homogene gesellschaftliche Schicht; sie erkennen sich, eben auf Grund der akademischen Bildung, als sozial Gleichstehende an. [. . .] Umgekehrt: wer keine akademische Bildung hat, dem fehlt in Deutschland etwas, wofür Reichtum und vornehme Geburt nicht vollen Ersatz bieten. [. . .] Und die Folge ist, daß die Erwerbung der akademischen Bildung zu einer Art gesellschaftlicher Notwendigkeit bei uns geworden ist, mindestens die Erwerbung des Abiturienten-zeugnisses, als des potentiellen akademischen Bürgerrechts.[8]

> (As a whole, professional people form a homogeneous social stratum; they recognize each other as social equals on the basis of their academic education. [. . .] Conversely: those without an academic education in Germany are being deprived of something for which wealth and noble birth cannot fully compensate. [. . .] As a consequence, the

acquisition of an academic education, at the very least the acquisition of the *Abitur* certificate, has become some kind of social necessity for us, a potential form of civil rights.)

Such a lofty definition of the mandarin class cannot disguise the fact that the holders of academic titles were under serious social and economic threat. They attempted to safeguard their position by joining the bandwagon of nationalist pride and imperialist ambition, symbolized in the massive Imperial Navy, and earning themselves the nickname 'Flottenprofessoren' (navy professors).[9] Increasingly more nationalist and anti-socialist, they saw themselves as the bulwark of the nation's culture, as *Kulturträger* (upholders of culture); their *Alldeutscher Verband* (Pan-Germanic League) excluded Jewish and other ethnically 'suspect' candidates from holding university chairs. At the outbreak of the First World War, with almost one voice, they celebrated the victory of nationalist sentiment over party politics. Their many chauvinistic speeches, known collectively as 'the Ideas of 1914',[10] unequivocally yoked German culture to the warmongering political and military leadership. Even relatively liberal-minded mandarins, such as Werner Sombart, succumbed to this atmosphere, comparing the German hero to the degenerate British grocer, the unfortunate victim of civilization, commerce and utilitarianism.[11]

At the end of the war, Allied attacks on German culture and the rapid deterioration in their social and economic position served to reinforce the mandarins' reactionary, anti-democratic spirit, with most of them strongly supporting monarchist, conservative political parties. The catastrophic deterioration in the social standing of the salaried classes during the period of high inflation, combined with the poor outlook for the funding of higher education, further alienated them from the Republic: a review of Oswald Spengler's *Der Untergang des Abendlandes* (The Decline of the West) exemplifies this attitude: 'Das Abendland geht unter, wenn es keine Dienstboten mehr gibt, wenn das Dienen als unwürdig gilt, wenn alle soziale Schichtung durch eine zugunsten des Strebens nach oben atomisierte Gesellschaft ersetzt wird.'[12] (The Western world is doomed if there is to be no servant class, if service is considered degrading, if all social stratification is to be replaced by an upwardly mobile atomized society.) The mandarins jealously guarded their social status, H. von Treitschke's comment 'keine Kultur ohne Dienstmädchen'[13] (no culture without a maid servant) being observed almost literally [Text 1].

Such pronouncements from the 1920s recall observations made during the cultural crisis of the 1890s, but with a nationalist, anti-democratic tone that had become shriller and more hysterical. By 1910, the liberal sociologist Alfred Weber was deploring the demise of traditional humanist culture in the face of conservative opportunism and *Realpolitik*.[14] Attempts by the mandarin class to 'correct' this decline in idealism can now be analysed, together with an examination of the development of technological and vocational education in the wake of German industrialization.

The Rise of the *Geisteswissenschaften*

Although influenced by J. S. Mill's *Logic* (1843), the *Geisteswissenschaften* are a specifically German phenomenon which, by the end of the nineteenth century, had overtaken the natural sciences and positivism in particular. At the same time, an effort was made to free this new discipline from metaphysical speculation and from the dominance of Hegelian idealism. Wilhelm Dilthey's *Einleitung in die Geisteswissenschaften* (1883) attempted to distinguish it from the natural sciences, stressing its anthropocentric, historical dimension and specifying in its definition a considerable measure of culture, with the aim of understanding rather than merely explaining our human environment. Dilthey wanted to accentuate the importance of 'Menschheit' and therefore attempted to describe, assess, and form judgements and concepts.[15] He referred specifically to hermeneutics,[16] to the need for positing the subject itself within the process of the investigation. It is within this general framework that *Geisteswissenschaften* were claimed to be the essential discipline for the scholarly pursuit of the arts and humanities. In contrast to natural sciences, they did not aim to be objective and to distance themselves from the subject under investigation, but accepted that it must first of all evoke our 'interest', our personal involvement in the subject-matter. One important attraction of Dilthey's method lay in his reinterpretation of history and nineteenth-century historicism in such a manner that the study of history could be integrated into the contemporary modern world, thereby liberating it from the blight of 'antiquarian' stagnation.[17]

A more problematic facet developed from the subjective nature of this discipline: once experience and interest were recognized as legitimate forces, the emergence of a specifically German *Weltanschauung* followed. This reinforced the nationalist, conservative and monarchist anti-democratic profile of the mandarin. Dilthey himself was not completely free of these tendencies: at the height of the *Schulstreit* (1890) he employed his criticism of natural sciences to inveigh against the general principles of the French Revolution and against socialism and democracy in particular[18] [Text 2 a]. Such observations do not belittle Dilthey's immense contribution to the development of a new epistemological awareness of the human dimension in the modernist search for truth claims, but they cannot be ignored in any broad analysis of the specifically German aspects of education. They contributed towards the establishment of a so-called German tradition of culture and, in particular, its exaggerated nationalism.

A second new discipline, *Kulturwissenschaften*, emerged, combining the arts, history, literature and the new *Lebensphilosophie* in a bid to define a specifically

German tradition. This discipline, initiated by the Neo-Kantian school and supported by Dilthey and Simmel, was eventually incorporated into the school curriculum as *Kulturkunde*, an integrated study of German language, literature, history, religion, geography and civics.[19] The German Youth Movement, imbued with a desire for a new beginning, a re-evaluation of all things German, made its own contribution towards growing nationalism, moving German *Bildung* further out of line with its Western neighbours. It contributed towards the retreat from modernism and affirmed its admiration for 'healthy heroism', for a nostalgic return to some rural, pre-industrialized *Heimat*.[20]

The Impact of Industrialization on the German Education System

The dramatic changes in Germany's economic and social structure after the unification of 1871 are well known. One or two examples will suffice to illustrate this development: between 1875 and 1915 the German population rose from 42.5 to 68 million, compared to an equivalent French expansion from 36.2 to 39.2 million.[21] While the agricultural workforce declined from 44 per cent to 32 per cent during the same period, not least as a result of rapid agricultural modernization, the industrial workforce continued to grow. Heavy industry provides a good example: in 1846, the Prussian state produced less coal than would have been needed to keep London's hearths burning; by 1910 the German *Reich* was producing more steel than France and Britain combined.[22] Expansion in the 'new' chemical and electrical industries was even more dramatic, with Germany gaining a virtual world monopoly.

The education system had to respond to these changes. The elementary school system, in particular, reacted in a very positive manner, to the extent that Prussia's victory over Austria in 1866 was said to have been achieved thanks to the superiority of Prussian schoolmasters.[23] We have seen how a reform movement, born in the spirit of Pestalozzi and fostered by Diesterweg, was halted by the *Stiehlsche Regulative* (1854). The class-room became once more an instrument for the education of subjects, not citizens, and religious instruction, loyalty to the crown, and secular Protestant virtues such as diligence, industriousness and discipline were judged of paramount importance. However, even if the liberal spirit of the 1848 Revolution had been defeated, the teachers' professional ethos was not destroyed. The educational legacy of Johann Friedrich Herbart (1776–1841) now came into its own, in an appropriate response to the new, post-revolutionary realism.

Although he was a contemporary of Humboldt, Herbart's philosophy was more rational and adaptable to the age of industrialization and early positivism:

Das Interesse geht aus von interessanten *Gegenständen und Beschäftigungen*. Durch den *Reichtum* derselben entsteht das *vielseitige* Interesse. Ihn herbeizuschaffen und gehörig darzubringen, ist die Sache des UNTERRICHTS, welcher die Vorarbeit, die von *Erfahrung und Umgang* herrührt, fortsetzt und ergänzt.[24]

(Interest is aroused by interesting *objects and activities*. The wealth of these *riches* in turn leads to *varied* interests. Their production and proper presentation is a matter for INSTRUCTION, continuing and completing the preparation which itself stems from *experience and familiarity*.)

The subjective, individualistic approach of Humboldt's idealism yielded to a more objective, practical framework, in which the curriculum played a major role. As a carefully organized curriculum could lead a young person to maturation, so the same principle, it was felt, could apply to society. Herbart approached education from two directions: firstly, by psychological means based on empirical studies, changing perceptions into reflective apperceptions and thereby directing human willpower within a predetermined *Gedankenkreis* (intellectual horizon). The second approach operated within a more normative, ethical framework, based on existing moral convention. This dual track produced a form of education based on instruction.[25] Herbart's followers transformed this philosophy into a system, the 'Formalstufentheorie', a formal framework, based on a curriculum which would support the political and social aspirations of the age. Although this new system was somewhat removed from Herbart's pedagogy, devised for individual tuition rather than the class-room, it served to restore a professional ethos to elementary teaching whilst at the same time supporting the vital tenets of the new industrialized German state. Coming under attack by the end of the century for a lack of originality and spontaneity, the system was superseded by a more subjective method which challenged society's conventions and values. Nevertheless, its contribution to the development of a new vocational concept of education was significant, giving rise to a general debate on its role in a modern industrialized society. In addition, Herbart was one of the first pedagogues to criticize the *Gymnasium* for its one-sided humanist pursuit of the classics, questioning the value of philology and advocating more emphasis on science and general knowledge within the syllabus.[26]

The Emergence of Vocational Education

Vocational education gained prominence during the second half of the nineteenth century, which witnessed a general change from the idealism and humanism of Humboldt and Hegel towards a new realism, manifested not only in liberal capitalism, but also in the Marxist view that man was the product of his environment. In general, this new realism gave pride of place to the 'object' and saw the subject as determined by objects. Friedrich Theodor Vischer's formula of the 'Tücke des Objekts'[27] (the duplicity of the object) is a good example, suggesting that we are moulded by the independent 'life' of the objects around us. Within such an environment the *Gymnasium* lost much of its prestige and, at university level, the faculty of philosophy lost ground to the positive sciences. *Realien* were now in demand, subjects with a vocational application, useful in 'real' life.

It was in this climate that vocational training regained its former position and became renowned for its typical German method of organization. Its origins can be traced back to the Sunday School movement of sixteenth- and seventeenth-century Württemberg, guiding a young man through the period from the end of elementary school education to adulthood, with a broad curriculum of general subjects. Later, basic crafts were added, together with German, history, geography and mathematics. From the late eighteenth century on, wealthy benefactors expressed an interest in improving the lot of the working man. The *Handelsschule* (trade school) came into being, with tuition moving from Sundays to weekday evenings. Instruction of between six to eight hours per week lasted for up to three years and eventually included some technical subjects. With the establishment of the German *Reich* (1871), *Gewerbefreiheit* (freedom of trade) was extended, a blow to the traditional craft training conducted by the guilds. The *Reich*'s new trade laws removed all restrictions: apprentices could now be taken on by anyone and their training lost its skilled craftsman status. As a result, the position of craftsmen deteriorated and they were no longer distinguishable from skilled or even semi-skilled factory workers. In the face of this decline their progressive, liberal attitude, a vital component of the 1848 Revolution and a contributory factor to the development of a trade union movement in the 1860s, now began to give way to a more conservative, even reactionary outlook. In common with the mandarin class, they, too, felt their status was threatened. In seeking to dissociate themselves from the growing class of factory workers, they came to be seen as potential allies in the fight against socialism. The *Handwerkerschutzgesetz* (trade protection law) of 1879 sought to re-establish the position of craftsmen. It became the cornerstone for a new type of vocational training and the Munich pedagogue Georg Kerschensteiner (1854–1932) can be seen as its progenitor.

Kerschensteiner's shaping of these schools falls within the period after 1901. He remains a controversial figure whose theories are indebted to the German humanist tradition, but also to certain aspects of the Youth Movement with its occasionally anti-industrial and even pre-fascist elements. Kerschensteiner is seen both as the founder of the German *Arbeitsschule* (activity school) and as an innovator in the dual education *Berufsschulsystem* (system of vocational education). His influential prize-winning essay bore the title 'Wie ist unsere männliche Jugend von der Entlassung aus der Volksschule bis zum Eintritt in den Heeresdienst am zweckmäßigsten für die staatsbürgerliche Gesellschaft zu erziehen?' (1901) (How can we best educate our young men for citizenship in the years between the end of elementary school and conscription?). He highlights a primary concern with moral and political issues and the specific fear that these young men may fall prey to socialism.[28] But, such fears apart, Kerschensteiner displays some ignorance of democratic political culture. More important to him than intellectual education is moral training. Physical work should be undertaken cheerfully as a service to the community; the aims of the individual should coincide with those of the state,[29] while political decisions remain the prerogative of political leaders. The apprentice must be guided to maturity via secondary virtues such as discipline, obedience and industriousness:

> Der Wert unserer Schulerziehung, soweit sie die großen Volksmassen genießen, beruht im wesentlichen weniger auf der Ausbildung des Gedankenkreises als vielmehr in der konsequenten Erziehung zu fleißiger, gewissenhafter, gründlicher, sauberer Arbeit, in der stetigen Gewöhnung zu unbedingtem Gehorsam und treuer Pflichterfüllung.[30]

> (The value of our education, in as far as the greater mass of the people will benefit from it, resides basically not so much in the development of an intellectual horizon, as in consistent instruction in conscientious, thorough, neat work, in the regular habits of absolute obedience and the faithful performance of duty.)

Paradoxically, such authoritarian, undemocratic views existed alongside more enlightened, practical and pragmatic considerations. Kerschensteiner had gained an insight into vocational education by visiting training centres in Austria and Switzerland. He sought to improve on these by including an element of general education and insisting on parity between academic and practical or technical education up to the age of fifteen and demanding compulsory attendance at vocational classes for another two or three years. In addition to their specific technical training, apprentices were given a broad, general education in civics, law, German, religion, hygiene and gymnastics, and also in commerce. Practical workshop training was to be the basis for the acquisition of all theoretical and general knowledge, intended for genuine self-education. A partnership was forged between schools and trade associations, which provided teachers from their master craftsmen or skilled workers, whilst the municipality financed school buildings, teachers' salaries, tools and machinery. Vocational education gradually moved into the working day, but in such a way as to cause the least inconvenience to the employer.

Practical education for girls took slightly longer to develop. By 1896 elementary schools had already introduced an optional eighth class where pupils received instruction in housekeeping, dressmaking, child-care, nutrition and other practical skills. In addition to these subjects, religion, hygiene and domestic book-keeping were introduced as compulsory subjects in the post-elementary school curriculum. Kerschensteiner's education programme was based on the theory that a women's responsibility was child-rearing, creating a good home and holding the family together. The stereotype of the three Ks ('Küche, Kinder, Kirche') owes much to Kerschensteiner's philosophy.

Much of Kerschensteiner's system of dual education still exists and some of the subsequent changes will be covered in later chapters. His system undoubtedly enhanced the status of crafts, trade and industry in Germany, but at the same time, some of its weaknesses still remain. Much of the actual specialist training, with its origins in a pre-industrial era, renders its vocational element of limited use in a modern high-tech age.[31] In particular, the belief that character building can be based on a system which subjects the individual to the wider authority of a hierarchical state system has had disastrous consequences: it not only reinforced the social differentiation between the intellectually talented and the less intellectually able but vocationally gifted children, but also diminished an individual's right to democratic self-determination. Kerschensteiner's subordination of the individual to state authority was, therefore, all too easily applied not only in Wilhelminian Germany, but also during the Third Reich, with some vestiges of this authoritarian attitude persisting into post-war German vocational training.

Education for Women: Reluctant Moves towards Equality in Education

As research in this area has been slow to develop, the image of women within the German education system has long suffered from the stereotyping of German women as being generally less emancipated than elsewhere. Whilst this perception cannot be entirely denied, it should also be recognized that a significant female emancipation movement, opposed to the traditionalist stance of the mandarin establishment, did exist. It should be viewed alongside the other modernist movement of the time, the emancipatory Youth Movement.

The initial impetus for women's education had arisen following the 1848 Revolution, alongside the demand for universal general education. Founded by Louise Otto-Peters, the *Allgemeiner Deutscher Frauenverein* took up these earlier demands, advocating access to vocational work and higher education for women in its programme.[32] Helene Lange and Gertrud Bäumer were of major importance within the field of women's education. Employing a strategy which emphasized feminine cultural values and the woman's role within the family and society, they succeeded in interesting a wider audience in the topic, gaining the support of influential groups in education and medicine. The *Frauenverein*'s 1872 conference in Weimar formulated ideas which, though hardly worthy of consideration in a modern feminist campaign, nevertheless prepared the ground for later reforms and looked to strengthen the role of women teachers [Text 3]. A strong impetus for women's equality in secondary education came from central and southern Germany, mainly from Baden, Hesse, Saxony and Württemberg, and from private schools in Prussia. Based on an initiative supported by the crown-princess, the daughter of Queen Victoria, the Berlin *Viktoria Lyzeum* offered special training for women teachers, as well as courses in Latin and mathematics, subjects not normally taught at state schools for women. Until 1908 the syllabus at girls' schools was still rather restricted, focusing on ethics and a general development of taste and style, to the exclusion of grammar, chemistry and most other sciences. Helene Lange organized special preparatory courses for women who wanted to take advantage of the more favourable opportunities for study in Switzerland (1889); she also founded an important pressure group, the *Allgemeiner Deutscher Lehrerinnenverein* (1890).

The fight for a woman's right to take the *Abitur* was of particular importance. This was achieved by 1908, when the *Lyzeum* curriculum was expanded to include courses corresponding to those of the existing *Gymnasium*, *Realgymnasium* and *Oberrealschule*.[33] In addition an *Oberlyzeum* was introduced to cater specifically for the vocational training of women teachers, and the teaching of home economics and social work [Text 4]. By then the ratio of women to men at the top end of the secondary sector was still approximately one to three. Professional opportunities were still subject to sexual discrimination: school leavers from the *Lyzeum* and *Oberlyzeum* were qualified to teach only in women's schools and to teach only art and home economics as well as to become middle-grade librarians; university entrance was restricted to the faculty of philosophy. Co-education during the last stage of secondary education had been adopted in the more progressive states by the beginning of the century; in Prussia it was permitted only after 1914.

The Impact of Technology and Commerce on Secondary and Higher Education

By the end of the century, Germany's educational system could no longer ignore the growing demands of industry. The established Humboldtian system had allied itself increasingly with the entrenched mandarin culture of the civil service and the army, whilst the 'newcomers', though far from being recent creations, were viewed with suspicion. We have already noted mandarin hostility to free trade and socialist positivism. Dilthey's polemics against the new scientific spirit are only one example amongst many. Even the newly crowned Kaiser Wilhelm II felt compelled to intervene in the debate, which became known as the *Schulstreit* (1890) (school dispute).[34] Once criticized for overloading its syllabus with too much material, the *Gymnasium*, was now accused of neglecting the 'national heritage',[35] of not concentrating sufficiently on German essay-writing, on national history and geography. The Kaiser, influenced by new trends in philosophy, particularly

Nietzsche's criticism of the *Gymnasium*, called for less erudition and more physical education and 'character building' in order to improve the quality of his officer class:

> Bedenken Sie, was uns für ein Nachwuchs für die Landesvertheidigung erwächst. [. . .], die Männer sollen nicht durch Brillen die Welt ansehen, sondern mit eigenen Augen und Gefallen finden an dem, was sie vor sich haben, ihrem Vaterlande und seinen Einrichtungen.[36]

> (Imagine what kind of new blood we will recruit for our national defence. [. . .], these men must not view the world through spectacles, but with their own eyes, and they must like what they see: their fatherland and its institutions.)

As a result of the dispute, the classics were whittled down, in particular Greek with its democratic and anti-Christian associations.[37] The German essay was to be the favoured subject, along with German history, notably that of the Hohenzollerns.[38]

Although the dispute favoured a more technologically orientated education, this came about more by default than by intention. Nationalist pressure, although directed against the spirit of Humboldt, still sought to retain the privileges of the *Berechtigungswesen* and the selection of children from the academic elites for university education.[39] At the same time, the *Gymnasium*'s rivals benefited from the new climate. Since gaining official recognition in Prussia in 1832, the *Realschule* had concentrated on instruction in German, French, mathematics, natural sciences, history and geography. As its leaving certificate did not qualify its holder for university entrance, nor for access to the middle strata of the civil service, it remained undervalued until the 1860s, managing to challenge the *Gymnasium*'s monopoly only when Latin was compulsorily introduced into its curriculum. It was subsequently renamed *Realgymnasium*. The 'domino effect' of this change led to a gap in the 'market' and the creation of a new type of school, the *Oberrealschule*. It did not include Latin in its syllabus and did not offer the *Abitur*.

The obvious need for engineering and technical education, as well as the rivalry between *Gymnasium* and *Realgymnasium*, benefited this new type of school. At the 1890 Schools' Conference in Kassel, the new Kaiser promoted it, as more active in its support for the national ideal and more vigorous in its opposition to socialism. By 1900, the three types of school received equal status, although university entrance still required Latin for all subjects except the natural sciences and mathematics. The mandarin faction, supporters of the humanist *Gymnasium*, were reduced to fighting a rearguard action, still insisting on the primacy of classical languages and the inculcation of discipline and logical thought as a status symbol for the Prussian civil service.[40] Despite this campaign, the demands of technology and industry were being met; the efficiency of German industry was guaranteed and with it 'Deutschlands Weltstellung in Frieden und Krieg'[41] (Germany's world position in peace and war).

The settlement of the *Schulstreit* saw defeat for the mandarins and victory for the champions of industry and commerce. The latter had changed in attitude from being the party of the Enlightenment and liberal ·democracy to being advocates of the monarchy and of imperialism; they had become politically acceptable. A considerable expansion in secondary education occurred, benefiting almost exclusively the new types of school and favouring the new social class of the bourgeoisie.[42]

Similar developments can be observed in higher education. The incentive came from that temple of positivism, the Paris *Ecole Polytechnique*, established towards the end of the eighteenth century. A generation later, similar institutions were introduced in Germany, but the level to which they aspired was not significantly higher than that of the existing trade schools. Berlin, Karlsruhe, Munich and Dresden witnessed the first of these foundations in the 1820s. Rapid industrialization after 1870 changed the outlook for technology within German higher education. At the Philadelphia World Exhibition in 1876, German products were still seen as cheap and badly made[43] and, in an effort to remedy this, technological education received a boost. The trademark 'made in Germany', introduced in Britain in 1887 as a method of discrimination, was soon to prove a sign of excellence, helping to outsell rival British products.[44] Amongst the new technological institutes, Karlsruhe was the first to gain university status. By 1899 all *Technische Hochschulen* were given the right to award doctorates in technological subjects, the acid test for university status in Germany (figure 5). And yet, by the end of the century, only 11 per cent of students were attending this type of institution, a majority of whom had come from the *Realgymnasium* or the *Oberrealschule*, indicating a background closer to the new industrial and commercial middle classes than to the traditional academic strata.

There were, at the same time, two further important developments: with the rise of the *Technische Hochschule* a gap was emerging in the education and training of technical experts below the rank of professional engineer, and the newly emerging *Fachschulen* rapidly filled this void. However, such was the reputation of general education, that even technical schools had to fall in line and include an element of general education. Max Maria von Weber, a leading railway engineer, stated the case. Maintaining that a fully trained engineer could only be grafted onto a fully developed person, he asserted:

Erzieht ganze Menschen, die an allgemeiner Bildung und Lebensform auf der Höhe des Völkerlebens [. . .] stehen, und macht aus ihnen dann Techniker – das ist das ganze Geheimnis und die alleinige Lösung des Problems.[45]

Figure 5 The *Technische Hochschule* Dresden (1870s). The machine room here illustrates the high level of expertise in electrical subjects attained by several such German *Technische Hochschulen*.

(Educate the whole person, who has reached [. . .] the peak of human perfection in terms of education and manners, and then turn him into a technical expert – this is the whole secret and the only solution to the problem.)

Technological education followed this Humboldtian principle well into the twentieth century and it is difficult to say whether the proximity of vocational and general education has been of benefit to society; the expansion of technological education and its associated practical skills in Wilhelminian Germany and since would suggest that it has. The predominance of a mandarin culture within the system as a whole would seem to indicate that the true driving force behind such a dual approach was the desire for status.

The Emerging Youth Movement and its Challenge to Education

It has already been seen that the traditional educational system was increasingly taking up a defensive stance against industrialization, positivism and the modernist movement of the declining century. The *Schulstreit*, though encouraging new forms of secondary education, ultimately failed to reduce the unwieldy syllabus and to allow young minds to develop freely. Paulsen was only one of many to criticize the *Gymnasium*'s syllabus for failing to promote logical argument, sensitivity, common sense and intellectual concentration.[46] A generation earlier, Nietzsche had already criticized the instrumentalist character of grammar school education, for channelling pupils into the civil service and contributing to the decline in humanist culture.[47] In many contemporary novels and plays the *Gymnasium* was castigated as a 'cramming school', a place for mechanical learning and authoritarian drilling, totally insensitive to the unique quality of young minds [Text 5].

The emerging youth culture reacted against such a suppression of individuality. The *Wandervogel* movement and the teaching of Gustav Wyneken are of particular interest. Whatever their shortcomings, they advocated the right of young people to independence, in a separate environment to that of adults, and, anticipating the findings of Freud, Wilhelm Reich and Erich Fromm, they introduced an awareness of the psychological sensitivity of adolescence. A comprehensive study of these movements, their history and fragmentation cannot be included here.[48] The general direction was towards opposition: opposition to Wilhelminian authoritarianism and militarism, to excessive drinking and loutish patriotism in student fraternities,[49] and to modernist tendencies in the new urban and industrial society. A broadly middle-class, Protestant movement, with centres in Berlin-Brandenburg, Thuringia, Lower Saxony and Hesse, the *Wandervogel* movement was both nostalgic and utopian, celebrating simple country life and folklore while working for the development of the individual within free communities.

Sociologists such as Ferdinand Tönnies contrasted industrial society with the rural community where the traditional values of friendship, family commitment, spontaneity and an inner 'warmth' were cultivated, values which were doomed in a modern, industrialized, urban society.[50] But while Tönnies, Georg Simmel and Max Weber employed critical analysis which afforded some kind of reconciliation with modernity, and were sympathetic towards the aspirations of the new working-class associations, the various leaders of the *Wandervogel* failed to appreciate the social complexities of a highly industrialized system, ultimately playing into the hands of extreme political parties. Following the patriotic Romanticism of *Turnvater* Jahn and rejecting the tradition of the Enlightenment, they inevitably drifted towards the Conservative Revolution and manifested an anti-intellectual, sentimental yearning for *Volksgemeinschaft* (ethnic community). Their essentially anti-semitic and anti-Catholic stance and an uneasy relationship with the working class led to the emergence of Jewish, Catholic and even left-wing splinter groups, though their influence was not much felt until after the war.

The pedagogical value of the movement, though perhaps not particularly out-standing, lies in its surprisingly modernist, emancipatory nature. It generated a general shake-up of the authoritarian, unimaginative, rigid school system and was part of an international movement opposed to an adult-centred stultified, pater-nalistic and sterile regime. As with many freedom movements, it tended to overshoot its original target and veered towards fundamentalism, thereby jeopardizing its own objectives. Several important pedagogues emerged from within its ranks, amongst them Ludwig Gurlitt, a teacher at the Steglitz *Gymnasium* where the whole movement had begun. He called for self-education and the development of the whole personality. In similar vein, Hermann Lietz developed the *Landerzie-hungsheim*, a concept based on the English school at Abbotsholme, designed to bring teacher and pupil more closely together and to encourage self-discipline, individual responsibility and leadership amongst his students.[51] The project of *Schülerselbstverwaltung*, student-centred self-government in schools, associated with Karl Wilker, incorporated American concepts of self-government, and was also influenced by ideas from Fichte and German Pietism. This project, in typically German fashion, was not so much directed towards the development of a democratic spirit, but concentrated on the rehabilitation of children with psychological or social problems. The Berlin *Lindenhof* became a centre for this reform programme, but – typical of the spirit of the whole Youth Movement – it collapsed on the departure of its founder.

Perhaps the most important stimulus from within the Youth Movement emerged with Gustav Wyneken. His own rather eclectic philosophy, indebted to Kant's idealism and Schopenhauer's voluntarism, as well as to Hegel's objective spirit, is of minor importance. It did, however, contribute to his belief in youth for youth's sake, defining adolescence, the age group from fourteen to twenty-one, as the third 'Septernium':

> Jugend ist nicht lediglich Vorbereitungszeit, sondern sie hat ihren eignen unersetzlichen Wert, ihre eigene Schönheit und infolgedessen auch das Recht auf eigenes Leben, auf die Möglichkeit der Entfaltung ihrer besonderen Art.[52]

> (Youth is not a mere period of preparation, it has its own unique value, its own beauty and consequently also the right to a life of its own, unfolding in its own way.)

Wyneken was the critical mind behind a declaration at the Hohe Meisner Meeting (1913), often seen as the climax of the Youth Movement and its last stand against *völkisch* nationalist ideas. He put his ideas into practice at the *Freie Schulgemeinde Wickersdorf* (Wickersdorf Free Community School), where pupils and teachers adopted the pseudo-medieval principle of *Gefolgschaft* (retinue), based on mutual commitment, comradeship and group loyalty. Critical of family ties and religion, the community nurtured a tacit homoeroticism, based on the conceptual framework of Freudian psychoanalysis, further developed by the Austrian psychologist Siegfried Bernfeld whose early publications Wyneken endorsed. The young Bernfeld and his Vienna circle influenced the periodical *Der Anfang*, published by Wyneken and written for students in secondary education. This relatively innocuous periodical aroused the fury of Catholics and Conservatives alike. It was denounced by parliamentarians within the Catholic *Zentrum* Party in Bavaria, Baden and Prussia, and by the conservative Berlin *Kreuzzeitung*, with accusations of revolutionary and subversive tendencies, of anti-clerical prejudice and of an anti-authoritarian, anti-nationalist ethos.[53] The young Walter Benjamin was a regular contributor, advocating the emancipation of young people in every sphere: 'Die Jugend [. . .] ist das Dornröschen, das schläft und den Prinzen nicht ahnt, der naht, es zu befreien.'[54] (Youth [. . .] is the Sleeping Beauty, unaware of the Prince, whose approach heralds liberation.) The periodical's intention was to arouse in young people a certain degree of awareness and intellectual appreciation, as a prelude to emancipation. The revolutionary aspect of such a platform was confirmed by the authority of the state itself: Bernfeld was accused of contravening the Austrian Penal Code by offending against 'die Einrichtungen der Ehe, der Familie oder der Rechtsbegriffe über das Eigentum'[55] (the institutions of marriage, the family or the legal status of property).

The outbreak of the First World War halted this emancipatory movement, crushing it under an overwhelming avalanche of chauvinism and war fever. Chapter 3 will consider to what extent it survived the war and how it influenced both the republican and the fascist elements in youth culture between 1919 and 1933.

Notes

1. Cf. statements by H. Baumgarten and J. Fröbel et al. in G. Bollenbeck (1994), *Bildung und Kultur. Glanz und Elend eines deutschen Deutungsmusters*, 2nd edn, Frankfurt/M., p. 236.
2. W. von Siemens (1893), *Lebenserinnerungen*, Berlin, p. 168.
3. Cf. H.-J. Hahn (1995), *German Thought and Culture. From the Holy Roman Empire to the Present Day*, Manchester, chap. 5.
4. Cf. F. Nietzsche (1962), *Werke in drei Bänden*, K. Schlechta (ed.), 2nd edn, Munich, vol. 1, p. 137; P. de Lagarde (1891), *Deutsche Schriften*, Göttingen, pp. 93f; J. Langbehn (1890), *Rembrandt als Erzieher. Von einem Deutschen*, 33rd edn, Leipzig, p. 248.
5. F. A. Lange [1866], *Geschichte des Materialismus und Kritik seiner Bedeutung in der Gegenwart*, Frankfurt/M. 1974, vol. 2, p. 535.
6. Cf. N. Elias (1992), *Studien über die Deutschen, Machtkämpfe und Habitusentwicklung im 19. und 20. Jahrhundert*, Frankfurt/M., pp. 61–6.
7. T. Mann (1956), *Stockholmer Gesamtausgabe*, Frankfurt/M., vol. 12, p. 103.
8. F. Paulsen (1902), *Die deutschen Universitäten und das Universitätsstudium*, Berlin, pp. 149f.
9. F. K. Ringer (1969), *The Decline of the German Mandarins, The German Academic Community 1890–1933*, Cambridge, Mass., pp. 139f.
10. Ibid., pp. 181f.
11. Ibid., pp. 183f.
12. G. von Below (1926), *Einleben in die Verfassung oder Verfassungsänderung*, Langensalza, p. 40.
13. Quoted from Bollenbeck, *Bildung*, p. 241.
14. A. Weber (1927), *Ideen zur Staats- und Kultursoziologie*, Karlsruhe, p. 76.
15. W. Dilthey (1958), *Gesammelte Werke*, 2nd edn, Stuttgart, vol. 7, pp. 79–81.
16. Cf. Chapter 1, p. 8.
17. Cf. Nietzsche's criticism of the 'antiquarischer Sinn', Nietzsche, *Werke*, vol. 1, p. 227.
18. W. Dilthey [1900], *Über die Möglichkeit einer allgemeingültigen pädagogischen Wissenschaft*, H. Nohl (ed.), Weinheim, pp. 85f.
19. Cf. Ringer, *Decline*, p. 312. By 1912 experiencing a further semantic modification as *Deutschkunde*, cf. W. Hofstaetter (1930), in *Sachwörterbuch der Deutschkunde*, Leipzig and Berlin, vol. 1, pp. 236f.
20. Cf. R. Hammann, J. Hermand (1973), *Stilkunst um 1900. Epochen deutscher Kultur von 1870 bis zur Gegenwart*, Munich, vol. 4, pp. 102–20 and 150–76.
21. For an excellent survey of German developments cf. C. Berg (ed.) (1991), *Handbuch der deutschen Bildungsgeschichte*, Munich, vol. 4, pp. 33–40 and

B. R. Mitchell (1992), *International Historical Statistics, Europe 1750–1988*, 3rd edn, New York.

22. Ringer, *Decline*, p. 43.
23. G. Büchmann (1912), *Geflügelte Worte*, 25th edn, Berlin, p. 534. For a fuller debate cf. K. A. Schleunes (1989), *Schooling and Society. The Politics of Education in Prussia and Bavaria 1750–1900*, Oxford, pp. 160f.
24. J. F. Herbart (1887), *Sämtliche Werke*, K. Kehrbach et al. (eds), Langensalza, vol. 2, p. 35.
25. Ibid., p. 10.
26. F. Paulsen (1921), *Geschichte des gelehrten Unterrichts*, 3rd edn, Berlin and Leipzig, vol. 2, pp. 551–3.
27. F. T. Vischer (1920), *Dichterische Werke*, 2nd edn, Munich, vol. 1, pp. 14–27.
28. Cf. H. Blankertz (1982), *Die Geschichte der Pädagogik von der Aufklärung bis zur Gegenwart*, Wetzlar, p. 208.
29. G. Kerschensteiner (1911), *Der Begriff der Arbeitsschule* (Lecture of 1911). Quoted from A. Reble (1992), *Geschichte der Pädagogik, Dokumentationsband*, 2nd edn, Stuttgart, pp. 524f.
30. Quoted from G. Wehle (1964), *Praxis und Theorie im Lebenswerke Georg Kerschensteiners*, 2nd edn, Weinheim, vol. 1, p. 34.
31. On the imbalance between training and industrial need cf. P. Raggatt, 'Quality Control in the Dual System of West Germany', in D. Phillips (ed.) (1995), *Education in Germany, Tradition and Reform in Historical Context*, London and New York, p. 194.
32. L. Otto-Peters [1865], 'Das erste Vierteljahrhundert des Allgemeinen Deutschen Frauenvereins', quoted from Berg (ed.), *Handbuch*, vol. 4, p. 280.
33. Berg (ed.), *Handbuch*, vol. 4, pp. 286f.
34. Cf. L. von Friedeburg (1992), *Bildungsreform in Deutschland*, Frankfurt/M., pp. 185–8.
35. O. von Bismarck (1932), 'Erinnerung und Gedanke', *Die gesammelten Werke*, 2nd edn, Leipzig, vol. 15, p. 5.
36. Quoted from Friedeburg, *Bildungsreform*, p. 186.
37. Cf. Blankertz, *Geschichte*, p. 168.
38. Cf. M. Kraul (1984), *Das deutsche Gymnasium 1780–1980*, Frankfurt/M., chap. 4.
39. Over half the students at Tübingen University between 1873 and 1877 came from an academic background. In Prussia between 1875 and 1899 22 per cent of *Gymnasium* graduates came from an academic background; the corresponding figure for the *Realgymnasium* was 7 per cent and for the *Oberrealschule* 4 per cent (Ringer, *Decline*, p. 40).
40. Cf. Friedeburg, *Bildungsreform*, pp. 192f.

41. Verein deutscher Ingenieure, quoted from E. Glöckner (1976), *Schulreform im preußischen Imperialismus*, Glashütten/Taunus, p. 110.
42. For a detailed analysis of changing patterns cf. Ringer, *Decline*, pp. 59f.
43. Cf. Blankertz, *Geschichte*, p. 179.
44. D. Head (1995), '"Made in Germany" in the 1990s', *German Monitor*, vol. 34, p. 172.
45. Quoted from Blankertz, *Geschichte*, p. 179.
46. Paulsen, *Geschichte*, p. 654.
47. Nietzsche, *Werke*, vol. 2, pp. 986f.
48. Cf. W. Laqueur (1984), *Young Germany, A History of the German Youth Movement*, 2nd edn, New Brunswick and London; P. D. Stachura (1981), *The German Youth Movement 1900–1945, An Interpretative and Documentary History*, London; T. Koebner et al. (eds) (1985), *'Mit uns zieht die neue Zeit', Der Mythos Jugend*, Frankfurt/M.
49. Cf. Chapter 3, pp. 59–61 for further discussion.
50. Cf. Ringer, *Decline*, pp. 162–71.
51. Cf. J. R. Schmid (1973), *Freiheitspädagogik. Schulreform und Schulrevolution in Deutschland 1919–1933*, Reinbek b. Hamburg; Glöckner, *Schulreform*, pp. 78ff.
52. G. Wyneken (1913), *Der Gedankenkreis der freien Schulgemeinde*, Leipzig, p. 10.
53. Cf. K. Laermann, 'Der Skandal um den *Anfang*. Ein Versuch jugendlicher Gegenöffentlichkeit im Kaiserreich', Koebner (ed.), *'Mit uns zieht'*, pp. 360–4.
54. *Der Anfang*, vol. 1, no. 3 (1913), p. 51; quoted from Laermann, 'Der Skandal', p. 366.
55. Laermann, 'Der Skandal', p. 373.

TEXTUAL STUDIES

1. Thomas Mann, *Unordnung und frühes Leid*

Zwischendurch ruft das Telephon im Arbeitszimmer des Professors, und die Großen laufen hinüber, denn sie wissen, daß es sie angeht. Viele Leute haben das Telephon bei der letzten Verteuerung aufgeben müssen, aber die Cornelius' haben es gerade noch halten können, wie sie die vor dem Kriege gebaute Villa bis jetzt noch haben
5   halten können, kraft des leidlich den Umständen angepaßten Millionengehalts, das der Professor als Ordinarius für Geschichte bezieht. Das Vorstadthaus ist elegant und bequem, wenn auch etwas verwahrlost, weil Reparaturen aus Materialmangel unmöglich sind, und entstellt von eisernen Öfen mit langen Rohren. Aber es ist der Lebensrahmen des höheren Mittelstandes von ehemals, worin man nun lebt, wie es

10 nicht mehr dazu paßt, das heißt ärmlich und schwierig, in abgetragenen und gewendeten
Kleidern. Die Kinder wissen nichts anderes, für sie ist es Norm und Ordnung, es sind
geborene Villenproletarier. Die Kleiderfrage kümmert sie wenig. Dies Geschlecht hat
sich ein zeitgemäßes Kostüm erfunden, ein Produkt aus Armut und Pfadfindergeschmack, das im Sommer beinahe nur aus einem gegürteten Leinenkittel und
15 Sandalen besteht. Die bürgerlich Alten haben es schwerer.
(Th. Mann (1958), *Erzählungen* [Stockholmer Gesamtausgabe], Oldenburg, p. 621)

Commentary

(numbers in parenthesis refer to line numbers in text)

An insight into the lifestyle of a professor's family during the Weimar Republic.
Note the contrast between the image society has of a mandarin's position and the
financial difficulty of living up to it. (1) Die Großen: the professor's two oldest
children. (5:) a millionaire at a time (1923) when one *Goldmark* was worth 2500
marks in paper money. (8) Iron stoves, connected to chimneys by long metal pipes,
replaced the pre-war central heating systems in order to save money. Only one or
two rooms were heated. (12) 'Villenproletarier': ironical description for those
accustomed to the lifestyles of the upper bourgeoisie, but now reduced to working-
class conditions. (13f) Pfadfindergeschmack: a reference to boy scouts, a variation
of the *Wandervogel* movement and its simple, natural lifestyle.

Vocabulary

daß es sie angeht = that it's for them; Verteuerung (f) = wave of price increases;
Ordinarius (m) = full-time professor; kraft = because of; leidlich = reasonably;
den Umständen angepaßt = under the circumstances; verwahrlost = neglected;
abgetragene und gewendete Kleider = worn clothing which has been turned inside
out.

2a. Wilhelm Dilthey, 'Abgrenzung der Geisteswissenschaften'

Ich gehe von dem umfassenden Tatbestand aus, welcher die feste Grundlage jedes
Räsonements über die Geisteswissenschaften bildet. Neben den Naturwissenschaften
hat sich eine Gruppe von Erkenntnissen entwickelt, naturwüchsig, aus den Aufgaben
des Lebens selbst, welche durch die Gemeinsamkeit des Gegenstandes miteinander
5 verbunden sind. Solche Wissenschaften sind Geschichte, Nationalökonomie, Rechts-
und Staatswissenschaften, Religionswissenschaft, das Studium von Literatur und
Dichtung, von Raumkunst und Musik, von philosophischen Weltanschauungen und
Systemen, endlich die Psychologie. Alle diese Wissenschaften beziehen sich auf
dieselbe große Tatsache: das Menschengeschlecht. [. . .]

10 Die Subjekte der Aussagen in den angegebenen Wissenschaften sind von
verschiedenem Umfang. [. . .] Es kann von ihnen erzählt, sie können beschrieben, es
können Theorien von ihnen entwickelt werden. Immer aber beziehen sich diese auf
dieselbe Tatsache: Menschheit zu bestimmen und von den Naturwissenschaften
abzugrenzen. Zudem ergibt sich aus dieser gemeinsamen Beziehung weiter ein
15 Verhältnis gegenseitiger Begründung der Aussagen über die in dem Tatbestand
'Menschheit' enthaltenen logischen Subjekte.
(W. Dilthey (1958), *Gesammelte Schriften*, 2nd edn, Stuttgart, vol. 7, pp. 4 & 6)

2b. Dilthey, *Schulreform* [1900]

Der naturwissenschaftliche Geist, der insbesondere in der modernen französischen
Literatur seinen Ausdruck gefunden hat, hat die abstrakten Prinzipien auf das
wirksamste unterstützt, welche in der Französischen Revolution so einflußreich
gewesen sind. Das abstrakte mathematische Denken, angewandt auf Gebiete des
5 gesellschaftlichen Lebens, wird stets das heranwachsende Geschlecht empfäglich
machen für die leeren Ideale eines Staates, der nach den Grundsätzen der Gleichheit
geregelt ist. [. . .] Frankreich hat den Sozialismus hervorgebracht. Ich frage Sie nun,
was in dem Unterricht einer Oberrealschule dem Fortschreiten dieses Geistes, seinem
Eindringen in unser Beamtentum, entgegenzuwirken vermag. [. . .] So kämpfen wir
10 für die Monarchie, indem wir die Entwicklung des geschichtlichen Bewußtseins als
die Vorschule des Juristen und des Beamten zur Geltung bringen.
(W. Dilthey [1900], *Über die Möglichkeit einer allgemeingültigen pädagogischen
Wissenschaft*, H. Nohl (ed.), Weinheim, pp. 85f)

Commentary

Both passages describe the need for a new and methodological approach to the
arts, in an age dominated by natural sciences. Whilst the first passage defines the
new concept of *Geisteswissenschaften* with a view to interpreting mankind in all
its complexities, the second passage strikes a much more nationalist and reactionary
note: it is directed against French literature and (French) socialism (St Simonism)
and against the principles of the Enlightenment.

Vocabulary

a. Räsonement (n) = reasoning; naturwüchsig = organic; gegenseitige Begründung (f) = reciprocal definition; **b.** empfänglich = responsive; hervorbringen = to
bring about; entgegenwirken = to counteract; zur Geltung bringen = to bring to
bear.

3. 'Denkschrift zur Organisation und Stellung des höheren Mädchenschulwesens'

[Es gilt] dem Weibe eine der Geistesbildung des Mannes in der Allgemeinheit der Art und der Interessen ebenbürtige Bildung zu ermöglichen, damit der deutsche Mann nicht durch die geistige Kurzsichtigkeit und Engherzigkeit seiner Frau an dem häuslichen Herde gelangweilt und in seiner Hingabe an höhere Interessen gelähmt
5 werde, daß ihm vielmehr das Weib mit Verständniß dieser Interessen und der Wärme des Gefühls für dieselben zur Seite stehe.

('Den hohen deutschen Staatsregierungen gewidmete Denkschrift der ersten deutschen Hauptversammlung von Dirigenten und Lehrenden der höheren Mädchenschulen. betr. eine gesetzliche Normierung der Organisation und Stellung des Höh. Mädchenschulwesens', quoted from C. Berg (ed.) (1991), *Handbuch der deutschen Bildungsgeschichte*, Munich, vol. 4, p. 281)

Commentary

Although designed to bring the education of girls into line with that of boys, the passage is biased, defining the role of a woman as that of a loving wife who finds her fulfilment as both intellectual and caring partner of her husband. (1) Weib, obs. for 'Frau', suggesting already a gender-specific role.

Vocabulary

Geistesbildung (f) = intellectual training; ebenbürtig = equal; Engherzigkeit (f) = pettiness; Hingabe (f) = devotion.

4. 'Studienanstalt für Mädchen' (1908)

18. Die Studienanstalt für Mädchen hat die Aufgabe, die Weiterbildung der Mädchen so zu fördern, daß die Schülerinnen in einer Reifeprüfung eine Bildung nachweisen, welche der durch die neunklassigen höheren Schulen für die männliche Jugend vermittelten gleichwertig ist, wenn auch mechanische Übereinstimmung nicht
5 besteht.[. . .]
22. Die Reifeprüfung der Studienanstalt, die in ihren drei Zweigen derjenigen der verschiedenen höheren Lehranstalten für die männliche Jugend entspricht, verleiht die Berechtigung der Oberschule, des Realgymnasiums oder des Gymansiums, soweit sie für Frauen in Betracht kommen. [. . .]

(Bestimmungen über die Neuordnung des höheren Mädchenschulwesens, 18 August 1908, in A. Reble (1992), *Geschichte der Pädagogik, Dokumentationsband*, 2nd edn, Stuttgart, pp. 566f)

Commentary

A comparison between this text and Text 3 reveals a remarkable step forward: equality between the sexes is aspired to, but in such a manner that some sexual stereotyping persists. (8f) suggests that some discrimination against women remains, as certain schools seem 'unsuitable' for girls.

Vocabulary

Studienanstalt (f) = secondary school; vermittelt = achieved; in Betracht kommen = to be considered.

5a. Thomas Mann, *Buddenbrooks* (1901)

Direktor Wulicke war ein furchtbarer Mann. Er war der Nachfolger des jovialen und menschenfreundlichen alten Herrn, unter dessen Regierung Hanno's Vater und Onkel studiert hatten, und der bald nach dem Jahre einundsiebenzig gestorben war. Damals war Doktor Wulicke, bislang Professor an einem preußischen Gymnasium, berufen
5 worden, und mit ihm war ein anderer, ein neuer Geist in die Alte Schule eingezogen. Wo ehemals die klassische Bildung als ein heiterer Selbstzweck gegolten hatte, den man mit Ruhe, Muße und fröhlichem Idealismus verfolgte, da waren nun die Begriffe Autorität, Pflicht, Macht, Dienst, Karriere zu höchster Würde gelangt, und der 'kategorische Imperativ unseres Philosophen Kant' war das Banner, das Direktor
10 Wulicke in jeder Festrede bedrohlich entfaltete. Die Schule war ein Staat im Staate geworden, in dem preußische Dienststrammheit so gewaltig herrschte, daß nicht allein die Lehrer, sondern auch die Schüler sich als Beamte empfanden, die um nichts als ihr Avancement und darum besorgt waren, bei den Machthabern gut angeschrieben zu stehen. [. . .] Bald nach dem Einzug des neuen Direktors war auch unter den
15 vortrefflichsten hygienischen und ästhetischen Gesichtspunkten mit dem Umbau und der Neueinrichtung der Anstalt begonnen und alles aufs glücklichste fertiggestellt worden. Allein es blieb die Frage, ob nicht früher, als weniger Komfort der Neuzeit und ein bißchen mehr Gutmütigkeit, Gemüt, Heiterkeit, Wohlwollen und Behagen in diesen Räumen geherrscht hatte, die Schule ein sympathischeres und segenvolleres
20 Institut gewesen war. . .
(Th. Mann (1974), *Buddenbrooks*, Fischer, pb. edn, p. 492)

Commentary
(numbers in parenthesis refer to line numbers in text)

A picture of grammar school education in the new Empire, with militaristic emphasis on secondary virtues (8) as opposed to the old system, still characterized by the Humboldtian spirit. Cf. the contrast between neo-classicism (6f) and German militarism (11); a reference to Kant whose ethics are perverted into harsh discipline and an emphasis on instrumentalist vocational skills instead of Humboldtian general education (9). (3) einundsiebenzig = beginning of the German Empire.

Vocabulary

berufen = to appoint; Selbstzweck (m) = end in itself; Dienststrammheit (f) = military discipline; bei den Machthabern gut angeschrieben zu stehen = to be in the good books of those in power; Neueinrichtung (f) = new equipment.

5b. W. Flitner, *Ideengeschichtliche Einführung in die Dokumentation der Jugendbewegung*

Vor allem war der Stil der Schule veraltet: es herrschte eine mechanische Disziplin, es gab keinen natürlichen Umgangston zwischen Lehrern und Schülern; die 'Pauker' wurden von den Schülern in den Reifungsjahren mißdeutet, verachtet, heuchlerisch behandelt; man fürchtete die willensstarken Lehrer und beugte sich, man hänselte und
5   verspottete die schwachen und gutmütigen. [. . .] Die Bildungspläne des humanistischen Gymnasiums stammten aus dem ersten Jahrhundertdrittel und waren veraltet; die neu entstandenen Realanstalten hafteten an den gleichen Methoden, die im Gymnasium üblich geworden waren, obgleich sie ganz andere Ziele hatten.
(Quoted from U. Herrmann, 'Die Jugendkulturbewegung. Der Kampf um die höhere Schule', in T. Koebner et al. (eds) (1985), *'Mit uns zieht die neue Zeit', der Mythos Jugend*, Frankfurt/M., pp. 225f)

Commentary

(numbers in parenthesis refer to line numbers in text)

To be read in conjunction with Mann's novel. Flitner also emphasizes mindless discipline (1) and lack of humanity (2), criticizing the hypocritical association with authority (3f). In contrast to Mann, Flitner blames outdated Humboldtian education for the malaise (5f).

Vocabulary

Pauker (m) = drill-bashing teacher; sich beugen = to give in to; hänseln = to tease; haften an = to adhere to.

3

The Weimar Republic: Reform and Reaction

Introduction: The Impact and Progress of 'Modernism'

Chapters 1 and 2 have provided an outline of the traditional German education system, how it developed during a period of neo-classical idealism, and how it was subsequently adapted to cope with the impact of industrialization. By the turn of the century the emerging picture revealed the standard-bearers of neo-classicism in the *Gymnasium* and the university taking up increasingly more conservative positions, whilst the reformers in the newer schools tried to revive some of the basic objectives of the traditional system, most notably the concept of general education. This traditionalism was in part a result of pressure from above, as the university sector sought to preserve the classics, and in part a desire to provide good-quality general education for social groups which had hitherto been denied the opportunity of all-round character development.

Following the general urbanization and industrialization of Germany at the end of the century, the concept of 'modernity' entered the intellectual debate, a development which coincided with the onset of a general crisis in values. Within the ranks of the mandarin class, which feared that the German concept of culture was under threat, this was reflected in a more pronounced reactionary attitude. In this context, the term 'modernism' is applied in its most wide and value-free sense, referring to those particular issues in education which eventually came to a head during the second half of the twentieth century or which brought the German system into line with recognized modern practice elsewhere. In its broadest, and perhaps even crudest, sense modernism in Germany became politically associated with the republican movement, in particular with social democracy, the anti-clerical movement and women's emancipation. It rejected *völkisch* and racist trends and, in terms of education policy, sought to extend compulsory schooling, develop a co-educational system, support the more technically orientated schools and broaden access to higher education. It was most firmly rooted in Prussia, the neighbouring states of Thuringia and Saxony, and in the free states of Hamburg and Bremen, whilst Catholic Bavaria remained the least progressive.

In common with other reform programmes, the new Republic's progressive education policy was soon plagued by the serious financial and economic problems which were to bring down the social-democratic MSPD-led coalition government and halt the reform movement in its infancy. The high point of the movement was the *Reichsschulkonferenz* of 1920; the general election of that same year, ousting the MSPD (Majority Social Democratic Party) from power, heralded the steady decline of the reform movement, delayed only by the progressive policies of Prussia. In addition to suffering financial and economic problems, the reform movement found itself in broad opposition to the country's cultural elite. The majority of university professors and an even larger proportion of students displayed a hostile attitude towards educational reforms and, in an attempt to retain their own privileges, allied themselves with anti-modernist factions.

The Socio-Intellectual Climate 1918–1924

While an overwhelming sense of relief greeted the end of the Second World War, with its unprecedented destruction and deprivation, the end of the First World War had been experienced quite differently. The material and psychological effects of the Versailles Treaty can hardly be overstated. The very existence of the German nation state, not yet fifty years old, was believed to be in peril; its potent symbol, the Hohenzollern dynasty, was replaced by a republic. Defeat in a war which had been regarded by many as a struggle to prove German cultural as well as military superiority resulted in a mood of profound pessimism, reinforcing the general impression that German culture had been seriously tarnished. This was made all the more evident by Germany's isolation and a widespread international condemnation of her cultural tradition. Indeed, defeat brought with it a significant rejection of German as a respected foreign language, particularly in the United States and Scandinavia, but also throughout the rest of Europe and in Russia. In this atmosphere Oswald Spengler's *Der Untergang des Abendlandes* (Decline of the West) (1922) struck a chord, predicting as it did the end of the 'Faustian civilization', which had lost its true direction and purpose only to indulge in the *Lebenslüge* (spuriousness) of Nietzsche's superman, Wagner's Bayreuth Festival and the general fabric of socialism.[1]

Now more than ever, the academic community was involved in a search for values, a quest for ideological commitment. A small group of modernists, mainly centred on the new universities of Cologne, Hamburg and Frankfurt and inspired by the sociologist Max Weber, challenged the main body of German academic traditionalists, who fiercely opposed the Weimar Republic and every Western influence that savoured of empirical and analytical positivism. This development has been comprehensively examined by Fritz K. Ringer,[2] some of whose findings are of particular relevance, especially in relation to the debate concerning values and the 'synthesis movement'. The latter, though dominated by traditionalists, was nevertheless based on one important tenet of modernity: the replacement of the individual by a greater entity, such as an ideology or the *völkische Gemeinschaft* (community). The concept of such an organically grown community, as opposed to the more rational, politically responsive and pluralist *Gesellschaft* (society),[3] even found favour among the less traditional circles of the mandarin class.

Both Weber and Ferdinand Tönnies distinguished between empirical analysis and any attempt to associate research with overt or covert values, with some kind of *Weltanschauung*. Weber's famous lecture 'Wissenschaft als Beruf' (Scholarship as a Vocation), delivered in 1919, a year before his premature death, questioned the orthodox view that specialization spelt the end of German *Wissenschaft*. In many respects his lecture was an attack on Dilthey and his school, who defined experience, inspiration and personality as the essential core for achieving general understanding. In particular, Weber opposed the orthodox notion that the fostering of scholarship must be justified in terms of an ultimate objective. In this, he anticipated the critical theory of *hinterfragen*, of exposing an underlying system of values. Weber no longer viewed scholarship in Humboldt's terms, as the essential pathway to *Bildung*, but as a vocation in itself, in the Western sense of research as an analysis of empirically verifiable facts, rejecting any form of *Kathederprophetie* (*ex cathedra* doctrines). Weber's polemics against 'the search for ultimate values in the cultural philosophy of the German Idealists'[4] evoked a massive response which occupied the German academic debate of the early 1920s. Without describing this debate in any detail,[5] mention should be made of the ultra-conservative protagonists, later National Socialists, Ernst Krieck and Philipp Lenard, and supporting the elitist *Lebensphilosophie*, Erich von Kahler, a friend of Stefan George and Friedrich Gundolf.

The Neo-Kantian school of philosophy attempted a synthesis between Weber's intellectualism and Dilthey's holistic hermeneutics. The majority of German academics at this time were preoccupied with the loss of status of German culture and the quest for spiritual renewal, and to this end they tended to attack overspecialization and positivism: 'In every discipline, scholars made war upon individualism, naturalism, mechanism, and the like. The new methods of the humanistic disciplines [the Dilthey school] spread like wildfire, along with intuitive and phenomenological approaches'[6] [Text 1]. This in turn made possible a specifically German form of 'reactionary modernism', a blending of the anti-modernist, irrationalist and mythical ideas, prevalent in nineteenth-century German thought as *Zweckrationalismus* (means–ends rationality), with an utterly functionalist employment of modern technology.[7]

Of particular importance in this respect were the economist Werner Sombart, the pedagogue-philosophers Eduard Spranger and Theodor Litt, and the philosopher Karl Jaspers. Prior to 1914, Sombart had already proffered some crude generalizations, contrasting the humanist concept of German scholarship with inferior

Western models, completely imprisoned in a cause-and-effect mechanism, unable to rise to man's nobler destiny. His own normative ideas were based on the mandarin tradition of establishing meaningful relationships, compatible with a conservative *Weltanschauung*. Taking up the theme of the antagonism between *Gesellschaft* and *Gemeinschaft*, Sombart associated the former with Christianity and the latter with Judaism. The capitalist order drew on both forces, but its unsavoury side, its calculating mechanism, was associated with the foreign, Jewish element.[8]

Spranger, a disciple of Dilthey and sympathetic to the Youth Movement, adopted a critical reactionary attitude to modern natural sciences and sought to return to neo-classical ideals in general and, in particular, to Humboldt's holistic concept of general education and of the individual's immersion in the 'world'. In an attempt to overcome the 'Polarität von Innerlichkeit und außerseelischer Welt'[9] (polarity between the inner and the external world) Spranger advocated reverting to the pre-war outlook of the mandarins. The student's character had to be developed as a whole, emphasizing personal experience within his own cultural tradition. Blinkered by his own narrow views, he enthusiastically welcomed Hitler's rise to power, only to be disillusioned a few years later. Karl Löwith described Spranger as a typical German professor who allowed his judgement to be affected by flawed idealism.[10]

Litt, Spranger's successor at Leipzig University, also sought to encompass education within the mandarin tradition, though in a more dialectical manner. In similar vein to Spranger, Litt posited the individual in his own age and society, underlining the importance of socialization.[11] As a result, education, in the form of *Kulturpädagogik*,[12] became a national concern: education set within the framework of the lifestyle of the whole nation. In essence, education of the individual corresponds to the collective cultural experience of the nation, an idea which attempted to correct some of the more individualistic aspects of *Reformpädagogik*. The teacher must guide his pupil, so that education is not merely a technical or scientific discipline but part of the *Geisteswissenschaften*, a response to man's natural unfolding, less concerned with empirical investigation than with the integration of the individual into a culturally defined community.[13] It is in this respect that Litt, though more of a modernizer than a traditionalist, became a champion of 'the mandarin heritage'.[14]

Similar observations hold true for Karl Jaspers, although he did more than most German mandarins to oppose *völkisch* nationalist trends. Jaspers's early work, specifically his *Die Idee der Universität*,[15] attempted a synthesis between Weber's critical and analytical stance towards scholarship and the post-Humboldtian German tradition. Like Weber, he sought to distance the university from any 'national idea'[16] by harnessing it to a convenient *Weltanschauung*. At the same time he tried to reconcile diverging disciplines and scholarly interests with the 'objective spirit', aiming for clarity of purpose and integrating scholarship into the 'whole of life':

Die scharfe Trennung von Sachkenntnis und Werturteil [. . .] wird doch als etwas empfunden, das nicht das letzte Wort sein kann. [. . .] So [. . .] drängt die Idee der Universität in ihrem Zentrum aus einer Epoche der Zersplitterung und Auflösung zu neuer Gestalt, [. . .] welche zu schaffen gemeinsame Aufgabe der gegenwärtigen Lehrer und Studenten ist.[17]

(The strict separation of factual knowledge and value judgement [. . .] is still felt to be something which cannot be the final word. [. . .] Thus [. . .] the essential idea of the university is urging us out of an epoch of disintegration and dissolution towards a new form, the creation of which is the joint task of the teachers and students of today.)

Jürgen Habermas interprets Jaspers's position as modernist, for it was not directed towards the particular interests of bourgeois society, but primarily towards a general, normative law of education which finds its justification within the 'objective spirit'.[18] And yet, the very formulation of such a normative law binds the university to the mandarin tradition. A good example is Jaspers's own definition of 'aptitude' in considering the ideal student for higher education, then still based on an elitist selection system. He recognized certain mechanical qualities such as memory, energy, quick-wittedness, accepting that actual intelligence was almost impossible to measure. He finally introduced two categories which were clearly related to the mandarin tradition, perhaps even to specific social strata: *Geistigkeit* (intellectuality) and *das Schöpferische* (creativity).[19] Jaspers equated the latter with genius which, according to him, was an entirely subjective category. We cannot take issue with Jaspers here, but it is surprising that a man of his insight apparently seemed unaware that his criteria for selection were so closely identified with the mandarin milieu, more likely to reinforce internal selection than to recruit new sources of academic energy.

This analysis of the Republic's intellectual climate is by no means comprehensive; no mention has been made of Carl Schmitt's anti-democratic, illiberal and racist position, nor have the scholarly contributions of historians or Germanists been included. A brief survey would, however, indicate the depth of the hostility of the majority towards the new Republic and how they yearned for a return to the mandarins' position in Imperial Germany.[20] The view of the judiciary and other academics was similarly reactionary.[21] Given such attitudes amongst Germany's academic elite, it is regrettable that the MSPD did not take a more revolutionary stance in 1918. By attempting to play the role of *Statthalter* (governor), rather than that of agent, in the 1918 revolution and by entering into coalition with liberal elements, the Social Democrats had targeted Bolshevism as the real enemy and tried to ingratiate themselves with the established forces of the former Empire. With hindsight, it is easy to condemn such a decision; in the autumn of 1918 the reality of the situation was confused and the coalition of socialist parties (MSPD and USPD), though uneasy, was still holding. A formal coalition (Stinnes–Legien Agreement) between industry and the trade unions appeared instrumental in preventing economic collapse and the army, under General Groener, seemed prepared to support the new political order. However, when the Majority Social Democratic Party (MSPD), with the support of the armed forces, connived to defeat the rebellious sections of the USPD (Independent Social Democratic Party), whose leaders Karl Liebknecht and Rosa Luxemburg were murdered by a faction of the army (January 1919), the political situation hardened and the MSPD fell victim to elements of the old bourgeoisie and to economic forces. The National Assembly elections denied the MSPD a clear majority, forcing it into a coalition with the Catholic Centre Party and the Liberals. An analysis of the education policy of the Republic will demonstrate how quickly the Social Democrats lost the political momentum and how genuinely modernist reform plans were taken up by more extreme left-wing groups, mainly in the free cities of Hamburg and Bremen and in the new state of Thuringia.

Education Policies during the Weimar Republic

Given Germany's traditional political culture with its strong emphasis on the civil service, it is perhaps not surprising that the social order in general and the education system in particular survived the upheavals of military defeat and the end of the monarchy. The MSPD was in favour of retaining the traditional establishment and only the city states of Bremen and Hamburg attempted far-reaching changes, based on grass-roots democratic principles, amongst them the abolition of church control in all schools, the abolition of voluntary religious education, the introduction of a collegiate system for teachers, with an elected headmaster, and the formation of teachers' councils (*Lehrerräte*). These reforms affected only the elementary system; the various *Gymnasien* had no part in any such reform plans.

Nevertheless, even the MSPD saw the need for radical reforms. The new Prussian government decreed: 'Ausbau aller Bildungsinstitute, insbesondere der Volksschule, Schaffung der Einheitsschule, Befreiung der Schule von jeglicher kirchlicher Bevormundung, Trennung von Staat und Kirche.'[22] (Expansion of all educational establishments, in particular of the elementary school, creation of the integrated school, liberation of education from any kind of church control, separation of State and Church.) The new *Reichs*-Constitution (11 August 1919) guaranteed certain minimal rights in education: equal access to education, complete equality between men and women, free education for eight years with an additional two-year period of vocational training, compulsory attendance during the first four years of elementary school, entrance to secondary education based on ability, stricter control of all aspects of education by the central government. The education of teachers was to be standardized; all teachers were to have a university education and be given the status of *Staatsbeamte* (civil servants). An *Elternbeirat* (parents' council) was introduced in all schools.[23] The new subjects of *Staatsbürgerkunde* (civics) and *Arbeitsunterricht* (work instruction) became obligatory and all religious and ethical convictions were accepted [Text 2]. A special school conference (1920) was to strengthen the new reform plans. Its resolutions, agreed after lengthy dialogue within the coalition and bitter debates with the Centre Party, still indicated a desire for modernization: compulsory attendance at elementary school for the first four years was reaffirmed, the old private *Vorschulen* (preparatory schools) were abolished. However, actual reforms were introduced with great reluctance and many of them were stalled or bypassed. Only a month after the *Reichsschulkonferenz* (national school conference), general elections brought disastrous results for the MSPD, forcing it into opposition and allowing the Centre Party to form a new coalition government. Though in coalition with the socialists since 1919, the Centre Party had always been a very reluctant partner in matters of education. Its overriding concern was the preservation and extension of religious control over education and the maintenance of church authority over private schools. Both churches supported the party in its objectives and the Prussian episcopacy issued an election declaration, read from every pulpit: 'Wer den Sozialismus unmittelbar oder mittelbar, durch eigenes Tun oder Nachlässigkeit oder durch Saumseligkeit unterstützt, versündigt sich an Christus und seiner Kirche.'[24] (Whoever supports socialism directly or indirectly, actively or passively out of apathy, sins against Christ and his Church.) An initial 'compromise' between the coalition partners led to the division of the *Volksschulen* into denominational, non-denominational (*Simultanschulen*) and secular schools, with parental pressure employed to secure the new ruling. As a consequence, by the end of the Republic, some 80 per cent of elementary education remained denominational.

Other extra-parliamentary reactionary forces[25] further weakened the position of the *Grundschule* (elementary school), including pressure from conservative and anti-republican parents and from the *Verband akademisch gebildeter Lehrer* (association of academically trained teachers), a grammar-school teachers' association. The *Grundschule* was allowed to prepare pupils for secondary education,[26] but selection for entrance was almost entirely at the discretion of the secondary sector itself, with the consent of the parents. The *Vorschule*, too, managed to survive, with pupils excused from the state sector on medical grounds; these schools were only gradually phased out, so that a majority of them were still in operation as late as 1933. Similarly disappointing was the training of elementary school teachers. Although the Constitution had decreed a similar type of training for both elementary and grammar school teachers, only the more progressive states of Thuringia, Saxony, Hesse, Hamburg and Bremen observed this law. The more conservative states in southern Germany did not implement it and pressure groups of grammar school and university teachers actively opposed it.[27] The main objections to the academic training of teachers came from those who feared that staff in rural schools might become overqualified and, once having enjoyed the academic freedom of university education, might not be so keen on dispensing religious instruction.[28] In spite of all these setbacks the new *Grundschulen* incorporated a number of the concepts that had emerged from the reform movement discussed in Chapter 2. In attempting to encourage 'die allmähliche Entfaltung der kindlichen Kräfte aus dem Spiel- und Bewegungstriebe zum sittlichen Arbeitswillen, der sich innerhalb der Schulgemeinschaft bestätigt'[29] (the gradual channelling of children's energies away from the orbit of games and movement into an ethical desire to work which will be established within the school community), it fulfilled the major tenets demanded by such representatives of reform as Ellen Key, Berthold Otto and Aloys Fischer.

While only a limited number of reforms were introduced in the secondary sector, two innovations must be mentioned. In northern and central Germany, the *Mittelschule* was further extended, leading to the qualification of *Mittlere Reife*, a replacement for the former *Einjährige* which, with the demise of the Empire, had lost its special importance for military service. The *Mittelschule* not only provided an additional pathway into the top level of secondary education, it also provided the standard entry qualification to the middle grades of the civil service.[30] The second important reform was the introduction of the *Deutsche Oberschule*. This type of school was introduced in 1922 as a fourth means of obtaining the *Abitur* and gaining entrance to university. It required the acquisition of two modern foreign languages, French and English, but concentrated on German and the appreciation of a specifically modern German culture. The secondary sector was the victim of a number of shortcomings and tensions: the proliferation of different schools prevented any attempt to integrate the various social strata. The *Volksschule* came to be seen as a *Restschule*, a school for all those whose academic development had ceased, a situation which can still be seen in today's *Hauptschule*. The existence of four types of 'upper' school not only increased the number of applicants entering university, again giving rise to the fear of a 'Bildungs- und Abiturienteninflation',[31] it also exacerbated the social divide: the different types of school were invested with different syllabuses: the traditional *Gymnasien* concentrated on the classics, the *Realgymnasien* on Western European civilization, the *Oberrealschulen* on natural sciences and the *Deutsche Oberschulen* on specifically 'German culture'. The new subject of *Kulturkunde*[32] was to provide a common element, allocating one third of the curriculum to the study of religion, history, geography and civics, emphasizing the specifically 'German' dimension in all these subjects. Not surprisingly, this strong emphasis on a national perspective rendered the younger generation within the secondary sector particularly easy prey to National Socialism.

The anti-Republican attitude within the universities has already been mentioned. Throughout the Republic's existence, controversies between a relatively progressive Ministry of Education and a reactionary university body abounded, particularly in Prussia, where Carl Heinrich Becker, supported by Konrad Haenisch, pursued a progressive modernist policy in higher education. Becker detected weaknesses in a German university system facing the twentieth century: a widening gulf between academic learning and the demands of real life, a serious lack of democratic structures, with titular professors reigning supreme and associate professors and lecturers in a quasi-feudal dependent position. The *ordentlicher Professor* or *Ordinarius*, the sole member of staff with full voting rights in the senate, was usually also director of his institute or *Seminar* (Section). The *Privatdozent* (associate professor), though qualified with the post-doctoral *Habilitation*, received no salary other than token fees from his students, had no pension rights and no vote at any university committee.[33] His career was almost entirely at the mercy of the titular professor, under whom he would normally have studied for his academic qualifications, and he remained financially dependent on his parents. A waiting period of ten years or more for the position of salaried professor was the rule, during which time associate professors and the *Assistenten* (lecturers) had to shoulder an increasing burden of basic teaching or menial scholarly work for their professor. A sharp rise in the numbers of *Privatdozenten* and *Assistenten* and only a slight increase in *Ordinarien* intensified the competition for promotion and, consequently, pressure to conform increased. Those who failed to conform, or were critical of nationalist attitudes rampant at German universities, were often forced to resign, even though they had the support of the Ministry of Education.[34]

Reactionary attitudes within the student body were even more extreme. While the post-war period between 1918 and 1923 saw a 30 per cent increase in students, they continued to be drawn from the same social strata. In the bleak economic situation, mass unemployment amongst graduates resulted: 'For the first time, a kind of academic proletariat grew up in Germany'[35] and universities were described as 'waiting rooms for the unemployed'.[36] Not surprisingly, nationalist and reactionary circles within the student body strengthened their position.

The student fraternities, amalgamated in the *Deutsche Burschenschaft* (1815) as a bulwark of liberalism, had become increasingly more reactionary, monarchist and nationalist. Their compulsive duelling and drinking contests, long commented on by foreign observers, had also become a focus for German writers[37] [Text 3]. Konrad H. Jarausch described a student subculture which had developed to fill a vacuum in the Humboldtian system, with its exclusive concentration on academic matters. As a result, the definition of academic freedom was broadened during the Empire to include a social and pseudo-legal code, allowing for the development of a student state within a state.[38] Guidelines for student morality were also included in a special *Commersbuch* (figure 6) that contained student songs. The prevailing

Figure 6 *Allgemeines deutsches Commersbuch* (1858). This contained a collection of student songs, but also various guidelines on *commercium*, the code of etiquette for social events and when representing one's *Verbindung* (student fraternity).

moral code had much in common with that of the officer corps, upholding a very narrow code of honour, the violation of which almost inevitably led to duelling (figure 7), either with sword or pistol, while turning a blind eye to debt, frequenting brothels or sexual relationships with women of a lower social class.

Student fraternities recruited their membership according to social status and subject. The most elitist and conservative were the *Corps*, whilst the *Lands-mannschaften*, though no less nationalist, catered more for the middle classes. The

Figure 7 The Student Fraternities' Duelling Day at Heidelberg University (1911). This picture reflects the para-militaristic spirit prevalent in the duelling fraternities, their obsession with ceremonial etiquette and their nationalistic attitude. This picture complements the text by Heinrich Mann. (Reproduced with the kind permission of Dr Tilmann Bechert, Duisburg.)

Verein deutscher Studenten, founded in 1881 and actively supported by Bismarck, became a mouthpiece for nationalist, anti-semitic and anti-feminist groups.[39] Since many members of student fraternities were war veterans and had grown up in a fiercely nationalist spirit, they were largely hostile to the new Republic. To combat ultra-conservative trends, the *Deutsche Studentenschaft* was founded in 1919, dedicated to representing student interests and organizing welfare activities such as the *Deutsches Studentenwerk* (1921). From this nucleus, democratically elected student committees developed at every university, including the *Allgemeiner Studentenausschuß* (*ASTA*) which is still in existence. Tensions were soon to develop between an increasingly nationalistic *Deutsche Studentenschaft* and the Prussian Ministry of Education, when students seeking to promote a 'Greater Germany' became involved in nationalist activities. Following a dispute over Jewish student membership, Becker, Prussian Secretary of Education, insisted that all students should have the right to join. The reactionary student fraternities, supported by former members and benefactors, the infamous *Alte Herren*, and partly with the aid of the Interior Minister, prevented this decision being implemented.[40] Several splinter groups emerged, a majority fiercely nationalist and anti-republican, such as the *Stahlhelm*, a league of war veterans, and the *Hochschulring deutscher Art*. These were opposed by a number of republican organizations such as the *Deutscher Studentenbund* and the *Republikanisches Studentenkartell*. In 1926, the *National-sozialistischer Deutscher Studentenbund* was founded and, by 1931, there was a National Socialist majority amongst student bodies at most universities, especially those in the smaller towns and at many technical universities.[41]

An example of nationalist fervour at the Republic's universities was the glorification of Langemarck, a First World War fortification in Flanders.[42] In November 1914 some German army units, containing many students, attempted to storm this fortification, their nationalist fervour reverberating to the sound of the *Deutschlandlied*, adopted after 1922 as Germany's national anthem. Severe loss of life was incurred and the attempt failed. Although this incident had no impact on the course of the war, it soon took on the mantle of a national legend, celebrated by Ernst Jünger, Baldur von Schirach and Adolf Hitler and hailed by countless minor nationalist figures as 'die Geburtsstunde des völkischen Deutschlands, des nationalen Sozialismus'[43] (the birth of *völkisch* Germany, of a national socialism). By the end of the 1920s, Langemarck had become the symbol of nationalist, anti-republican sentiments, incorporating the ideals of the Youth Movement, such as leadership and physical heroism, with nationalist militarism and anti-intellectual xenophobia [Text 4]. The *Deutsche Studentenschaft* initiated the building of a special memorial at Langemarck, a move later 'hijacked' by the Nazis for the Hitler Youth movement.

The Position of Women in Education

By the end of the Empire women had attained a position of equal status with men, as far as obtaining the *Abitur* was concerned. The prudent policies of Helene Lange and Gertrud Bäumer had brought about significant improvements for women in education, even if some sexual discrimination still featured in the general curriculum and overall policies. After 1901 women were admitted to some universities (Heidelberg, Freiburg) and from 1908 this was extended throughout Prussia. The Weimar Constitution placed women's education on an equal footing with that of men. The compulsory *Grundschule* reduced the length of the *Lyzeum* course to six years, with a four-year common core for both sexes. From 1923, the *Oberlyzeum* gave access to university education, offering modern languages, but no Latin. In line with opportunities at the *Oberrealschule* and *Reformrealgymnasium*, similar pathways for the education of women were created. The proportion of women students at universities rose from 7.5 per cent (1914) to 20 per cent (1932) and, from 1920, women were eligible for the *venia legendi*, enabling them to become university professors. By 1925, women accounted for 100,000 teachers, 2,572 medical doctors, 4,000 dentists, 2,720 pharmacists and 1,000 chemists.[44]

A comparison of the percentage within a particular age group would suggest that women were not lagging far behind men and, given their short period of access to high-school education, their achievements look even more remarkable. An analysis of pupil numbers for boys and girls in upper schools in the mid-1920s suggests a difference of some 3–5 per cent.[45] By 1930 nearly half the women in secondary education were at the *Oberlyzeum*, indicating an increasingly more academic orientation on their part.

However, these relatively positive figures seem to apply only to the more progressive aspects of women's emancipation. There is still much evidence to suggest that society resisted any further expansion of secondary and higher education for women. The *Frauenschulen*, though by now less popular, were still designed to introduce women 'in die besonderen Aufgaben der Frau in Familie und Volksgemeinschaft'[46] (to the special tasks of women within the family and the *völkisch* community). Even Baden's liberal Secretary for Education observed in 1925 that neither cultural enrichment, nor enhanced intellectual lifestyles had been achieved through the academic education of women. He believed that women should concentrate on the more sublime, intuitive and irrational aspects of culture; mathematical and linguistic instruction could therefore be reduced.[47] Fritz Lenz, Professor for Racial Hygiene in Munich, resented women in the professions, believing that they deprived men of employment and thereby prevented them from establishing families.[48] In essence, the fourteen years of the Republic's existence was too short a period for sustained and effective progress, considering the tremendous economic, ideological and international problems confronting the government. Moreover, previous reforms carried out under the Empire should not be underestimated; we can now discern in them a more modernist, reformist trend than previous research would have led us to expect.

On the whole, the Weimar Republic arouses more interest on account of its contradictions rather than its genuine reform projects. Many of its progressive ideas had their origins under the Empire, while its truly modernist phase was confined to the first two or three years of its existence. At the same time, the Republic must be seen as providing a springboard for developments which were to foreshadow racist and fascist advances during the Third Reich. Here, too, care must be taken not to disregard the potential which had accumulated prior to Hitler's rise to power. Chapter 4 will discuss to what extent the mandarin community can be held responsible for the decline into barbarity.

Notes

1. O. Spengler (1923), *Der Untergang des Abendlandes*, 33rd edn, Munich, vol. 1, pp. 468f.
2. Cf. F. K. Ringer (1969), *The Decline of the German Mandarins, The German Academic Community 1890–1933*, Cambridge, Mass., chaps 4, 6, 7.
3. Cf. F. Tönnies (1887), *Gemeinschaft und Gesellschaft: Abhandlung des Communismus und des Socialismus als empirischer Culturformen*, Leipzig; H. Plessner (1924), *Grenzen der Gemeinschaft*, Bonn.
4. Quoted from Ringer, *Decline*, p. 356.
5. For a more detailed study cf. R. H. Samuel and R. Hinton Thomas (1949), *Education and Society in Modern Germany*, London, pp. 122f.
6. Ringer, *Decline*, p. 387.
7. J. Herf (1984), *Reactionary Modernism. Technology, Culture and Politics in Weimar and the Third Reich*, Cambridge, chap. 1.
8. Ibid., chap. 6.
9. E. Spranger (1928), *Der deutsche Klassizismus und das Bildungsleben der Gegenwart*, 2nd edn, Erfurt, p. 5.
10. K. Löwith (1989), *Mein Leben in Deutschland vor und nach 1933. Ein Bericht*, Frankfurt/M., p. 114.
11. F. Nicolin (1978), 'Theodor Litt', in J. Speck (ed.), *Geschichte der Pädagogik des 20. Jahrhunderts*, Stuttgart, vol. 2, p. 80.
12. Ibid., p. 82.
13. T. Litt (1919), *Individuum und Gemeinschaft*, Leipzig.

14. Ringer, *Decline*, p. 408.
15. K. Jaspers (1923), *Die Idee der Universität*, 1st edn, Berlin.
16. Ibid., pp. 49, 79.
17. Ibid., p. 61.
18. J. Habermas (1987), 'Die Idee der Universität – Lernprozesse', in *Eine Art Schadensabwicklung*, Frankfurt/M., p. 74.
19. Jaspers, *Idee*, p. 129.
20. A wealth of literature here, including the contributions by K. Ziegler (pp. 144–60) and H. Bausinger (pp. 125–44) in A. Flitner (ed.) (1965), *Deutsches Geistesleben und Nationalismus. Eine Vortragsreihe der Universität Tübingen*, Tübingen.
21. For a satirical critique cf. K. Tucholsky (1929), *Deutschland, Deutschland über alles*, Berlin; for a more critical approach cf. K. Sontheimer (1971), *Deutschland zwischen Demokratie und Antidemokratie*, Munich, pp. 38–114.
22. 'An das preußische Volk' [1919], quoted from C. Führ (1972), *Zur Schulpolitik der Weimarer Republik*, 2nd edn, Basel, p. 31.
23. 'Die Schulartikel der Reichsverfassung vom 11. August 1919', in A. Reble (1992), *Geschichte der Pädagogik, Dokumentationsband*, Stuttgart, pp. 568f.
24. G. Grünthal (1968), *Reichsschulgesetz und Zentrumspartei in der Weimarer Republik*, Düsseldorf, p. 58.
25. L. von Friedeburg (1992), *Bildungsreform in Deutschland, Geschichte und gesellschaftlicher Widerspruch*, Frankfurt/M., p. 225.
26. *Grundschulgesetz* (28 April 1920), § 1, in B. Michael and H. H. Schepp (eds) (1974), *Politik und Schule von der Französischen Revolution bis zur Gegenwart. Eine Quellensammlung zum Verhältnis von Gesellschaft, Schule und Staat im 19. und 20. Jahrhundert*, Frankfurt/M., vol. 2, p. 76.
27. Cf. G. Wyneken at the *Reichsschulkonferenz* 1920, in Friedeburg, *Bildungsreform*, p. 224.
28. Friedeburg, *Bildungsreform*, p. 251.
29. *Preußische Richtlinien von 1921 für die Grundschule*, quoted from Friedeburg, *Bildungsreform*, p. 230.
30. H.-G. Herrlitz et al. (1993), *Deutsche Schulgeschichte von 1800 bis zur Gegenwart*, Weinheim and Munich, p. 133.
31. Ibid., p. 138. For a fuller discussion cf. K. H. Jarausch (1982), *Students, Society, and Politics in Imperial Germany. The Rise of Academic Illiberalism*, Princeton, pp. 49–77.
32. Cf. Chapter 2, p. 30.
33. Cf. Samuel and Hinton Thomas, *Education*, p. 124, and Ringer, *Decline*, pp. 54–7.
34. Samuel and Hinton Thomas, *Education*, p. 127.
35. Ringer, *Decline*, p. 65.

36. S. D. Stirk (1946), *German Universities – through English Eyes*, London, p. 31.
37. Cf. Mark Twain (1982), *A Tramp Abroad*, Hippocrene Books, US, chaps 4 and 5; J. Schlaf, *Ein Tod*, in A. Holz, J. Schlaf [1889], *Papa Hamlet. Ein Tod*, Reclam Nr. 8853/54, Stuttgart; H. Mann (1958), *Der Untertan*, Hamburg.
38. K. H. Jarausch (1991), 'Universität und Hochschule', in C. Berg (ed.), *Handbuch der deutschen Bildungsgeschichte*, Munich, vol. 4, p. 333.
39. B. vom Brocke (1980), 'Hochschul- und Wissenschaftspolitik in Preußen und im Deutschen Kaiserreich 1882–1907. Das "System Althoff"', in P. Baumgart (ed.), *Bildungspolitik in Preußen zur Zeit des Kaiserreichs*, Stuttgart, pp. 9–118.
40. Friedeburg, *Bildungsreform*, pp. 362f.
41. Samuel and Hinton Thomas, *Education*, p. 130.
42. Cf. U.-E. Ketelsen (1985), '"Die Jugend von Langemarck", ein poetisch-politisches Motiv der Zwischenkriegszeit', in T. Koebner et al. (eds), *'Mit uns zieht die neue Zeit'. der Mythos, Jugend*, Frankfurt/M., pp. 68–97 and Jarausch, *Students, Society, and Politics*, pp. 395f.
43. W. Matthießen, Geleitwort, in W. Dreysse, *Langemarck 1914*, quoted from Ketelsen, '"Die Jugend"', p. 82.
44. B. Beuys (1980), *Familienleben in Deutschland*, Reinbek b. Hamburg, pp. 459f.
45. M. Kraul (1984), *Das deutsche Gymnasium 1780–1980*, Frankfurt/M., p. 150.
46. 'Übereinkunft der Länder' [1931], in Führ, *Zur Schulpolitik*, p. 302.
47. W. Hellpach (1925), *Die Wesensgestalt der deutschen Schule*, Leipzig, pp. 150f.
48. Beuys, *Familienleben*, p. 460.

TEXTUAL STUDIES

1. Alfred Weber, 'Die Bedeutung der geistigen Führer in Deutschland'

[. . .] Es ist gar keine Frage, daß die Bedeutung der Menschen dieser Art [geistige Führer] und damit auch das Gewicht der von ihnen vertretenen geistigen Güter bei uns in Deutschland in den letzten hundert Jahren in geradezu unerhörter Weise gesunken ist; man möchte sagen wie in einer Katastrophe zusammengebrochen, wenn
5 nicht das Merkwürdige wäre, daß der Gewichtsverlust nicht plötzlich, sondern gewissermaßen schrittweise und beinahe systematisch geschehen ist. [. . .]
    Die Antwort, welche vielleicht am besten ihren allgemeinen Untergrund aufdeckte, wird sein: es ist die unentrinnbare Formation des modernen Lebens, das seine äußere und innere Gesamtstruktur, aus der sie folgt: Mechanisierung, Verapparatung,

10 Massenqualität des Daseins, Losgerissenheit seiner Formationen vom Gewachsenen
und Umgeformtwerden aller Daseinsgebilde in praktische Zweckeinheiten, die auf dem
cash nexus beruhen, [. . .] was soll darin anderes gedeihen als Materialisierung und
chaotische Zerbrochenheit vom Geistigen her gesehen? [. . .]
[. . .] Es hat bei uns ganz ohne Frage weitgehend an der nötigen Auslese der starken
15 Kräfte für das geistige Leben gefehlt, – das rein geistige sowohl, wie das politisch-
geistige –, vor allem an dem Aufstieg der kräftigen Talente, die von **unten** kommen.
[. . .] Es hat weiter an der nötigen Verbindung des geistigen Lebens mit dem politischen
und öffentlichen Leben überhaupt gefehlt, an den nötigen Zwischenstufen und Treppen
von dem einen zum andern, der Beweglichkeit in ihnen, die den ursprünglichen und
20 universellen Begabungen die Wege geebnet hätten, um anerkannte, geistiges Handeln
und Praxis gleichmäßig umfassende Führer des Volkes zu werden. [. . .] Unser
Erziehungssystem, auf das wir in mancher Beziehung – vor allem in der Volksschule
– stolz sein durften, war und ist in den höheren Stufen [. . .] von Entleerungen,
Bürokratisierungen, Vertrocknetheiten und Rückständigkeiten heute behaftet [. . .]. Es
25 entläßt die von ihm ausgelesenen Kräfte so weitgehend ohne Verbindung mit dem
großen öffentlichen Leben, ja, mit den geistigen Bewegungen der Zeit, daß sie die
nicht fürs Praktische bestimmten Teile ihrer sogenannten Bildung [. . .] beim Übergang
zur Universität [. . .] als lästiges Gepäck wegwerfen und auf ihre eigene Weise den
geistigen Anschluß an das Allgemeine suchen, oder [. . .] auf einen solchen geistigen
30 Anschluß überhaupt verzichten und durch feuchtfröhliche Karriere-Institutionen ohne
geistigen Inhalt hindurch 'ihren Eintritt in das öffentliche Leben' vollziehen in
hoffnungsloser geistiger Eingeschränktheit.
[. . .] Denn überall dreht es sich darum, eine neue **Totalanschauung** der lebendigen
Kräfte zu gewinnen, die hinter jenem Zivilisatorisch-Mechanistischen und gleichzeitig
35 über ihnen stehen, einen neuen lebendigen Kosmos zu erblicken. Nur aus einer Vision,
einer Erfahrung von einer **wirklichen**, **sichtbaren** lebendigen Gesamtheit konnte das
an irgendeiner Stelle wachsen, in irgendeinem Volk entstehen. [. . .]
(*Die Neue Rundschau* 29 (1918), pp. 1249, 1251, 1263f, 1265)

Commentary

(numbers in parenthesis refer to line numbers in text)

The author, Max Weber's younger brother, professor of sociology and culture, and
sympathetic to the Youth Movement, reflects on the inadequate intellectual leadership given by his mandarin class. He reiterates the typical cultural pessimism of
the time (3–6), combined with a profound distrust of materialism (13) and the
advent of the 'masses'. His criticism of the German education system focuses on
the sterility of selection which separates its leaders from the *Volk* (16) and, at the
same time, dilutes spiritual and cultural values to such an extent that they are no
longer taken seriously (22–33), leading to mere careerism (30). He pleads for a
new all-embracing vision (33), a move towards synthesis, based on *völkisch* values.
(7) Antwort: the answer to the cultural malaise. (8) die unentrinnbare Formation

des modernen Lebens: an anti-modernist, anti-Western sentiment, blaming materialism (cash nexus (12)) for some of the problems. (17f) Verbindung . . . mit dem politischen und öffentlichen Leben überhaupt: recognizes the isolation of the mandarin classes, not only from other social strata, but also from the public domain.

Vocabulary

Gewichtsverlust (m) = weight loss; 'Umgeformtwerden . . . Zweckeinheiten = transformation of all essential life forms into practical units of purpose; Zwischenstufe (f) = intermediate stage; geebnet = levelled off; behaftet = to be afflicted with; lästiges Gepäck = burdensome luggage; feuchtfröhlich = boozy; Eingeschränktheit (f) = limitation.

2. *Schulartikel der Reichsverfassung vom 11. August 1919* (excerpts)

Art. 143. [. . .] Die Lehrerbildung ist nach den Grundsätzen, die für die höhere Bildung allgemein gelten, für das Reich einheitlich zu regeln. Die Lehrer an öffentlichen Schulen haben die Rechte und Pflichten der Staatsbeamten.

Art. 145. Es besteht allgemeine Schulpflicht. Ihrer Erfüllung dient grundsätzlich die
5 Volksschule mit mindestens acht Schuljahren und die anschließende Fortbildungsschule bis zum vollendeten achtzehnten Lebensjahre. Der Unterricht und die Lernmittel in den Volksschulen und Fortbildungsschulen sind unentgeltlich.

Art. 146. Das öffentliche Schulwesen ist organisch auszugestalten. Auf einer für alle gemeinsamen Grundschule baut sich das mittlere und höhere Schulwesen auf. Für
10 diesen Aufbau ist die Mannigfaltigkeit der Lebensberufe, für die Aufnahme eines Kindes in eine bestimmte Schule sind seine Anlage und Neigung, nicht die wirtschaftliche und gesellschaftliche Stellung oder das Religionsbekenntnis seiner Eltern maßgebend.

Art. 148. In allen Schulen ist sittliche Bildung, staatsbürgerliche Gesinnung, persönliche
15 und berufliche Tüchtigkeit im Geiste des deutschen Volkstums und der Völkerversöhnung zu erstreben. Beim Unterricht in öffentlichen Schulen ist Bedacht zu nehmen, daß die Empfindungen Andersdenkender nicht verletzt werden. [. . .]
(A. Reble (1992), *Geschichte der Pädagogik, Dokumentationsband*, 2nd edn, Stuttgart, pp. 568f)

Commentary
(numbers in brackets refer to the articles of the Constitution)

The section on education contains many modernist principles, including teacher training at universities [143] and free compulsory education up to eighteen [145].

Selection according to ability should not be influenced by class or religion [146], a claim which could not be sustained, especially with increased parental involvement in schools (November 1919). Similarly, the religious issue hindered the claim for tolerance, basic instruction in ethics and national reconciliation [148], threatening to undermine the whole education policy of the Republic.

Vocabulary

einheitlich = uniformly; Erfüllung (f) = fulfilment; Lernmittel (pl) = schoolbooks and equipment; ausgestalten = to organize; maßgebend = decisive; staatsbürgerliche Gesinnung (f) = civic thinking; Bedacht nehmen = to take into consideration.

3. Heinrich Mann, *Der Untertan* (1918)

Und für diesen Posten fühlte er sich bestimmt. Er sah sich in einen großen Kreis von Menschen versetzt, deren keiner ihm etwas tat oder etwas anderes von ihm verlangte, als daß er trinke. Voll Dankbarkeit und Wohlwollen erhob er gegen jeden, der ihn dazu anregte, sein Glas. Das Trinken und Nichttrinken, das Sitzen, Stehen, Sprechen
5 oder Singen hing meistens nicht von ihm selbst ab. Alles ward laut kommandiert, und wenn man es richtig befolgte, lebte man mit sich und der Welt in Frieden. [. . .] Man breitete sich, vom Biertisch her, über die Welt aus, ahnte große Zusammenhänge, ward eins mit dem Weltgeist. Ja, das Bier erhob einen so sehr über das Selbst, daß man Gott fand. [. . .] Nicht Stolz oder Eigenliebe leiteten Diedrich: einzig sein hoher Begriff
10 von der Ehre der Korporation. Er selbst war nur ein Mensch, also nichts; jedes Recht, sein ganzes Ansehen und Gewicht kamen ihm von ihr. Auch körperlich verdankte er ihr alles: die Breite seines weißen Gesichts, seinen Bauch, der ihn den Füchsen ehrwürdig machte, und das Privileg, bei festlichen Anlässen in hohen Stiefeln mit Band und Mütze aufzutreten, den Genuß der Uniform! [. . .] Seine Männlichkeit stand
15 ihm mit Schmissen, die das Kinn spalteten, rissig durch die Wangen fuhren und in den kurz geschorenen Schädel hackten, drohend auf dem Gesicht geschrieben – und welche Genugtuung, sie täglich und nach Belieben einem jeden beweisen zu können! (Heinrich Mann (1958), *Der Untertan*, Hamburg, pp. 30f)

Commentary
(numbers in parenthesis refer to line numbers in text)

An ironic account of life in a duelling student fraternity at the end of the nineteenth century. Of particular interest is the complete disintegration of the personality of the protagonist, Diedrich: he becomes an integral part of his fraternity (3–8), sacrificing not only his will, but also his moral principles and self-respect. The text shows similarities with *Biertischpolitik* (saloon-bar politics) (7) and with the subservience of the *Spießbürger.*

(14) Band . . . Uniform: the uniform of duelling student fraternities, going back to the *Burschenschaften* and the Wars of Liberation. A love of uniforms in general subverts the individual. Duelling scars (15), inflicted despite some protection, contribute to the picture of a person who needs to bolster his weak personality and feels the necessity to prove himself (16f).

Vocabulary

befolgen = to comply with; erheben = to raise; Korporation (f) = student fraternity; Breite (f) = width; Fuchs (m) = fresher in student society; Schmiß (m) = duelling scar; rissig = chapped; Wange (f) = cheek; Genugtuung (f) = satisfaction.

4. Walter Flex, *Der Wanderer zwischen beiden Welten, ein Kriegserlebnis*

Im Eisenbahnwagen kamen wir ins Gespräch. Er saß mir gegenüber und kramte aus seinem Tornister einen kleinen Stapel zerlesener Bücher: ein Bändchen Goethe, den Zarathustra und eine Feldausgabe des Neuen Testaments. 'Hat sich das alles miteinander vertragen?' fragte ich. Er sah hell und ein wenig kampfbereit auf. Dann lachte er. 'Im
5 Schützengraben sind allerlei fremde Geister zur Kameradschaft gezwungen worden. Es ist mit Büchern nicht anders als mit Menschen. Sie mögen so verschieden sein, wie sie wollen – nur stark und ehrlich müssen sie sein und sich behaupten können, das gibt die beste Kameradschaft.' [. . .] Aus allen seinen Worten sprach ein reiner, klarer, gesammelter Wille. So wie er die Anmut des Knaben mit der Würde des Mannes
10 paarte, war er ganz Jüngling [. . .]. 'Sind Sie nicht Wandervogel, Wurche?' fragte ich ihn aus meinen Gedanken und Vergleichen heraus, und sieh, da hatte ich an die Dinge des Lebens gerührt, die ihm die liebsten waren! Aller Glanz und alles Heil deutscher Zukunft schien ihm aus dem Geist des Wandervogels zu kommen, und wenn ich an ihn denke, der diesen Geist rein und hell verkörperte, so gebe ich ihm recht . . ..
(Walter Flex (1936), *Gesammelte Werke*, vol. 1, 9th edn, Munich, pp. 193, 196)

Commentary
(numbers in parenthesis refer to line numbers in text)

Written in 1916, a year before the author's death on the Russian front, this short story became a best-seller. His role model was his friend Wurche (10) who combined a Protestant, missionary zeal with that of a patriotic warrior. The selection of books (2f) seems authentic and represents a strange blend of humanism, piety and hero worship. The emphasis is placed on the unifying power of war and comradeship (5–8). The extolling of will power (9) leads directly to the *Wandervogel* movement (10) which itself was centred on such sentiments and – by 1916 – had abandoned cosmopolitanism in unconditional service to the fatherland (12–14).

Vocabulary

kramen = to rummage about; Tornister (m) = knapsack; zerlesen = well-thumbed; Feldausgabe (f) = combat edition; sich miteinander vertragen = to get on with each other; Schützengraben (m) = trench; sich behaupten = to survive; Anmut (f) = gracefulness; gerührt = moved.

—4—

Education and Ideology under
National Socialism

Introduction: National Socialism and the Modernist Debate

Education under the Nazis is a very complex issue, fraught with contradiction and controversy, not least because the historical interpretation of National Socialism itself is still in a process of fermentation, which this brief analysis cannot hope to clarify. The very phenomenon of Hitler's rise to power has been the subject of many different interpretations: revolution, counter-revolution or some kind of *coup d'état*, and these interpretations have been broadened in order to assess this phenomenon from either a modernist or anti-modernist point of view.

Hitler and his party described their rise to power as a 'nationale Erhebung' (national uprising), thus defining their movement in nationalist–*völkisch* terms. Given the speed of the uprising and some of its objectives, it might well be described as a revolution.[1] In the wider context in which it sought to overthrow the republican tenets of 1919, it might even be seen as a counter-revolution, though it did little to reinstate the old imperial order. Yet another version might suggest an interpretation of the events of 1933 as a *coup d'état*, in as much as Hitler replaced the Weimar Constitution, *de facto* though not *de jure*, with a one-party system. The label 'revolution' would apply in the context of the national and aggressive impetus of this movement; it might also indicate why no effective resistance seemed to emerge.

All these questions relate, moreover, to an understanding of the Nazi rise to power in terms of its modernist or anti-modernist context, a debate which, with the demise of socialism in Eastern Europe and in the light of some post-modernist interpretations, has gained a new urgency. Where representatives of the Critical Theory define modernism in a normative context as a 'project of modernity', inseparably linked to the tradition of the Enlightenment and its emancipatory dimension, post-modernist interpreters would criticize such a Hegelian, teleological approach for leaning too heavily towards Anglo-American ideals and for branding German developments with the stigma of a *Sonderweg*, whilst ignoring the many changes which the Western liberal systems themselves had undergone.[2] Hans Mommsen, opposed to such a reductionist, descriptive definition of modernism, suggests that National Socialism lacked the intellectual force which might have accorded it the status of an ideology and that it failed to live up to a more normative application of 'modern'.[3] A middle position is adopted by Jeffrey Herf who interprets the technical, cultural and political development of Weimar *and* the Third Reich as 'reactionary modernism', observing 'an embrace of modern technology by German thinkers who rejected Enlightenment reason'.[4] The problem of this approach is that it equates two components which are anything but equal, reminiscent of the old cliché which sought to justify the Third Reich on the grounds that it built the autobahns.

If we now discuss briefly the nature of National Socialism and ask whether it can be defined as an ideology, some of the issues raised earlier may become clearer. The view, expressed by Herf and others, that 'Hitler's *Weltanschauung* was both fanatically coherent and politically decisive',[5] is difficult to sustain. The individual constituents of Nazism: nationalism, racism, Teutonic mysticism, blood-and-soil fanaticism, considered in concert, hardly constitute a holistic ideology, let alone a modern one. Utopian palingenesis[6] may suffice to explain the hero worship bestowed on Hitler, but it must also be held responsible for those irrational, truly insane decisions which plunged Germany into war and resulted in the policy of 'final victory'. Conclusive evidence exists to demonstrate that the Germanic mysticism of Alfred Rosenberg can be linked to those aspects of the German tradition which are most often associated with Germany's *Sonderweg*: the anti-intellectualism of the Youth Movement, faith in the Nordic inventor (Spengler), a fierce rejection of Western Enlightenment (Langbehn) together with all its liberal associations (Lagarde). These elements, however, were not always strictly observed by Hitler and Goering.

Further complications arise from the relatively short duration of the Nazi dictatorship, and the fact that six of its twelve years covered the war period, an exceptional phase in itself, which almost certainly distorted the implementation of a planned reorganization and had of necessity to accord priority to the war effort.

The issues raised in this introduction will be dealt with heuristically by examining educational changes and policies not only in relation to the Empire and the Weimar Republic, but also in connection with their modernist and revolutionary impact or – conversely – with their anti-modernist, reactionary nature. Firstly, we shall analyse the reception given to early National Socialist educational policies by the intelligentsia; secondly, we shall examine the common links between National Socialism and the Youth Movement, including those aspects where a definitive departure from *völkisch* Romanticism can be discerned. Finally, we shall discuss the education policy of the Third Reich as it affected different levels of education, in an attempt to discover a common denominator. In conclusion we return full circle to those aspects discussed in the introduction, hoping to have shed some light on many unanswered questions.

The National Socialist Rise to Power and the Intelligentsia

In Chapter 3 we examined the response of the German mandarin class to defeat in the First World War and to the modernizing tendencies of the Weimar Republic. This chapter will pursue some of the arguments rehearsed earlier, in order to illustrate the extent to which these mandarins shared responsibility for the rise of National Socialism.

Even the most cursory glance at this period will demonstrate that university students reacted much more radically and with considerably more enthusiasm to the 'events of 1933' than did their professors. Social and economic pressures played a major part in this response, linked as it was to protests against the Republic, condemning it for having betrayed the German people. Strong Nazi representation in student bodies such as the *Deutscher Hochschulring* and the *Nationalsozialistischer Deutscher Studentenbund* made it inevitable that violent disturbances occurred at most universities even before Hitler seized power, with anger directed against Jewish professors and Social Democratic pacifists. In Halle, Heidelberg and Breslau, teachers were suspended, whereas Munich University withstood student pressure. The burning of books, orchestrated by the Nazi ideologist Alfred Bäumler, reached its climax in May 1933 and targeted all socialist, Semitic, pacifist and even humanist writers.[7] The journal *Der deutsche Student* commented on such incidents with strangely prophetic words: 'Politische Soldaten in Uniform rücken auf die Hochschule; der Intellektuelle fürchtet sich vor solchem Barbarentum; die junge Generation aber freut sich, daß sie zum Urwald zurückfand.'[8] (Political soldiers in uniform march on the university; the intellectual is afraid of such barbarism; the younger generation, however, rejoices at having found its way back to the jungle.) Anti-semitism became the overriding, official policy. The 'Zwölf Thesen gegen den undeutschen Geist' (Twelve Theses against the anti-German Spirit) (April 1933) led to a mass expulsion of Jewish professors and urged that in future Jews should only be permitted to publish in Hebrew.[9] The Student Corporations were won over by the Nazis when duelling was restored and they gained representation in the Constitutional Assembly of the *Deutsche Studentenschaft*.[10] Besotted by the desire for 'national unity and national freedom', and explicitly invoking the liberal patriotic spirit of 1817, the *Burschenschaften* declared their support for Hitler and vowed to jettison everything that had previously separated them from the Nazis. Ironically, this promise was fulfilled in 1935, when the Corporations were dissolved by the Nazis and integrated into the *Nationalsozialistischer Studentenbund*. A final *Gleichschaltung* (political co-ordination) was accomplished in November 1935 when all student organizations were compelled to merge with this Nazi organization.[11]

University teachers joined in this *völkisch* hysteria, resurrecting the 'Ideas of 1914' with all their anti-liberal and anti-individualist tendencies. This anti-Western attitude, which cannot be explained merely by reference to military defeat or the injustices inflicted on Germany at the Versailles Peace Treaty, lies at the very heart of the mandarin tradition of 'unpolitical detachment from the state and unpolitical adulation of power'.[12] As a result, these academics failed to see the need to participate in party politics or to employ a system of pluralist lobbying, describing such practices as the murky work of party squabbles. They admired the Hegelian 'étatist' tradition[13] and revered Renaissance Caesarism as propounded by Nietzsche, Lagarde and Spengler, but supported also by such civilized humanists as Ernst Robert Curtius, who had hoped for national unification under the banner of 'culture' [Text 1]. Exploiting such a tradition, the *Machtergreifung* (seizure of power in January 1933) failed to ring the alarm bells which would have been sounded in academic circles steeped in liberal democracy. And it was this illiberal German tradition, rather than craven or base opportunism, which accounted for the mandarins' *völkisch* stance. Even the speech in May 1933 by Wilhelm Frick, Minister of the Interior, failed to arouse dissent in academic circles. In it he blamed liberal-inspired pedagogy for the wholesale corruption of education:

Die individualistische Bildungsvorstellung hat wesentlich zu der Zerstörung des nationalen Lebens in Volk und Staat beigetragen und vor allem in ihrer hemmungslosen Anwendung in der Nachkriegszeit ihre völlige Unfähigkeit erwiesen, die Richtschnur der deutschen Bildung zu sein.[14]

(The individualistic concept of education has been the main contributor to the destruction of national life within society and state and in particular its unrestrained application in the post-war era has demonstrated its utter inadequacy as a guiding principle for German education.)

Here again Eduard Spranger provides an example of this mandarin mentality. He welcomed 'the national movement of 1933' as the embodiment of Kant's ethos of duty, as freedom closely bound up with the greater national will of the people, rejecting both Marxist materialism and Western ideals of 'Wohlfahrt und Glück-seligkeit' (well-being and happiness); Kant's equally strong commitment to the Enlightenment and to individual emancipation from self-willed immaturity is conveniently overlooked. Spranger welcomes the new militancy as one of the positive stimuli resulting from the First World War and expresses his support for a voluntary labour service, greater leadership in youth education and a measure of co-operation between the War, Labour and Education Ministries. The Nazi advance to power is seen as a positive step, though he regrets an 'exaggerated anti-semitism'. However many excuses have been made for such misjudgements, the following excerpt from an article by Spranger seems to place him squarely amongst the advocates of Nazism:

Auch der Sinn für den Adel des Blutes und für Gemeinsamkeit des Blutes ist etwas Positives. Bewußte Pflege der Volksgesundheit, Sorge für einen leiblich und sittlich hochwertigen Nachwuchs (Eugenik), bodenständige Heimattreue, Wetteifer der Stämme und Stände [. . .] gehören zu den Kräften, die neu belebt sind und die in eine bessere Zukunft weisen.[15]

(Also a sense of the nobility of blood and of the bond of blood is something positive. A conscious cultivation of the health of the people, concern for the high physical and ethical quality of the future generation (eugenics), love of one's homeland, rooted in the soil, rivalry between individual regions and classes [. . .] are the prerogative of those powers which have been given a new lease of life and point towards a better future.)

However, correspondence between Spranger and his fellow editors of the journal *Die Erziehung* expresses an early reluctance to become more deeply involved with the Nazi movement, especially since his co-editors, Theodor Litt and Wilhelm Flitner, seem to have preserved a greater sense of detachment than Spranger.[16] And yet, many other intellects of the highest calibre gave enthusiastic support to the Nazis. The eulogy on the Nazi state, given by the philosopher Martin Heidegger at his inauguration as *Rektor* of Freiburg University, is perhaps the best-known example. In this infamous speech, Heidegger rejects the concept of academic freedom in favour of service to the German nation.[17] He was also prominent among some thousand German academic signatories of the infamous manifesto which attempted to justify 'die völlige Umwälzung unseres deutschen Daseins' (the complete transformation of our German existence), subjecting scholarship and knowledge to the 'higher ideals' of the *Volk*.[18] The declaration, also endorsed by eminent scientists, anticipates the assertion that the scientist must be, above all, a servant of the nation, at the same time rejecting non-Aryans in the service of German scholarship.[19] S. D. Stirk, an Oxford graduate, who spent the first three years of Hitler's dictatorship at Breslau University, has examined the Nazi attack on 'the idea and methods, and consequently the reputation, of German "Wissenschaft"',[20] despite a sensitivity towards the issue of a value-free *Wissenschaft*, which he notes in Alfred Rosenberg's *Der Mythos des 20. Jahrhunderts*. Both Rosenberg and Ernst Krieck, two of the most unsavoury of all Nazi professors, were to conclude that scholarship without presuppositions was no longer desirable in the new state. According to Stirk, the Reich Leader of University Teachers declared in 1938: 'The German university is solely the creative act of Aryan and Germanic man. "Wissenschaft" must only serve the community of the people, and nobody else; in this service it is free.'[21]

Professors of German played a particularly important role, having already been seriously infected by nationalist stirrings. Strenuous efforts were made to reinterpret Goethe in an Aryan, Nordic mould. German literature in general was rewritten; its more cosmopolitan, enlightened and rationalist aspects were ignored or dismissed, as in the work of Heine, whose Jewish background was held responsible for his hostile attitude towards burgeoning nationalist issues. The anti-Western, barbaric, irrational elements of German literature were extolled; its individualistic features were replaced by an exaggerated emphasis on folklore, hero worship and the glorification of war. A special type of Caesarism expressed itself as the glorification of Germanic greatness, especially as seen in the veneration of the *Hildebrandslied* and the *Nibelungenlied*, but also in the admiration of the late eighteenth-century man of genius (Goethe's *Faust*). These values hark back to the very origins of German literary studies and anticipate the National Socialist thesis of the German master race.[22]

Not withstanding the profoundly illiberal and anti-democratic mandarin tradition, universities put up some opposition to the new regime, even if only at the very modest level of passive resistance and indifference. There was some unease with the new climate which rejected the independence of learning and other time-honoured academic traditions. By the end of 1933 some 15 per cent of the teaching faculty had been replaced[23] and by the end of the war a third of staff had been removed, mainly for racist or political reasons. The best-known resistance groups came from within the *Kreisauer Kreis* and the *Weiße Rose* group around Hans and Sophie Scholl in Munich, the former of a somewhat conservative nature, the latter closely associated with Catholicism.[24] Resistance in both cases emerged relatively late and was, to some extent at least, motivated by the desire to avert Germany's total defeat.

National Socialism and the Reform Movement

Amongst the many continuing traditions reaching far back into Germany's cultural and intellectual past, the Reform Movement is just one facet, albeit a prominent one. The strong emphasis given to *Gemeinschaft* (community) and the concurrent scepticism towards rational intellectualism were essential links between the Reform Movement and National Socialism. The encouragement of healthy physical exercise, against a background of romantic camp fires and nostalgic German folk-songs, were features eagerly exploited by the Nazis, who channelled them into a slightly more militaristic and nationalist direction. Baldur von Schirach, leader of the *Hitlerjugend*, made the Hitler Youth Movement's leadership principle the chief organizational axiom, encapsulated in the formula 'Jugend muß durch Jugend geführt werden'[25] (youth must be led by youth). The traditional scepticism towards society and its allegedly degenerate influence was another powerful theme which developed into Nazi doctrine [Text 2]. A strong emphasis on community spirit was perverted into totalitarian collectivism, illustrated by the numerous mass rallies where youth groups took a prominent role, hailed as 'Symphonie von Jugend, Musik,

Kraft und Schönheit des männlichen Körpers'[26] (symphony of youth, music, power and beauty of the male figure). Such commitment to the unity of form, so typical also of other contemporary mass movements, was to become symbolic of the new Germany, united behind its leader and bound together in a faithful 'retinue'. The acclamation of eternal youth also implied that, within such a myth, the process of growing up and of maturation was unthinkable. The 'future' was completely enveloped in this myth of eternal youthfulness, which itself became subsumed in the mythical worship of 'ein Reich, ein Volk, ein Führer'[27] (one empire, one people, one leader).

The Youth Movement's anti-intellectual attitude, decrying traditional schooling as 'Lern und Wissensschule'[28] (learning and knowledge schools), led to a reduction in the academic content of the curriculum at every level, while the *Staatsjugendtag* (1934–6) excused members of the HJ from attending school on Saturdays. Replacing the old *Bildungsbürger* and their traditionally humanist education, a new official policy initiated a training programme geared towards war and discipline, aimed at promoting the very antithesis of the 'Jewish intellectual'.[29] Applied to the *Hitlerjugend*, this policy ensured that Schirach gave priority to emotion over understanding, and that unquestioning belief in the *Führer* eliminated any risk of producing 'a highly educated aesthete who dampens every stirring of his weak feelings with rational considerations'.[30] The special elitist Nazi schools, in particular, cultivated the collectivist, anti-intellectual approach first mooted in the pre-1933 Youth Movement: both the *Nationalpolitische Erziehungsanstalten* (*Napolas*), introduced in 1933 under the aegis of Reich Education Secretary Bernhard Rust, and the *Adolf-Hitler-Schulen*, initiated in 1937 by Schirach and Robert Frey, chief Nazi Party organizer, were devotees of an education system and indebted to educational concepts dating from the Reform Movement. Both schools rejected formal academic reports in favour of character assessment, encouraged self-reliance and responsibility through unsupervised examinations, emphasized physical training, but not competitiveness, supported artistic and musical activities to strengthen community spirit, together with various paramilitary exercises such as gliding, motorsports and the construction of model aeroplanes, this latter concept adapted from the *Arbeitsschule*.[31]

Some younger representatives of *Reformpädagogik* at first saw these developments as a continuation of their work, just as they had viewed their own policies as heir to the 'German Movement' in the tradition of Herder, Humboldt, Schleiermacher and Dilthey. Hermann Nohl forged these ideas into a dialectical system, based on Humboldtian individualism, with the Youth Movement as its antithesis and the nationalist uprising of 1933 as its synthesis, where both individualism and the community spirit espoused service to the nation.[32] Nohl formulated these ideas in 1933 and saw no reason to distance himself from them when his work was republished in 1949. However, he always remained aloof from the Nazis and his efforts, for all their weaknesses, could be seen as a conscious attempt to uphold an element of individualism and personal integrity. Similar observations apply to Wilhelm Flitner who believed the *völkisch* community spirit had to be protected from the pluralist separation of state power, from the particularist interests of political parties and from divisive pressure groups.[33] His zeal was directed against a perceived European crisis and against the decadent heritage of the Wilhelmine Empire, which had severed the bond between individual and community:

Wer diese Zeit besteht und Träger des Staates werden soll, der muß anders durchgebildet werden als der Mensch der Vorkriegszeit, der sich auf eine stetig fortschreitende städtisch-kapitalistische Welt vorbereitet. Jetzt handelt es sich um den Menschen der europäischen Krisis, des politisch bedrohten Deutschland, der zerfallenden kapitalistischen Wirt-schaftsordnung – um den Menschen, der eine neue und *echte Volksordnung mitzutragen* bereit und fähig ist.[34]

(Whoever wishes to survive this age in order to become a supporter of this state must be formed differently from the man of the pre-war period, preparing for an urban and capitalist world of continuous progression. We are now concerned with the man of the European crisis, of a politically threatened Germany, of a collapsing capitalist economic order – with the man who is ready and capable of *joint commitment to a genuinely new völkisch order*.)

Whilst such sentiments differ only marginally from those expressed by mandarins such as Spranger and Heidegger, they tend to retain an element of individualism and personal responsibility and can be used to highlight certain differences between the Youth Movement and the Nazi Party. Representatives of the Youth Movement were too autonomous in their general outlook to accept any form of *Gleichschaltung* which might have integrated them into a totalitarian regime. At the same time, they were too divided to organize effective opposition. As a result, the Nazis managed to infiltrate the *Bündische Jugend*, the most prominent youth organization. In April 1933, a Hitler Youth detachment took over their Berlin headquarters and, shortly afterwards, the youth hostel organization as well.[35] Some *Bündische Jugend* groups expressed resentment at overt Hitler Youth regimentation, whilst others kept a low profile in an attempt to remain independent. However, by the end of 1933, the *Bündische Jugend* had been swept aside, opposition to the Hitler Youth now being confined mainly to Catholic youth organizations. Recruitment to the Hitler Youth was, however, by no means universal, with resistance centred in industrial and Catholic regions. By December 1936, when membership became compulsory, nearly 30 per cent of young men in the ten-to-eighteen age group, some 4 million, were still not registered. Even by 1939 1 million youngsters had managed to remain outside the Hitler Youth or the *Bund Deutscher Mädchen* (*BDM*), the equivalent organization for girls.[36] These figures are of some relevance, since they indicate that, although there was virtually no active resistance to the Nazi dictatorship, there was an attempt on the part of some groups not to become involved in Nazi barbarism.

Educational Policies under the Third Reich

The main thrust of specific educational policies, as distinct from general National Socialist totalitarianism, falls within the period 1938–42. The years before 1938 were characterized by *ad hoc* decisions and by *Gleichschaltung* pressure aimed at breaking up the existing order and replacing it by a mass *Führer* cult; the post-1942 period was increasingly dominated by the war effort, which imposed its own economic strictures on education. Despite the brevity of the effective lifetime of this educational policy, its results were, nevertheless, severe and far-reaching. Several early statements on education, published in party manifestos or government proclamations, had promised a general modernization: free universal education, the special promotion of gifted children from a lower social background,[37] streamlining of different types of school and a university-level teacher-training programme. In the final analysis, however, these measures proved ineffective: fewer children from a disadvantaged social background benefited from education under Hitler than had been the case in the Republic. Most teacher training remained below university standard and the *Gymnasium*, though reduced in status, attracted more children from the academic middle classes than before.[38]

One of the first changes in education affected the cultural autonomy of the individual *Länder* (January 1934).[39] This measure had effectively been anticipated in April 1933, when a Reich law reintroduced civil service status for all teachers, thereby creating a pretext for excluding non-Aryan and politically undesirable teachers.[40] Schools were now empowered with the education of the politically conscious young German, 'der in allem Denken und Handeln dienend und opfernd in seinem Volke wurzelt und der Geschichte und dem Schicksal seines Staates ganz und unabtrennbar zu innerst verbunden ist'[41] (whose every thought and action is rooted in the service and sacrifice of his people and who is inalienably and inseparably bound to the history and destiny of his state). The general tenor of these proclamations was anti-liberal and anti-intellectual, a theme already apparent in Hitler's *Mein Kampf* [Text 3]. Other anti-democratic measures included the abolition of the collegiate system amongst teachers and the concentration of power in the hands of the headteacher, the abolition of parents' associations and their replacement by a Hitler Youth Leader.[42] In violation of the Concordat with the Vatican (1933), church schools were abolished and school leavers no longer received a copy of the Weimar Constitution. Crude measures were employed to solve the problem of university overcrowding, despite statistical evidence of a downturn in applications prior to Hitler's seizure of power.[43] Taken together, these initiatives appear to share an exaggerated concern for national solidarity, for the *Führer* principle; they also contributed to the general atmosphere of anti-intellectualism and contempt for democracy.

The second phase of education policy, from 1938 to 1942, focused in particular on the reorganization of the secondary sector. There was a return to some of the ideas first raised in September 1933, envisaging plans for a radically new system, the creation of an ideologically comprehensive school to replace the 'liberal confusions' of the existing system.[44] Accordingly, the existing range of secondary schools was reduced to two types of *Oberschulen*, educating boys and girls separately. Access to the *Gymnasium*, now exclusively for boys, was restricted to students with a special interest in classics. Secondary education followed four or six years of elementary education, continued in special *Aufbauschulen* (feeder schools) for pupils from rural areas, enabling them to join the last stage of the *Oberschule*. Secondary schooling was reduced to eight years in total and English became the first foreign language at the *Oberschule*. The final three years were divided into a science–mathematics or a languages stream. Physical education enjoyed a prominent role, with five hours per week timetabled throughout the full eight years.[45]

If an overall, non-ideological view is taken, a somewhat contradictory picture emerges: whilst separation of the sexes appears reactionary, many other measures appear progressive and in line with international developments. Only detailed scrutiny will expose this modern outlook as nothing more than a veneer, disguising a system which, regardless of its short period of existence, failed to provide the educational resources necessary for a modern industrial state. A closer analysis of its five major features will bear this out:

(a) *The introduction of secular state education.* The liberation of education from private privilege and clerical tutelage was an aim that could be traced back to Humboldt. It also formed the cornerstone of the Republic's early reform plans. The *Reichsschulpflichtgesetz* (1938) had formally abolished private prep schools and made attendance at the *Volksschule* obligatory.[46] Religious education for the two major Christian traditions was still guaranteed under Article 149.3 of the Weimar Constitution, but now reflected a religious policy of 'positives Christentum'. The *Verordnung zum Schutz von Volk und Staat*[47] ensured that religious education should uphold and endorse the policies of the existing government. The reorganized secondary sector produced no new syllabus for religious instruction, but reiterated the principle of 'positivism', and that the uniformity of education must not be jeopardized.[48] The uniformity claim meant that religious education had to conform to official anti-semitism and was subject to other coercions of the totalitarian system, so that any liberal claim for religious tolerance was little more than window dressing.

(b) *Moves towards a comprehensive education system.* Demands for a classless, comprehensive type of education can be traced back to Fichte's concept of patriotic education; they had been made repeatedly since then in attempts to overcome a socially divisive method of selection. The term 'comprehensive' is used here in its widest sense, including the demand for university education for all teachers and for the greatest possible access to university for school-leavers from every type of secondary school. Official guidelines seemed keen to promote these tendencies. Secondary schools took on the task of dismantling that concept which sought to distinguish between educated and uneducated people, redefining education as a bridge between the past and the future of a nation, as a living entity rather than an accumulation of knowledge.[49] The *Aufbauschule*, established during the Republic, was further expanded in order to give children from rural areas access to secondary education.[50] The training of elementary school teachers seemed to realize the long-standing aim for equality between teachers in elementary and secondary schools: Prussia reorganized its teacher-training colleges into *Hochschulen für Lehrerbildung* (1933), eventually to be extended across the rest of Germany. From 1936, trainee secondary school teachers spent their first year at these institutions, thereby ensuring a uniform ideology throughout the teaching service.[51] By 1941 the pressure of war already enforced the closure of the new *Hochschulen*. As a result, poorly qualified teachers entered the profession, after a one-year training course for holders of the *Abitur* and a five-year course for candidates from the *Volksschule*.

Apart from such cosmetic changes, the old tripartite system was preserved and became even more essential in order to meet the country's growing employment needs.[52] Even the redefined *Arbeitsunterricht* was not, as during the Reform Movement, designed to promote independent practical learning, but was downgraded to foster secondary virtues such as discipline, hygiene and cleanliness.[53]

(c) *Curriculum development.* Seen from an administrative, instrumentalist angle, many of the curricular reforms continued the modernist trends observed during the Reform Movement and under the Weimar Republic. Subjects were no longer taught in isolation, but grouped together to form larger units in an attempt to further interdisciplinary understanding. *Kulturkunde* was extended to include art and music in addition to German, history and geography in order to create a 'zusammen-haltende Klammer unseres nationalen Gebäudes'[54] (a consolidating brace for our national edifice). Its true propaganda value lay in the claim that the Aryan race had attained the highest political and cultural standards,[55] thereby turning the curriculum into yet another instrument of totalitarian *Gleichschaltung*. Such indoctrination started with the elementary education primer: 'It [the primer] goes on, page after page, with no other purpose than to fill little children with hatred for the "enemies of Germany", which include, aside from the Jews, everyone not in complete accord with the plans and methods of the Führer.'[56] German lessons were frequently the keystone in such indoctrination. The famous Goethe specialist Hermann August Korff greeted the new era as 'Aufbruch des deutschen Geistes aus langer Fremdherrschaft und eine Einkehr in das eigene Wesen'[57] (liberation of the German spirit from prolonged foreign domination and a return to its own essence). Amongst contemporary works exemplifying this idea were the writings of Ernst Jünger, Hans Grimm, Hans Johst, Walter Flex and Paul Ernst [Text 4].

History, too, became instrumentalized, presenting to the younger generation the ideology of the front-line fighter: 'Der behördlich geregelte Patriotismus ebensowohl wie die Kräfte, die sich ihm gegenüberstellen, müssen von einem dämonisch aus allen Schichten auflodernden Glauben an Volk und Vaterland verschlungen, jeder anders Fühlende muß mit dem Brandmahl des Ketzers behaftet und ausgerottet werden.'[58] (Officially regulated patriotism as well as its opposing forces must be demonically devoured by a blazing faith in nation and fatherland, apparent in all social classes; anyone who feels differently must be branded as a heretic and must be eradicated.) The dividing line between history and mythology became blurred, both consumed in the battle of the Aryan race against a fictitious Judaeo-Bolshevik world revolution. Within the curriculum, history now spawned the new subjects of *Wehrgeschichte* (defence history) and — in association with geography and biology — *Grenzlandkunde* (frontier studies).

Even the natural sciences conformed, with biology gaining prominence as *Rassenkunde* (race studies). The modernist approach of endowing individual subjects with personal experience and intuition had become perverted: instead of awakening intellectual curiosity through the excitement of personal discovery, a stultifying indoctrination had taken over, generating militarism, hatred and racial hysteria.

(d) *The humanist tradition.* Chapter 2 sought to illustrate how, by the end of the nineteenth century, the humanist tradition seemed to have reached a crisis, accused of overburdening students with mechanically assimilated knowledge rather than scholarship. This criticism, though justified by concern for the students' academic aspirations and personal self-fulfilment, was nevertheless nurtured by an illiberal, nationalist spirit; precisely the same spirit which provided Nazi educators with much of their ammunition. Hitler opposed the assimilation of knowledge, regarding it as a degenerate influence since it stunted character development. He particularly derided the 'einseitige Ausbildung des Geistes'[59] (one-sided intellectualism), associating it with Jewish and Bolshevik decadence, to be countered by physical education which would strengthen will-power and deter-mination.[60] Once he was in power, his hostility towards the neo-humanist tradition became more focused: the Hellenic spirit, hailed as a fertile tension,[61] was at the same time distanced from neo-humanist scholarship. 'In ganz anderer Weise, als der Neuhumanismus es vermochte, hat die nationalsozialistische Revolution uns Hellas, seinen Begriff vom Leibe, von der Kunst, vom politischen Leben nahegerückt.'[62] (In a manner quite different from that of neo-humanism, the National Socialist Revolution, in its notion of the body, of art, of political life, brought Hellas closer.) The Humboldtian concept of education was criticized for its individualism and its emphasis on intellectual aspirations, which were perceived as factors weakening the *völkisch* community spirit. The notion of general education, condemned as the pathway to pure intellectualism [Text 5], was to be replaced by a structure forged from within a community of true conflict.[63]

(e) *Education for girls.* This is an area where the Nazis have always been seen as pursuing a reactionary policy, blindly guided by their racist obsessions. *Mein Kampf* had already proclaimed the ultimate aim of female education to be motherhood.[64] Accordingly, segregation of the sexes was strictly adhered to and home economics became the main stream in the new *Oberschule für Mädchen*, directing its pupils towards the role model of German womanhood as mother and guardian of the Nordic race.[65] Only 5 per cent of girls entered secondary education and of these some 40 per cent selected this type of school.[66] Such policies led to a drastic reduction in the number of women in higher education: by 1939 only 6,342 women were registered at university, leading to a serious shortage of teachers and necessitating a massive U-turn by 1942, when some 42,000 women, 64 per cent of the student population, were matriculated at German universities.[67] Economic and logistic demands had obviously overridden doctrinal considerations and forced the regime to revise its reactionary policies.

This discussion of National Socialist educational policies has demonstrated that, though many of its initiatives followed a semi-ideological direction, they resulted in nothing more than short-term measures, producing a patchwork based on resentment and opposition to liberal and intellectual traditions. As such, they can hardly be described as modern, even if certain features seem to link up with a liberal-modernist tradition favouring further emancipation and rational enlightenment. The example of women's education reveals how industrial and military necessity forced the system to abandon its reactionary policies, while attempts at a comprehensive teacher-training scheme failed for similar reasons, compelling the system to adopt a more traditionalist course. It follows, therefore, that National Socialism lacked any coherent concept of education which went beyond crude indoctrination. Based on its educational policies, the movement hardly deserves the name of revolution. At the same time, sentiments and reactions displayed during this period by the educated classes illustrate certain continuities, which have already been observed in earlier chapters: a reluctance to embrace democracy and to exercise critical involvement in political issues which go beyond personal concerns, together with an exaggerated reverence for irrational and, in particular, *völkisch* themes. Chapters 5–8 will examine the extent to which these essentially anti-modernist traditions were overcome and where we may still detect shortcomings in Germany's transformation into a liberal industrial society.

Notes

1. Cf. J. Fest (1982), *Hitler*, Harmondsworth; I. Kershaw (1993), *The Nazi Dictatorship, Problems and Perspectives of Interpretation*, 3rd edn, London; D. Schoenbaum (1968), *Die braune Revolution*, Cologne; R. Zitelmann (1987), *Hitler*, Hamburg.
2. R. P. Sieferle (1995), *Die Konservative Revolution*, Frankfurt/M., pp. 198–221.
3. H. Mommsen, 'The Nazi Regime: Revolution or Counterrevolution', in R. Rürop (ed.) (1998), *The Problem of Revolution in Germany; German Historical Perspectives*, Berg, Providence.
4. J. Herf (1984), *Reactionary Modernism*, Cambridge, p. 1.
5. Ibid., pp. 193f.
6. R. Griffin (1991), *The Nature of Fascism*, London.
7. K. H. Jarausch (1984), *Deutsche Studenten 1800–1970*, Frankfurt/M., p. 168.
8. W. Klose (1967), *Freiheit schreibt auf Eure Fahnen – 800 Jahre deutsche Studenten*, Oldenburg and Hamburg, p. 229.
9. H. P. Bleuel (1968), *Deutschlands Bekenner – Professoren zwischen Kaiserreich und Diktatur*, Bern, Munich and Vienna, p. 217.
10. Jarausch, *Deutsche Studenten*, pp. 166f.
11. Ibid., p. 172.
12. K. D. Bracher (1975), *The German Dilemma*, New York, p. 87.
13. K. Sontheimer (1990), *Deutschlands politische Kultur*, Munich, pp. 36f.
14. H.-G. Herrlitz et al. (1993), *Deutsche Schulgeschichte von 1800 bis zur Gegenwart*, Weinheim and Munich, p. 149.
15. U. Herrmann (1988), '"Die Herausgeber müssen sich ändern". Die "Staatsumwälzung" im Frühjahr 1933 und die Stellungnahmen von *Eduard Spranger*, *Wilhelm Flitner* und *Hans Freyer* in der Zeitschrift "Die Erziehung". Mit einer Dokumentation', *Zeitschrift für Pädagogik* 22, Beiheft, Weinheim and Basel, p. 287.
16. Ibid., p. 290.
17. M. Heidegger (1983), *Die Selbstbehauptung der deutschen Universität*, Frankfurt/M., pp. 14f.
18. H. Pross (1959), *Die Zerstörung der deutschen Politik*, Frankfurt/M., pp. 98–100.
19. J. Stark (1934), *Nationalsozialismus und Wissenschaft*, Munich, p. 10.
20. S. D. Stirk (1946), *German Universities – through English Eyes*, London, p. 44.
21. Ibid., p. 46.
22. Cf. K. Ziegler (1965), 'Deutsche Sprach- und Literaturwissenschaft im Dritten Reich', in A. Flitner (ed.), *Deutsches Geistesleben und Nationalismus. Eine Vortragsreihe der Universität Tübingen*, Tübingen, p. 157.

23. Bracher, *German Dilemma*, p. 95.
24. H. Roth (ed.) (1959), *Katholische Jugend in der NS-Zeit*, Düsseldorf, pp. 59f; K. Sontheimer (1991), 'Die Bedeutung des Widerstands der Weißen Rose für die deutsche Universität', in H. Siefken (ed.) (1991), *Die Weiße Rose, Student Resistance to National Socialism 1942/1943*, Nottingham, pp. 183–94.
25. B. von Schirach (1938), *Revolution der Erziehung*, Munich, p. 116.
26. Quoted from J. Schmitt-Sasse (1985), '"Der Führer ist immer der Jüngste", Nazi-Reden an die deutsche Jugend', in T. Koebner et al. (eds), *'Mit uns zieht die neue Zeit'. Der Mythos Jugend*, Frankfurt/M., p. 130.
27. Ibid., p. 138.
28. P. C. Hartmann (1972), 'Jugendbewegung und nationalsozialistische Bildungs-vorstellungen', in H. Steffen (ed.), *Bildung und Gesellschaft*, Göttingen, p. 43.
29. B. Zymek (1980), 'War die nationalsozialistische Schulpolitik sozial-revolutionär? Praxis und Theorie der Auslese im Schulwesen während der nationalsozialistischen Herrschaft in Deutschland', in M. Heinemann (ed.), *Erziehung und Schule im Dritten Reich*, vol. 1, Stuttgart, pp. 266f.
30. B. von Schirach (1934), *Die Hitlerjugend, Idee und Gestalt*, Leipzig, p. 130, quoted from P. D. Stachura (1981), *The German Youth Movement, 1900–1945, An Interpretative and Documentary History*, London, p. 145.
31. H. Blankertz (1982), *Die Geschichte der Pädagogik von der Aufklärung bis zur Gegenwart*, Wetzlar, pp. 276f.
32. H. Nohl (1949), *Die pädagogische Bewegung in Deutschland und ihre Theorie*, 3rd edn, Frankfurt/M., pp. 218f.
33. Herrmann, '"Die Herausgeber müssen sich ändern"', p. 290.
34. Ibid., p. 291.
35. Cf. Stachura, *German Youth Movement*, p. 123.
36. Ibid., pp. 134f.
37. 'Programm der NSDAP', quoted from G. Giese and W. Treue (1961), *Quellen zur deutschen Schulgeschichte seit 1800*, Göttingen, p. 279.
38. M. Kraul (1984), *Das deutsche Gymnasium 1780–1980*, Frankfurt/M., p. 171.
39. B. Michael (1994), *Schule und Erziehung im Griff des totalitären Staates*, Göttingen, p. 5.
40. Ibid., p. 11. Cf. also B. Ortmeyer (1996), *Schulzeit unterm Hitlerbild*, Frankfurt/M., p. 31.
41. W. Frick (1933), *Kampfziel der deutschen Schule*, Langensalza, p. 24, quoted from Michael, *Schule und Erziehung*, p. 3.
42. Michael, *Schule und Erziehung*, p. 8.
43. Cf. Herrlitz et al., *Deutsche Schulgeschichte*, p. 148.
44. B. Rust, *Völkischer Beobachter*, 28.9.1933, quoted from Michael, *Schule und Erziehung*, p. 65.

45. 'Amtlicher Teil, Neuordnung des höheren Schulwesens', *Deutsche Wissenschaft, Erziehung und Volksbildung*, vol. 4 (1938), pp. 54f.
46. Cf. Giese and Treue, *Quellen*, p. 289.
47. Cf. P. C. Bloth (1989), 'Kreuz oder Hakenkreuz?', in R. Dithmar (ed.), *Schule und Unterrichtsfächer im Dritten Reich*, Neuwied, p. 91.
48. 'Amtlicher Teil', p. 47.
49. Ibid., p. 49.
50. Ibid., p. 53.
51. Herrlitz et al., *Deutsche Schulgeschichte*, p. 152.
52. Cf. Zymek, 'War die nationalsozialistische', pp. 266f.
53. Reichs- und Preußisches Ministerium für Wissenschaft, Erziehung und Volksbildung (ed.) (1938), *Erziehung und Unterricht in der Höheren Schule*, Berlin, p. 22.
54. 'Amtlicher Teil', p. 48.
55. R. Eilers (1963), *Die nationalpolitische Schulpolitik, eine Studie zur Funktion der Erziehung im totalitären Staat*, Cologne and Opladen, p. 15.
56. E. Mann (1939), *School for Barbarians. Education under the Nazis*, London, p. 54.
57. H. A. Korff (1933), 'Die Forderung des Tages', *Zeitschrift für Deutschkunde*, p. 341.
58. German reader for 8th form, quoted from K. I. Flessau (1977), *Schule der Diktatur*, Munich, p. 180.
59. A. Hitler (1942), *Mein Kampf*, 743–747th edn, Munich, pp. 258, 277.
60. Ibid., p. 469.
61. 'Amtlicher Teil', p. 51.
62. Reichsministerium (ed.), *Erziehung und Unterricht*, p. 207.
63. 'Amtlicher Teil', p. 49.
64. Hitler, *Mein Kampf*, p. 460.
65. Reichsministerium (ed.), *Erziehung und Unterricht*, pp. 1f.
66. Kraul, *Das deutsche Gymnasium*, p. 172.
67. Jarausch, *Deutsche Studenten*, p. 203.

TEXTUAL STUDIES

1. Ernst Robert Curtius, *Deutscher Geist in Gefahr*

Der deutsche Geist hat nicht entfernt in demselben Maße wie der Franzose oder der Engländer den Rückhalt an einer klar aufgebauten Gesellschaft und an wohlgefällig ausgebildeten Lebensformen. Aber dafür hat er in viel stärkerem Maße als die Westvölker ein metaphysisches Bedürfnis, einen philosophischen Drang zum Wesensurgrund

5   aller Dinge. Die Elemente, die Gründe und Sinnzusammenhänge der Natur, der
Geschichte und des übergeschichtlichen Geistes, das ist das große Thema des deutschen
Denkens, und mit diesen Aufgaben ringt es und in diesem Ringen trägt es Siege davon,
die den Rationalismus der Westvölker unendlich überflügeln. [. . .] Ich schließe daraus,
daß wir heute in Deutschland den wahren Nationalismus noch gar nicht haben. [. . .]
10 Ich gestehe niemanden [*sic*] und keiner Partei ein Monopol nationaler Gesinnung zu.
Ich behaupte vielmehr umgekehrt, daß alle diejenigen *nicht national genug* sind, die
sich auch jetzt noch nicht entschließen können, ihre Parteiwünsche und Parteiinteressen
dem heiligen Gebot des nationalen Zusammenschlusses unterzuordnen. Was im August
1914 möglich war – keine Parteien mehr, nur noch Deutsche – das muß auch im
15 Frühling 1932 möglich sein.
     (E. R. Curtius (1932), *Deutscher Geist in Gefahr*, Stuttgart)

Commentary

(numbers in parenthesis refer to line numbers in the text)

Ernst Robert Curtius (1886–1956), one of Germany's most eminent professors of
French literature, friend of Hofmannsthal and sympathizer with the Conservative
Revolution, working towards an elitist synthesis of German *Geist* with Christian
(Catholic) and humanist ideals. Although his kind of nationalism was opposed to
that of the Nazis, he expressed the hope that 1932 would see a decisive change for
the better! The text discusses the danger in which the German spirit finds itself
and shares the widely held belief that a division exists between *Geist* and *Macht*,
with the spirit being the hypostasis of power, a quasi-divine element. Curtius
discusses the difference between German culture and other Western cultures; he
recognizes that German culture lacks a certain amount of social integration and
realism (2f), but interprets this as an advantage for the Germans, since it allows
greater metaphysical depth and greater powers of abstraction (4–7). He thus
demands a 'true nationalism', based on the national spirit and not on political parties
(9–13). The rejection of party politics betrays a typical form of German political
culture and Curtius refers specifically to August 1914 and the Kaiser's statement
that Germans should rise above party politics (14). Other passages in Curtius's
book refer to a national and socialist union, based more on the ideas of Italian
fascism and cultural elitism than on Hitler's racism. He fails to support the Republic
for which he has nothing positive to say.

Vocabulary

Rückhalt (m) = support; 'Drang zum Wesensurgrund aller Dinge' = urge to get to
the bottom of everything; Sinnzusammenhang (m) = sense context; ringen = to
wrestle; überflügeln = to surpass.

2. *Hitler auf dem Reichsparteitag 1933*

Ihr seid noch jung. Ihr habt noch nicht die trennenden Einflüsse des Lebens ken-
nengelernt. Ihr könnt euch noch so unter- und miteinander verbinden, daß euch das
spätere Leben niemals zu trennen vermag. Ihr müßt in eure jungen Herzen nicht den
Eigendünkel, Überheblichkeit, Klassenauffassungen, Unterschiede von reich und arm
5   hineinlassen. Ihr müßt euch vielmehr bewahren, was ihr besitzt, das große Gefühl der
Kameradschaft und Zusammengehörigkeit.
(Julius Streicher (ed.) (1934), *Reichstagung in Nürnberg 1933*, Berlin, pp. 210f)

Commentary

Note the emphasis on a generation not yet spoilt by a potentially degenerate society.
The emphasis is again on *Gemeinschaft*, comradeship which will overcome all
divisions in life. The vices (from line 4 onwards) suggest an arrogant and divisive
intellectualism which the Youth Movement also sought to combat.

Vocabulary

trennend = divisive; vermag = can; Eigendünkel (m) = self-conceit; Klassenauf-
fassung (f) = class consciousness.

3. **Hitler,** *Mein Kampf*

Der völkische Staat hat in dieser Erkenntnis seine gesamte Erziehungsarbeit in erster
Linie nicht auf das Einpumpen bloßen Wissens einzustellen, sondern auf das Heranzüchten kerngesunder Körper. Erst in zweiter Linie kommt dann die Ausbildung der
geistigen Fähigkeiten. Hier aber wieder an der Spitze die Entwicklung des Charakters,
5   besonders die Förderung der Willens- und Entschlußkraft, verbunden mit der Erziehung
zur Verantwortungsfreudigkeit, und erst als letztes die wissenschaftliche Schulung.
   Die gesamte Bildungs- und Erziehungsarbeit des völkischen Staates muß ihre
Krönung darin finden, daß sie den Rassesinn und das Rassegefühl instinkt- und
verstandesgemäß in Herz und Gehirn der ihr anvertrauten Jugend hineinbrennt. Es
10   soll kein Knabe und kein Mädchen die Schule verlassen, ohne zur letzten Erkenntnis
über die Notwendigkeit und das Wesen der Blutreinheit geführt worden zu sein.
(Adolf Hitler (1942), *Mein Kampf*, 743–747th edn, Munich, pp. 452 and 475f)

Commentary

Note the emphasis on a *völkisch* community spirit, on the primacy of physical
health over knowledge, of character development over intellectual training, of ethnic
purity.

Vocabulary

Erkenntnis (f) = perception; Einpumpen (n) = impression; einstellen = to employ, enlist; Heranzüchten (n) = breeding; kerngesund = thoroughly healthy; Förderung (f) = promotion; Entschlußkraft (f) = decisiveness; Verantwortungsfreudigkeit (f) = readiness to take on responsibility; Krönung (f) = culmination; Rassesinn (m) = race consciousness; verstandesgemäß = rational; anvertraut = entrusted; hineinbrennen = to instil into; Blutreinheit (f) = blood purity.

4. Paul Ernst, 'Rasse'

Wir leiden in unserem heutigen Deutschland unzweifelhaft unter einer Herrschaft der Juden; diese ging vor der Revolution auf Kunst, Theater, Schriftstellerei, Presse; nun geht sie auch auf unser gesamtes staatliches Sein. Zu diesem Geistigen kommt die wirtschaftliche Macht. Sie wissen, ich bin nicht Antisemit im gewöhnlichen Sinne;
5 aber schließlich bin ich doch ein Deutscher und nicht ein Jude; und als Staatsmann muß ich mir klar werden, durch welche Mittel die Deutschen wieder von der Judenherrschaft frei werden können.
(Paul Ernst (1931), *Erdachte Gespräche*, Munich, pp. 348f)

Commentary
(numbers in parenthesis refer to line numbers in the text)

This rather extreme passage is taken from a collection of fictitious conversations between statesmen, philosophers and poets, classified as 'Repräsentanten des Menschengeschlechts' who discuss 'wesentliche Dinge'. The passage is both anti-semitic and anti-intellectual; anti-semitic in the perceived threat to Germany's future: Jews are seen to be infiltrating German literature and culture (2f), and eventually the state and the economy (4). The speaker maintains that he is not anti-semitic in the 'ordinary sense' (4), but is seeking ways to liberate Germany from Jewish domination.

Vocabulary

unzweifelhaft = without a doubt; Judenherrschaft (f) = Jewish domination.

5. 'Erziehung und Unterricht in der Höheren Schule'

Die nationalsozialistische Revolution der Weltanschauung hat an die Stelle des Trugbildes der gebildeten Persönlichkeit die Gestalt des wirklichen, d.h. durch Blut und geschichtliches Schicksal bestimmten deutschen Menschen gesetzt und an Stelle der

humanistischen Bildungsideologie, die bis in die jüngste Vergangenheit fortgelebt hatte,
5   eine Erziehungsordnung aufgebaut, die sich aus der Gemeinschaft des wirklichen
Kampfes entwickelt hatte. Nur aus dem Geist dieser politischen Zucht kann auch
echte Bildung als die zentrale Aufgabe der kommenden Schule erwachsen, die die
Begeisterungsfähigkeit des jungen Deutschen nicht lähmt, sondern steigert und zur
Einsatzfähigkeit fortführt.

('Amtlicher Teil, Neuordnung des höheren Schulwesens, Anlage: Grundlagen',
Deutsche Wissenschaft, Erziehung und Volksbildung, vol. 4 (1938), p. 49)

Commentary

(numbers in parenthesis refer to line numbers in the text)

The official argument against neo-classicism becomes clear if we focus on the antithesis between certain key words: the image of the educated person is an illusion (2), based on the concept of a humanist education (4); the destiny of the true German (3) is determined by blood (race) and history (2f); his education is grounded in community struggle (5), in discipline (6) and in a zeal (8) which will optimize his capacity for self-sacrifice (9).

Vocabulary

jüngst = recent; erwachsen = to develop; lähmen = to maim; steigern = to increase.

Re-education after 1945

Introduction

Until recently there was a virtual consensus as far as the results of Allied attempts at re-educating Germany were concerned. The established view suggested that a complete re-education programme was successful only in the Soviet zone and that the Western occupation powers achieved at best only limited success within their territories in refashioning the education system in accordance with modern democratic principles.[1] This rather negative view is as much the result of exaggerated expectations as of an underestimation of the forces of reaction, reaching much further back into German history and culture than the twelve years of Nazi rule. If we look at Germany from a more recent vantage point, it must be acknowledged not only that it is now fully integrated into Western political culture, but that its democratic structures have demonstrated an ability to embrace modern concepts and problems. Germany has developed a pluralist, tolerant response to political and public pressures and, especially amongst its younger generation, produced a protest culture which, in general, has been beneficial to the nation's social and political life.

Such a change could not have happened overnight. The experiences of war and nationalism and the 'ideological activity' of the previous age produced a 'sceptical generation' with an instinct to shun the public stage and to withdraw into the secure obscurity of private life.[2] This prevalent scepticism resulted in the rejection of all forms of idealism in favour of personal stability, with practical considerations such as career prospects uppermost in their minds [Text 1]. In contrast, the almost immediate and apparently successful transformation which many thought was evident in East Germany was perhaps less total than propagandist literature might have suggested and – in the aftermath of the collapse of the GDR – a re-evaluation of its social and educational reforms would therefore seem in order.

In view of the availability of a wealth of detailed studies on Allied education policies in the four occupation zones, this chapter will not consider each zone separately. It will attempt to focus on common problems such as the potential supersession of the old elite by a new one and will analyse the German response to Allied proposals for educational reform, examining specific interest groups such as the churches and the mandarins and the emerging political parties. In addition, problems common to all sectors will be discussed. Berlin will be treated as a special case study, for it was here that the four occupation forces had the most direct contact and where the ideological confrontation, brought about by the emerging Cold War, became most visible.

Initial Responses to the Forces of Occupation

In contrast to the situation in 1919, when most Germans failed to comprehend that their country had been defeated, that the Reich was demolished and that they must accept the diktat of an apparently unjust peace, the end of the Second World War was accepted with fatalism or even welcomed. The desperate material situation of the final months undoubtedly contributed to this emotional climate; regional administrations had lost faith in the political leadership, and unofficial reports from the front painted a bleak picture.[3] In view of such despair and with a fundamental breakdown in law and order, unconditional surrender was greeted with some relief. Whilst few Germans were optimistic enough to believe in a political future for their country, they were, nevertheless, grateful that they had survived. Thornton Wilder's play *The Skin of our Teeth* (1942), published in the US-controlled *Die Neue Zeitung* (December 1945) as *Wir sind noch einmal davongekommen*, was seen as a reflection of the German situation: the Antrobus family, having survived the Ice Age, the Flood and modern warfare, though destitute and starving, were yet again prepared for a new beginning, adjusting to an existence amongst the ruins, unsure but heedless as to whether this time they would fare much better than before.

Virtually all Germans suffered almost unimaginable material deprivation and this concentrated their disaffection on the leadership of the Third Reich. Slogans, such as the one daubed on the ruins of a devastated Berlin: 'Dazu brauchte Hitler 12 Jahre Zeit'[4] (This took Hitler twelve years), sought to place the blame for the catastrophe entirely on the Nazi leadership. An urgent need to obliterate the immediate past brought a burgeoning desire for new sensuous experiences, found in eroticism, jazz and expressionist poetry, constituting the other side of the 'sceptical generation', though this was perhaps limited to the more creative elites of the country.[5] The recognition of an inherent German guilt for the heinous crimes against humanity was slow to dawn in this post-war society; slower still was the awareness that much of this inhumanity was deeply rooted in Germany's history and culture. In contrast to the younger, sceptical generation, but possibly for similar reasons, the older generation attempted to salvage as much as possible of Germany's cultural tradition. With hindsight, we find it paradoxical that leading German academics such as Friedrich Meinecke advocated the founding of 'Goethe circles' in order to restore 'einen deutschen Charakter indebilis'[6] (a German character free of debility). The establishment of literary groups in many cities reflected the belief that, by concentrating on the 'human element' to the exclusion of all political and social factors, German culture could be rehabilitated. Once again it is the mandarin class, in a tradition almost unbroken since the Second Empire, which sought to re-establish German culture, unwilling to accept the influx of Western rationalism or an American 'subculture'.

The university establishment emerged as a stronghold of this mandarin tradition and few Nazi professors lost their posts. Others, although accepted as non-Nazis, 'stood firm in the long tradition of undemocratic or even anti-democratic thought'.[7] Of the forty-three professors of German literature who had actively participated in the Nazi 'Kriegseinsatz deutscher Hochschulgermanisten' (university Germanists in support of the war), twenty-nine continued in post after 1945, ten had either died or retired, and only two were actually dismissed.[8] With regard to the scrutiny of German Studies pertaining to the Nazi period – and we have seen in Chapter 4 how heavily the subject was steeped in *völkisch* traditions – little concern was expressed in reports and surveys about any deviation from the norms of scholarly integrity, reflecting once again the problematic nature of an often all too subjective *Geisteswissenschaften*. Seminal histories of German literature continued to praise 'faustisch-nationale Bluts- und Gemeinschaftsmetaphysik' (a Faustian-national metaphysical community of blood), deploring the 'Verlust an gemeinschaftlichem Denken und Gestalten, das Ausbleiben führender Kräfte, die einen Mittelpunkt der Orientierung bedeuten können'[9] (loss of community thinking and creativity, a lack of the leadership which could constitute a rallying point) and dismissing the 1933–45 period as a break in cultural continuity.[10] A leading handbook of German Studies excused the academic perversions of Nazi professors as the outcome of irrational tendencies which had already manifested themselves in the first decades of the twentieth century, concluding that by now (1957) they had been overcome, 'durch eine genau prüfende Verbindung der festen Traditionen wissenschaftlichen Verfahrens'[11] (through a strict scrutiny of the relationship of the firm traditions of scholarly practice).

A closer analysis of the issue would indicate that a majority of German Studies professors had escaped into aestheticism, thereby avoiding a discussion of the socio-political relevance of their subject. The first post-war conference of Germanists in Munich advocated a retreat from rational order in favour of pure poetry, which was considered to be 'wirklicher als die Wirklichkeit'[12] (more real than reality). Not content with a defence of their activities during the Third Reich, these professors, with almost breathtaking hypocrisy, displayed a reactionary scepticism towards the post-war era, seeing fit to warn of a crisis in the 'Humanitätsideal' (ideal of humanism) and anticipating the disintegration of the Christian faith – all this during a period which was just emerging from the horrors of National Socialism! Such statements were also to be found issuing from amongst the representatives of the 'inner exile', intellectuals who had remained within the borders of the Reich but had not supported the Nazis. They appear to have failed to register international developments since 1933, enabling Thomas Mann, with specific reference to Curtius, to describe such men as intellectually degenerate and politically quite impossible.[13] Even in the few exceptional instances where men of integrity made an honest effort to confront the past, their contribution seemed out of touch with the immediate situation. Karl Jaspers exemplifies this in his book *Die Idee der Universität*. Rewritten in May 1945 and intended as a complete revision of the 1923 edition, the author apparently felt no compulsion to change his basic assumptions. Despite recognizing the moral decline of German universities during the preceding fifty years, with a near moral collapse during the Third Reich, he nevertheless concludes: 'Bei der Wiedererrichtung der Universität ist die Rückkehr zu unseren besten Überlieferungen durch gegenwärtige Neuschöpfung eine Schicksalsfrage unseres geistigen Lebens überhaupt.'[14] (The return to our best traditions with the re-establishment of the university, through the current regeneration, has become a vital issue, affecting the whole of our cultural destiny.) His analysis of the humanist traditions of university life makes no attempt to encompass modern social and democratic concerns. The reader searches in vain for any references to student participation or for the need for wider access to higher education. Instead, *Bildung* is related to historical ideals such as that of the gentleman,[15] whilst the introduction of student grants is rejected on the grounds that they would only promote mediocrity.[16] Similar fears surface regarding the remuneration of junior university teachers, a practice said to militate against personal sacrifice whilst encouraging passive contentment.[17] Richard Hinton-Thomas, looking at German universities from a British perspective and writing at about the same time, saw clearly the weakness of the German tradition:

> The system of the unsalaried 'Privatdozent' is still in operation, theoretically on the grounds that it attracts only the most devoted scholars and so weeds out mere careerists. But it is based on the conception of the cultural mission of the well-to-do middle class, and its supporters are often motivated, even though unconsciously, by the consideration that it discourages men from the lower classes who cannot afford this unlucrative apprenticeship. Furthermore, its maintenance helps to uphold the authority of the professor, and the average German professor, to-day as in the past, is a conspicuous seeker after power and social prestige.[18]

It is hardly surprising, therefore, that General Lucius Clay, military governor of the US occupation zone, perceived that the old universities were bent on impeding the development of a democratic spirit and delaying the replacement of Nazi professors by democratic candidates, and he expressed regret that they had been reopened.[19]

Greater discrimination was observed in the selection of students: active Nazis or leaders of the Hitler Youth Movement were not admitted, nor were professional officers, SS volunteers and former pupils of special Nazi schools. The number of applicants far exceeded the available places, and the material needs of most students were so severe that they took priority over any implementation of a process of democratic participation. Anticipating the term 'sceptical generation', a British University Control Officer made the following comment with regard to his role in supporting and advising the students: 'They needed guidance in simple democratic procedures, such as electing their officers and committee, setting up committees dealing with problems of accommodation and student welfare, and how to chair a meeting. They were inclined to wait for orders from someone.'[20] Unlike the students of the Weimar Republic, this post-war generation showed little interest in politics but, where public debate touched on sensitive issues, a reactionary response ensued [Text 2]. In January 1946, Martin Niemöller, a leading member of the *Bekennende Kirche* (Confessing Church) and courageous opponent of the Third Reich, gave a lecture at Erlangen University. In reminding his audience of the Holocaust and of German war crimes committed in Poland and the Soviet Union, he provoked vehement criticism.[21]

Many of the observations made about the university sector also applied to the *Gymnasium*. A wholesale cleansing of the Nazi past was to be achieved by a return to humanist and Christian values, but only at the expense of political realism. Admission to the *Gymnasium* was dependent on passing an entrance examination at the age of ten and Latin was promoted as the first foreign language. Occasionally such elitist concepts were based on eugenic considerations, as in Lower Saxony, where a study in 1948 established a correlation between social status and genetic predisposition.[22] The revival of classics, German literature and music occurred at the expense of training in logical argument, public debate or student involvement in school life. Reform of the elementary sector, on the other hand, was more successful. As a result of the chaotic situation that had prevailed since the winter of 1944/5, many ten- and eleven-year-olds could hardly read or write. The enormous dearth of suitable teachers and school buildings resulted in unacceptably high pupil–teacher ratios, reaching 1:83 in Bavaria, with an average age for teachers of fifty-two.[23] Despite these material and logistical problems, most children in the age group 6–14 had returned to school by the autumn of 1945. A further disadvantage, common to teachers in every institution, was their complete isolation from international developments. Nazi propaganda, severe foreign currency controls and the war had cut them off from any debate on pedagogics and curriculum development, as well as from modern concepts of socialization and psychology. As a result, Allied support and guidance were essential, not merely in the material sense of building up libraries and forging international contacts, but also for the active suppression of fascist doctrines.

The Emerging Shape of German Post-War Education

The Potsdam Agreement transferred responsibility for Germany's re-education to the control of the Allied powers: 'German education shall be so controlled as completely to eliminate Nazi and militarist doctrines and to make possible the successful development of democratic ideas.'[24] This policy was explained in *Die Neue Zeitung*, a US Forces publication. It regarded the re-education programme as crucial for the rebuilding of Germany, clearly distancing itself from the 1944 Quebec Conference which had advocated reducing Germany to an agricultural backwater:

> [. . .] Die kulturelle und geistige Umerziehung des Volkes muß daher Hand in Hand gehen mit einer Politik, die darauf berechnet ist, die Stabilität einer deutschen Friedenswirtschaft wiederherzustellen und die Hoffnung auf eine zukünftige Wiedergewinnung der nationalen Einheit und nationalen Selbstachtung lebendig zu erhalten.[25]

> ([. . .] The cultural and intellectual re-education of the nation must, therefore, go hand in hand with a policy calculated to re-establish a stable German peace-time economy and to keep alive the hope for a restoration of national unity and self-respect in the future.)

Despite this declaration of goodwill, many newly established German authorities distrusted the Allies and sought to circumvent or sabotage their attempts at re-education, especially where the cherished selective tripartite system was at stake.

It was natural that the four Allied powers approached the problem very much from the point of view of their own indigenous systems. Furthermore, the denazification process was handled differently by each power: amongst the three Western powers, the Americans were the most stringent in this respect, apparently reflecting the 'punitive spirit' of earlier strategies,[26] in marked contrast to their very positive youth policies. The British approach was more pragmatic, seeking early personal contacts with German teachers and encouraging exchange programmes. Both powers attempted to restrict church control over schools, expand primary education and oppose any reintroduction of school fees. Their efforts were largely unsuccessful, since the reactionary elements within their zones soon gained political influence in the shape of the newly founded Christian Democratic Union (CDU).

The French authorities, too, promoted their own national education policies, especially their great concern with cultural matters and a desire for a centralized administration. But the French attitude also reflected their own recent history: denazification was carried out less stringently than in other zones. There was evidence that teachers, dismissed in the American Sector, found employment in the French

Zone. Every effort was made to enthuse Germans with the French *mission civil-isatrice*, hoping to instil into them a love of freedom and individualism: 'a compulsory daily period of French was regarded as the appropriate medium for fostering independence of mind and clarity of judgement'.[27]

The Soviet-occupied Zone introduced the most far-reaching reforms. Even prior to the cessation of hostilities, German *émigré* teachers, together with the Soviet authorities, had set to work on new school textbooks and to establish a new education system. The *Nationalkomitee Freies Deutschland* (National Committee for Free Germany) was guided by the German Communist Party conference decisions that had first seen the light in 1935 (Brussels) and 1939 (Berne).[28] Reforms were not only determined on a 'cleansing of education from fascist filth',[29] they also aimed to eliminate all capitalist and imperialist influence and, in particular, to break the upper-class monopoly within the sphere of education.[30] Attempts to revitalize the Reform Movement were soon rejected in favour of Marxist-Leninist pedagogics.[31] Some 40,000 new teachers were recruited from amongst the working classes, while teachers already in post were assessed as to their suitability for the new system and underwent retraining. It would be tempting to conclude that the Soviets were the most conscientious in adhering to the Potsdam Agreement and that their harmonious co-operation with German officials – in contrast to wide-spread disagreement and bickering in the Western zones – led to the successful establishment of a new and democratic education system. In fact, as early as April 1944, Communist leaders had already decided on very specific measures, including a three-month course for new teachers, as part of their general policy of indoc-trination. With the enforced amalgamation of the Social Democrats (SPD) and the Communists (KPD) into the Socialist Unity Party (SED) in April 1946, an element of coercion became evident which, whatever the merits of the socialist education reforms, damaged the free and open discussion of new ideas and, in contrast to developments in the Western zones, probably stifled long-term progress. The *Gesetz zur Demokratisierung der deutschen Schule*[32] (Law for the Democratization of the German School System) of May/June 1946 set the seal on a radical departure from German tradition. The school system already in existence, based on selection at the age of ten, was replaced by an integrated eight-year period of schooling, followed by a further four years of education, either at the *Berufsschule* (vocational school) or the *Oberschule* (secondary school). The former type was vocational and afforded access to technical college, the latter prepared pupils for university.

The provision of new textbooks was a problem which confronted the whole of occupied Germany. The existing book stock was completely unsuitable and books in use under the Weimar Republic proved unacceptable in their nationalist, militaristic or openly National Socialist proclivities. In 1944, Western forces had already begun to examine German textbooks, available in American and Swedish libraries. By December 1945, approved German teachers were being co-opted onto textbook committees. Figures from the British Zone indicate that, in elementary education, the ratio of pre-1933 reprints to new books was 1:1.4, compared to the secondary sector's ratio of 1:0.3.[33] A British report on 'German Textbook Literature' describes how every effort was made to eliminate nationalism, racism, militarism, violence and cruelty, as well as hostility towards international world organizations reminiscent of attitudes prevalent in the Wilhelmine period.[34] The same report also observes trends in the Soviet Zone: whilst acknowledging its superior textbook provision, it is critical of the many references to 'militarism, descriptions of war, fighting, militant heroes, traditionalism, folk-conscious nationalism [. . .], the defamation of other countries',[35] all reinforcing Marxist-Leninist propaganda. Even allowing for Cold War rhetoric, any casual glance at East German textbooks would vindicate these observations.

The Situation in Berlin: A Case Study

Educational policy in Berlin came under the control of the Four Power Kommandatura. Right from the outset, education was dominated by Soviet and East German Communist authorities. An analysis of their policies would suggest that early differences between the Eastern and Western sectors of the city were resolved by the joint determination of all four powers to modernize the system, even though their efforts were ultimately destroyed by Cold War tensions. Initial Communist proposals met with the approval of the US administration, which also favoured a twelve-year period of comprehensive education. The Americans even insisted that primary and secondary education should be under the same roof and that pupils should be taught by a joint body of staff.[36] These policies also had the support of most teaching unions, not least because Berlin was witnessing the return of many teachers who had, in the past, been keen supporters of *Reformpädagogik* and had long advocated a comprehensive system. Social Democrats and Liberals, too, preferred a system which guaranteed free access to education, regardless of parental background, and, aware of the reactionary role played by the Catholic Church during the Weimar Republic, they sought to exclude religious education from the official syllabus. Communist, socialist and liberal elements expressed a common interest by forming the *Kulturbund zur demokratischen Erneuerung Deutschlands* (1945) (Cultural Federation for the Democratic Renewal of Germany) in an attempt to create a progressive forum for culture and education.[37]

However, this atmosphere of co-operation did not last very long; as early as 1947, ideological cracks became visible. It is difficult to assess to what extent these divisions were the direct result of Cold War tensions. Early administrative rifts developed in the wake of Communist retraining policies, creating social tensions between individual districts. The more affluent Western districts of Zehlendorf, Charlottenburg and Steglitz enjoyed a relatively favourable pupil–

teacher ratio, whereas the Soviet-controlled areas suffered from a severe teacher shortage, partly the result of a rigorous de-nazification policy.[38] In order to overcome this problem, but also for ideological reasons, *Schulhelfer* (auxiliary teaching assistants) were recruited, usually committed Communists with little pedagogical expertise. Western districts were compelled to accept these assistants, often at the expense of professional teachers.

By the end of 1947, the Catholic Church, supported by the CDU in opposing the secularization of the school system, had succeeded in gaining the support of the influential American Cardinal Francis Spellman. He protested to the US authorities about the exclusion of religious education from the curriculum and the closure of private schools.[39] Both measures were deemed to offend against the democratic principle of minority rights; they were also seen as a rebuff to a middle-class public which, it was felt, had yet to be won over to the democratic process. By May 1948 a compromise formula had emerged: religious education was still excluded in the public sector, but private schools were reinstated, 'limited to those which have been authorized up to the present time, and to the small number which may be authorized according to the same procedure as was used in the case of the existing ones'.[40]

Controversies over the selection of a history textbook, acceptable to all parties, had already highlighted serious ideological divisions. By the summer of 1946, the resumption of German history lessons had been scheduled and the Communist school authorities, supported by the Soviet military administration, had proposed a curriculum which was unacceptable to the Western powers: its Marxist view of history blamed monopoly capitalism for the rise of National Socialism and for the outbreak of the Second World War. The Americans, rejecting an historical interpretation based exclusively on economic factors, wished to stress the liberal, democratic tendencies in the German tradition.[41] The US authorities now openly discussed a split in the administration of the city in order to facilitate education 'along democratic lines'.[42] The Berlin Blockade put an end to any meaningful co-operation and by December 1948 education policy followed a *de facto* political reality.

One important consequence of this increasing tension and of growing ideological divisions in higher education was the establishment of the Free University of West Berlin. The Eastern Sector wished to see an expansion in the number of working-class children entering higher education with a strengthening of the vocational element at university level. Within the first two years of its reopening, the number of working-class students enrolling at the renamed Humboldt University had risen from 9 to 25 per cent[43] and selection for higher education followed strictly ideological guidelines. Student representatives with no working-class or Communist background felt discriminated against. In one incident, the editors of the student paper *Colloquium* were expelled over a reference to the new *Rektor*'s Nazi past.[44]

This punitive action was supported by the Senate and a majority of the professors. A large demonstration in April 1948 led to demands for permission to set up a new university. General Lucius Clay, commander of the US Forces, secured American funds and books and, despite the extreme deprivation suffered by the blockaded Western sectors during the winter of 1948/9, the Free University was founded, consisting of just over 2,000 students and 128 faculties.[45] In a break with German convention, the new university had a democratic structure with student participation at all levels [Text 3]. Intended as a beacon of Western democratic freedoms, it was often held up as a model for university reform. Unfortunately it did not retain its democratic status for very long, unable to withstand the pressures of the mandarin tradition. Nevertheless, it took centre stage in the student protests of the late 1960s, and the extent to which this can be ascribed to its liberal constitution will be examined in Chapter 6.

Forces of Reaction

The controversies in Berlin over comprehensive education, religious instruction and private schools were reflected throughout Germany, developing into altercations between the German authorities and the occupation forces in the Western zones. In contrast, the Soviet Sector imposed its own preferred solution, often against the will of the majority of Germans. In the West, the debates re-enacted disputes which had raged during the period of the Weimar Republic, involving the churches, the mandarins and – on a more general level – the *Bildungsbürgertum*, all advocating a reactionary, restrictive policy. The forces of modernism were once again defeated, ending any hope of a comprehensive and secular education system, based on the concepts of *Reformpädagogik*.[46] The end of the Second World War saw reactionary elements regaining a prominent position, partly through their claims of alleged suppression by the Nazis. Paradoxically, however, their own anti-modernist policies often continued precisely those trends which the Nazi regime itself had encouraged. The surviving members of the 20 July Resistance Group serve as just one such example. Often against the wishes of the occupying authorities,[47] they advocated a return to traditional German values in family life, church influence in education and the restoration of a humanist culture. This found a ready response within some newly established political circles which were informed by the policies of the Catholic Church or by the views of the *Kreisauer Kreis*, which in 1943 was already advocating a strictly Christian concept of education, based on conservative family values and embedded within a humanist, European tradition.[48]

The churches played a leading part in such policies: even before hostilities had ceased, they were preparing to regain their hold in every aspect of education. The World Council of Churches, supported by British and American bishops, facilitated contacts with other churches. The key role played by priests and pastors during the de-nazification process is well known, their testimony leading to the reinstatement of many teachers.[49] The Catholic Church, in particular, fought hard to regain the position it had enjoyed during the Weimar Republic, using Cold War rhetoric to achieve its aims. An Episcopal Decree of 1948 described inter-denominational education as a 'constant de-Christianization of the school', seeing the ideological interlacing between the German Trade Union Congress, the Social Democrats and the teachers' unions as a general move towards a Bolshevik takeover.[50] Cardinal Frings of Cologne sought to extend church influence beyond school into teacher-training colleges, aiming to control the syllabus, in line with the 1929 Encyclical of Pope Pius XI, laying down the Church's 'inalienable right' to control education 'in all institutions [. . .] in regard to every other branch of learning and every regulation in as far as religion and morality are concerned'.[51]

Bavaria became a centre for Catholic reaction, restoring mono-confessional schools immediately after the war, ostensibly in line with a Bavarian royal decree dating back to 1883.[52] Interdenominational schools, which had been set up after 1933, were abolished or converted into mono-confessional schools and religious orders were granted a licence to establish new private schools. The newly formed Christian Socialist Union (CSU) supported such policies, and it was not until 1968 that interdenominational schools became the rule in Bavaria. Alois Hundhammer, the minister responsible for education, rejected the substantial reform plans proposed by the US military government and, in the ensuing battle between the CSU and the US authorities, the Catholic Church, in association with Catholic teaching unions and the universities, resisted all American pressure for change, employing delaying tactics until the end of the occupation era (1949).[53] Similar patterns, though less extreme, were evident in most Western zones. In North Rhine–Westphalia and in the Rhineland–Palatinate mono-confessional schools became the norm, although in Baden and in Rhineland–Hesse they were opposed, despite the support of the governing CDU. The most crucial damage caused to the modernization of education was in the sphere of elementary schooling, where these policies encouraged the selection of children at the age of ten and denied to whole sections of society the opportunity to enter the *Gymnasium* and thereby higher education.

A second reactionary voice came from within the staff of the *Gymnasium*, represented by the *Philologenverband*, the professional association of grammar school teachers. Like the churches, they also sought some redress from alleged Nazi victimization. They insisted on their independence from other teacher organizations, both as far as teacher training and any envisaged development towards comprehensive education was concerned. Selection at the age of ten remained the rule, except in Schleswig-Holstein and the city states of Hamburg, Bremen and Berlin, where primary education was extended to the age of twelve, with foreign-language tuition introduced in the final year.[54] The period of study at the *Gymnasium* was again gradually extended to nine years. The US 'Zock Commission' criticized the undemocratic nature of the 'aristocratic-militarist tradition'[55] fostered in the *Gymnasium*, with its elitist selection ensuring a tripartite school system which rejected 90 per cent of an age group and discriminated against those social strata which were already disadvantaged in economic, social and cultural terms[56] [Text 4]. Bavaria, once more the most reactionary region under CSU Education Minister Hundhammer, rejected US-inspired reforms on genetic grounds! Only a limited number of pupils, predominantly from the higher social strata, were to benefit from grammar schools: 'Diese biologisch gegebene Ungleichheit kann durch keine zivilisatorischen Maßnahmen beseitigt werden, auch nicht durch die Änderung unseres sogenannten zweispurigen Schulsystems zugunsten eines Einheitsschulsystems.'[57] (This biologically established inequality cannot be eliminated by civilizing measures, not even by a change to our so-called two-tier school system in favour of a unitary system.) Any such move would be seen to undermine the centuries-old tradition in education and revive National Socialist education policies. The old demand that *Volksschullehrer* should benefit from university education was likewise rejected, on the basis of arguments from the time of the Weimar Republic and going back to the days of Ferdinand Stiehl and 1850s Prussia. An inflated higher education for teachers entrusted with the task of educating useful citizens was believed to undermine the democratic (!) education of the German people.[58] No attempt was made to explain the curious contradiction that while higher education for the privileged minority was designed to overcome the legacy of National Socialism, such an education was apparently not in the interests of democracy when applied to the lower social classes. Such entrenched opinions gained the full endorsement of the churches and the universities, both of which attempted, for different reasons, to deprive large sections of an age group of a more academic, intellectually liberating form of education.

A third reactionary force in post-war education was centred on the *Elternrecht*, the right of parents to decide on a child's education. Since the autonomy of parents in general, and of the family in particular, had been severely infringed by the Nazis, all politicians in the West, in alliance with the occupation forces, sought to respect parental choice. However, the term itself was deceptive in so far as most vocal and politically aware parents belonged to the middle social strata and, crucially, to that academic elite which displayed a natural interest in self-perpetuation. The lower social strata, particularly in the traditionally more Catholic regions such as the Rhineland, Westphalia and Bavaria, found that their 'right' was being manipulated by the Church in favour of mono-confessional education and small rural schools (figure 8). Another factor in the exercise of parental choice was the tripartite system itself. Selection for the *Gymnasium* was based on the decision of parents rather than on the professional judgement of teachers or any other assessment of educational suitability. As late as 1953, a legal ruling in Hamburg gave priority to

Figure 8 A rural *Einklassenschule* of the early 1960s. This type of school remained in existence until the mid-1960s. One teacher taught the complete curriculum and took responsibility for all children in the age group six to fourteen. Usually taught together, pupils were separated only for classes in arithmetic and German and often received only two to three hours' tuition per day. (Reproduced with the kind permission of Walter Weller, Neubronn.)

parental choice, a factor deemed vital to the development of the student's personality.[59] A decisive element in the court's verdict may have been the fact that German schools, then as now, usually release their students at midday, ensuring that parental involvement in supervision of homework and private study is essential. As a result of such policies, the education system in the Western zones did little to change the social composition of the existing system. The term *nivellierte Mittelstandsgesellschaft*[60] (a levelled-out middle-class society), often applied during the early years of the Federal Republic, proved to be largely cosmetic, as became apparent a decade later when the debate on *Begabungsreserven* (educational reserves) was to highlight the many serious inequalities and injustices affecting the rural population and the working classes.

Conclusion

With this discussion focusing mainly on the Western Sectors, an analysis of developments in the Soviet Sector will be given in Chapter 7. The resolutions of the Potsdam Agreement, as applied in the West, were only partially fulfilled. Whilst there was little evidence of a new spirit of German militarism in the immediate post-war period, there was also no genuine or far-reaching desire to democratize the education system. Universities upheld their authoritarian structures, the *Gymnasium* was more concerned with the pursuit of its 'humanist' tradition than with democratic values, thereby favouring the traditional *Bildungsbürgertum*, whilst parents, frequently under the influence of the churches, were intent on the restoration of an anti-democratic, conservative system which had previously hindered progress under the Weimar Republic. The rare attempts at a genuine democratization of the system were haphazard and half-hearted. Only the SPD-governed city states, together with Hesse, Lower Saxony and Schleswig-Holstein, attempted to postpone the selection process by extending the period of primary education. Elsewhere, councils were established to assist teachers in internal organizational matters, but far-reaching structural change was neglected. And yet it was probably unrealistic to expect a radical change in the direction of a Western-style society, given that the educational system had traditionally upheld authoritarian undemocratic structures.[61]

A restructuring of the youth organizations may have been one such modest social reform. Protestant and Catholic youth groups were established in the immediate post-war period, followed by the relaunch of the reformist *Bündische Jugend* and, shortly afterwards, by liberal, social-democratic and socialist or trade union-sponsored youth organizations. The US Sector inaugurated the German Youth Activities programme, stimulated by initiatives on the part of the US Army to win over German youth and keep them out of trouble.[62] Youth exchange programmes followed, particularly with the United States, where it was intended that young

Germans should experience a working democracy, thereby encouraging them to recognize the mistakes of their parents' generation. However, a genuine coming-to-terms with the Nazi past did not occur. It needed more time in order to succeed and it was too high an expectation of a still traumatized people. The post-war period, moreover, was characterized by 'anti-historical' tendencies on an international scale, brought about by an enthusiasm for technological innovation, a strong sense of security, egalitarian trends and a generally universalist, supra-national attitude.[63] A wider-ranging analysis of literary trends would reveal that a genuinely serious commitment to democracy and a meaningful debate on education under the Nazis did not begin until the mid-1960s, culminating in the student revolution of 1968. Indeed, the ghost of the *unbewältigte Vergangenheit* (the past with which Germany has not yet come to terms) is still not laid. The concept of a *zweite Schuld*[64] (second guilt) has emerged, which attempts to cover up the 'first' guilt, a phenomenon best illustrated by the scandal surrounding Michael Verhoeven's film *Das schreckliche Mädchen* (The Terrible Girl), which portrays the hostility of the authorities and citizens of Passau towards a young girl who attempts to uncover the truth about events in her own community during the Third Reich.[65]

Notes

1. K.-H. Füssl (1994), *Die Umerziehung der Deutschen. Jugend und Schule unter den Siegermächten des Zweiten Weltkriegs 1945–1955*, Paderborn, p. 15.
2. H. Schelsky (1960), *Die skeptische Generation. Eine Soziologie der deutschen Jugend*, 4th edn, Düsseldorf and Cologne, pp. 84f.
3. H. Glaser (1995), *1945, ein Lesebuch*, Frankfurt/M., p. 34.
4. H. Glaser (1989), *Kulturgeschichte der Bundesrepublik Deutschland, zwischen Kapitulation und Währungsreform, 1945–1948*, vol. 1, Munich, p. 36.
5. Glaser, *1945*, pp. 160–2.
6. F. Meinecke (1946), *Die deutsche Katastrophe. Betrachtungen und Erinnerungen*, Wiesbaden, p. 176.
7. R. H. Samuel and R. Hinton Thomas (1949), *Education and Society in Modern Germany*, London, p. 175.
8. W. Dahle (1969), *Der Einsatz einer Wissenschaft. Eine sprachinhaltliche Analyse militärischer Terminologie in der Germanistik 1933–1945*, Bonn, p. 66.
9. F. Martini (1958), *Deutsche Literaturgeschichte. Von den Anfängen bis zur Gegenwart*, Stuttgart, pp. 556 and 592.

10. H. A. and E. Frenzel (1966), *Daten deutscher Dichtung*, Munich, vol. 2, pp. 256f.
11. J. Dünninger (1957), 'Geschichte der deutschen Philologie', in W. Stammler (ed.), *Deutsche Philologie im Aufriß*, 2nd edn, vol. 1, Berlin, column 197.
12. W. Höllerer (1951), 'Die erste deutsche Germanistentagung in München', *Germanisch-Romanische Monatsschrift*, vol. 32/3, p. 147, quote attributed to E. Ruprecht.
13. Th. Mann (1963), *Briefe 1937–1947*, Frankfurt/M., p. 569.
14. K. Jaspers (1946), *Die Idee der Universität*, 2nd edn, Berlin and Heidelberg, Vorwort.
15. Ibid., p. 31.
16. Ibid., p. 119.
17. Ibid.
18. Samuel and Hinton Thomas, *Education and Society*, pp. 179f.
19. Glaser, *1945*, p. 173.
20. G. Bird (1978), 'Universities', in A. Hearnden (ed.), *The British in Germany. Educational Reconstruction after 1945*, London, p. 151.
21. Glaser, *1945*, p. 176.
22. K. V. Müller (1948), 'Begabung und Begabungseigenart im schulischen Nachwuchs. Erster Bericht über die Niedersächsische Begabtenuntersuchung nach den Ergebnissen der Auszählung des Regierungsbezirks Hannover', *Die Wandlung*, no. 3, pp. 360–70, esp. p. 363.
23. G. Giese (1961), *Quellen zur deutschen Schulgeschichte seit 1800*, Göttingen, p. 295.
24. 'Protocol of Proceedings of the Berlin Conference, July 17–August 2, 1945, II, 7', quoted from H. Feis (1960), *Between War and Peace. The Potsdam Conference*, Princeton, p. 341.
25. Quoted from Giese, *Quellen*, p. 292.
26. *1945 Directive to the Commander in Chief, U.S. Forces of Occupation*, quoted from A. Hearnden (1974), *Education in the Two Germanies*, Oxford, p. 36.
27. E. Vermeil (1949), 'Notes sur la Rééducation en Zone Française', in H. Liddell (ed.), *Education in Occupied Germany*, Paris, pp. 65f.
28. H. Klein (1974), *Bildung in der DDR*, Reinbek b. Hamburg, p. 50.
29. *Dokumente und Materialien zur Geschichte der deutschen Arbeiterbewegung*, Serie 3, Berlin 1959, vol. 1, p. 19, quoted from K.-H. Günther and G. Uhlig (1973), *History of the Schools in the German Democratic Republic 1945 to 1968*, Berlin, p. 13.
30. F. Rücker (1966), 'Die Arbeit der Lehrer im Nationalkomitee "Freies Deutschland" und die schulpolitisch-pädagogische Arbeit des Nationalkomitees', in *Protokoll der Konferenz 'Die Lehrer im antifaschistischen Widerstandskampf der europäischen Völker (1933–1945)'*, Potsdam, pp. 158ff.
31. L. Gläser (1970), 'Die deutsch–sowjetischen Beziehungen auf schulpolitischem

und pädagogischem Gebiet in den ersten Nachkriegsjahren – Ausdruck einer konsequenten marxistisch-leninistischen Bildungspolitik', *Vergleichende Pädagogik*, vol. 2, p. 119.

32. B. Michael and H. H. Schepp (eds) (1993), *Die Schule in Staat und Gesellschaft. Dokumente zur deutschen Schulgeschichte im 19. und 20. Jahrhundert*, Frankfurt/M., pp. 341–5. Cf. also Klein, *Bildung in der DDR*, p. 50.
33. K. S. Davis, 'The Problem of Textbooks', in Hearnden (ed.), *The British in Germany*, p. 112.
34. Ibid., p. 115.
35. Ibid., p. 116.
36. L. Froese (ed.) (1969), *Bildungspolitik und Bildungsreform*, Munich, p. 111.
37. Cf. H.-J. Schmitt (1983), 'Literaturbetrieb als Staatsmonopol', in H.-J. Schmitt (ed.), *Hansers Sozialgeschichte der deutschen Literatur*, Munich, vol. 11, p. 52.
38. Füssl, *Die Umerziehung*, p. 301.
39. Ibid., p. 322.
40. Minutes of Berlin Kommandatura Deputies, 4 May 1948, quoted from Füssl, *Die Umerziehung*, p. 323.
41. Füssl, *Die Umerziehung*, p. 311.
42. Office of Military Government, Berlin Sector, 29 November 1948, quoted from Füssl, *Die Umerziehung*, p. 324.
43. U. Schlicht (1980), *Vom Burschenschaftler bis zum Sponti. Studentische Opposition gestern und heute*, Berlin, p. 40.
44. Ibid., pp. 42f.
45. Ibid., p. 45.
46. Hearnden, *Education in the Two Germanies*, p. 42.
47. Cf. Füssl, *Die Umerziehung*, p. 91, who quotes from the US National Archives on US reaction to the 20 July Resistance Group's programme for a new government in Germany.
48. Cf. J. Hohlfeld (ed.) (1953), *Dokumente der deutschen Politik und Geschichte von 1848 bis zur Gegenwart*, Berlin and Munich, vol. 5, pp. 439ff.
49. M. Kraul (1984), *Das deutsche Gymnasium 1780–1980*, Frankfurt/M., p. 190.
50. W. Klafki (1971), 'Restaurative Schulpolitik 1945–1950 in Westdeutschland. Das Beispiel Bayern', in S. Oppolzer and R. Lassahn (eds), *Erziehungswissenschaft zwischen Herkunft und Zukunft der Gesellschaft*, Wuppertal and Ratingen, p. 158.
51. Quoted from Samuel and Hinton Thomas, *Education and Society*, p. 169.
52. 'Verordnung vom 26. August 1883 über die Errichtung von Volksschulen', quoted from Klafki, 'Restaurative Schulpolitik', p. 145.
53. M. Heinemann (ed.) (1981), *Umerziehung und Wiederaufbau. Die Bildungspolitik der Besatzungsmächte in Deutschland und Österreich*, Stuttgart, chapter by J. F. Tent, 'Education and Religious Affairs Branch', pp. 68–85.

54. Hearnden, *Education in the two Germanies*, p. 44.
55. K. E. Bungenstab (1970), *Umerziehung zur Demokratie? Re-education-Politik im Bildungswesen der US-Zone 1945–1949*, Düsseldorf, p. 51.
56. Kraul, *Das deutsche Gymnasium*, p. 186.
57. Intermediary report to US Military Government by A. Hundhammer (7 March 1947), quoted from Klafki, 'Restaurative Schulpolitik', p. 153.
58. Letter by Ministerpräsident Hans Ehard to US Military Government (January 1947), quoted from Klafki, 'Restaurative Schulpolitik', p. 157.
59. Cf. L. von Friedeburg (1992), *Bildungsreform in Deutschland. Geschichte und gesellschaftlicher Widerspruch*, Frankfurt/M., p. 299.
60. H. Schelsky (1953), *Wandlungen der deutschen Familie in der Gegenwart*, Stuttgart, p. 332.
61. Samuel and Hinton Thomas, *Education and Society*, p. 181.
62. Cf. Füssl, *Die Umerziehung*, pp. 148–67.
63. K. Sontheimer (1971), *Deutschland zwischen Demokratie und Antidemokratie*, Munich, pp. 13–16.
64. R. Giordano (1987), *Die zweite Schuld*, Hamburg.
65. B. Ortmeyer (1996), *Schulzeit unterm Hitlerbild*, Frankfurt/M., pp. 168f.

TEXTUAL STUDIES

1. Helmut Schelsky, *Die skeptische Generation*

Diese dem jugendlichen Wesen recht unangemessenen Erfahrungen des Krieges und seiner Folgen haben nicht nur die Identifikationsbereitschaft mit bestimmten politischen Systemen, etwa dem Nationalsozialismus oder dem Nationalismus, erschüttert, sondern die politische Glaubensbereitschaft und ideologische Aktivität, die die vorige Gener-
5 ationsgestalt der Jugend insgesamt kennzeichnete, an der Wurzel vernichtet. [. . .] Indem für diese Jugend [. . .] der Bereich der 'primären' Sozial- und Gruppenbindungen, der Ausgangsbereich ihrer kindlichen Verhaltensheimat, zutiefst verunsichert und gefährdet wurde, ging ihr Streben nach Verhaltenssicherheit und Bewahrung des Vertrauten auch auf die Festigung dieser persönlichen und privaten Lebensverhältnisse aus. [. . .] Wir
10 haben uns dafür entschieden, den ebenfalls von allen Beurteilern dieser Jugend zugeschriebenen skeptischen und nüchternen Wirklichkeitssinn, der sie von der romantischen Geisteshaltung der Jugendbewegung und dem ideologischen Denken der 'politischen Jugend' unterscheidet, zu ihrer vorläufigen Kennzeichnung zu wählen, und sprechen daher von der 'skeptischen Generation', eine Benennung, die eine größere
15 zeitliche Distanz oder ein anderes Verhältnis dieser Jugend bestätigen mag oder nicht.
(H. Schelsky (1960), *Die skeptische Generation. Eine Soziologie der deutschen Jugend*, 4th edn, Düsseldorf and Cologne, pp. 85–8)

Commentary

(numbers in parenthesis refer to line numbers in the text)

Schelsky's description of the post-1945 generation analyses a process of de-politicization and de-ideologization which makes any personal identification with a political system or ideology impossible (1–5). As a result, the new generation has retreated into the private sphere (9) and has developed a new sceptical sense of realism. Schelsky's observations could be backed up by a similar analysis of post-war literature which also avoided any reference to romantic notions and ideals, attempting instead the portrayal of life as realistically as possible.

Vocabulary

Wesen (n) = nature; Identifikationsbereitschaft (f) = readiness to identify; erschüttert = shaken; Glaubensbereitschaft (f) = readiness to believe; Generationsgestalt (f) = generation; Ausgangsbereich (m) = starting base; Verhaltensheimat (f) = behavioural background; Beurteiler (m) = judge; zugeschrieben = attributed to.

2. Karl Barth, 'Der deutsche Student'

[. . .] Aus der Erkenntnis, daß die Welt es nun einmal ablehnt, 'am deutschen Wesen genesen' zu sollen, wird gerade er gewiß nicht die Folgerung ziehen dürfen, daß der Deutsche nun am amerikanischen oder russischen Wesen zu genesen hätte. Er wird aber auch scharfe Wache darüber halten müssen, daß es nicht zu neuen, tiefsinnigeren
5 oder ebenso humorlosen Wiederholungen jener alten Parole komme. [. . .] Die dritte Gefahr, die den deutschen Studenten bedroht, ist [. . .] die immer noch fast hermetische Abschließung Deutschlands dem Ausland gegenüber. [. . .] Zum Heranwachsen einer neuen besseren Akademikerschicht trägt sie jedenfalls nichts bei. Es tut dem deutschen Studenten nicht gut, in dem Ghetto zu leben, in das er jetzt mit seinem ganzen Volke
10 verwiesen ist. Daß ihm gerade die wichtigsten Anregungen im Blick auf seine Zukunft entgehen müssen, solange die deutschen Universitäten vom Ausland her nicht wieder frei und allgemein besucht werden können und solange die ausländischen Universitäten den deutschen Studenten [. . .] verschlossen sind, das ist höchst wahrscheinlich. Und höchst wahrscheinlich ist auch dies, daß die Isolierung, in der der deutsche Student
15 jetzt studieren muß, der Neubildung eben der geistigen Autarkie, eben der deutschen Introvertiertheit, Vorschub leisten muß. [. . .]
Die vierte Gefahr ist die ältere Generation, die dem deutschen Studenten besonders in der Gestalt der Mehrheit seiner Professoren entgegentritt. [. . .] Und es ist klar, daß die wenigen, die hier zu nennen wären, viele andere aufwiegen. Aber es sind zu viel
20 dieser anderen, die der 'Denazifikation' unter irgendeinem Titel entkommen sind und die dennoch viel zu wenig gelernt und viel zu wenig vergessen haben, als daß sie der akademischen Jugend gerade bei der für ihre Zukunft so dringend nötigen Klärung

des Verhältnisses von deutscher Vergangenheit und Gegenwart und zu einer wirklichen
Aufgeschlossenheit für neue Fragestellungen hilfreich sein können: keine Bösewichte,
25 keine Nazis, nur unverbesserliche Nationalisten in der Art derer, die das zum erstenmal
frei gewordene Deutschland 1918–1933 dem neuen Verderben entgegengeführt, es
schlicht ans Schlachtmesser geliefert, dann sich als 'anständige Leute' aufs Grollen
und wohl aufs Komplottieren gegen Hitler verlegt haben und nun längst wieder zu
mehr oder weniger vernehmlichem Grollen gegen die letztlich nicht gänzlich ohne
30 ihre ganz besondere Mitschuld entstandene Lage übergegangen sind.
(Karl Barth, 'Der deutsche Student', *Die neue Zeitung*, 8 December 1947)

Commentary

(numbers in parenthesis refer to line numbers in the text)

Karl Barth (1886–1968), a famous Swiss theology professor and existentialist
philosopher, took a special interest in the reform of German intellectual life. His
argument has, of necessity, to be shortened here. Barth recognizes that the 'new'
Germans cannot be colonized by the Allies (1–3), but he also sees four specific
dangers which might hinder progress towards democratization: catastrophic material
needs which weaken the resolution to participate in a democratic community, the
presence of Allied troops who frequently do not act as exemplary leaders and
educators, isolation from international academic life (5–16) and the presence of
the older generation of German professors who, though not active Nazis, passively
encouraged inroads into democracy and are still opposed to change (17–25). Barth
recognizes the help given by the Allies in opening up Germany and the readmittance
of students into a wider international community as decisive. 'Am deutschen Wesen
genesen' (1f), a phrase used by the poet E. Geibel (1871) and rendered famous in
a speech by Kaiser Wilhelm II in 1907.

Vocabulary

Wache (f) = guard; tiefsinniger = more profound; Akademikerschicht (f) = class of
academics; verwiesen = relegated; Vorschub leisten = to encourage; aufwiegen =
to make up for; Aufgeschlossenheit (f) = openness; Fragestellung (f) = formulation
of a question; Bösewicht (m) = villain; Verderben (n) = disaster; Grollen (n) =
wrath; Komplottieren (n) = conspiracies.

3. *Gründungsaufruf zur Errichtung der Freien Universität Berlin*

Es geht um die Errichtung einer freien Universität, die der Wahrheit um ihrer selbst
willen dient. Jeder Studierende soll wissen, daß er sich dort im Sinne echter Demokratie
frei zur Persönlichkeit entfalten kann und nicht zum Objekt einseitiger Propaganda

wird. Jeder Dozent soll hier frei von Furcht und ohne einseitige Bindung an partei-
5 politische Doktrin lehren und forschen können. Aus dem Geiste der Selbstbehauptung
heraus, mit der sich Berlin gegen die über die Stadt verhängte Blockade erhob, soll
diese Universität erstehen und als geistiger Mittelpunkt des freiheitlichen Berlin der
Gesundung Deutschlands dienen.
(L. von Friedeburg et al. (1968), *Freie Universität und politisches Potential*, Berlin,
p. 48)

Commentary

Although the Free University of Berlin arose out of the Cold War confrontation
between – mainly – US and Soviet forces, its liberal spirit was to become a beacon
for other German universities, indicating to German students what a modern Western
university should be. For the first time in their history, German university students
had an active role in the running of the university (cf. E. Heilmann, 'The Students'
Role in the Free University', in *The American-German Review*, vol. 18, no. 2
(December 1951), p. 12). Unfortunately the forces of reaction did much to undermine this free and democratic spirit (cf. Chapter 6).

Vocabulary

Selbstbehauptung (f) = self-assertion; verhängt = declared.

4. *Übergangsrichtlinien für die bayrischen Volksschulen*

Entgegen dem vielfach festzustellenden Drang nach neuen Methoden und aufzeigbaren
Effekten müssen im Volksschulunterricht vor allem Ruhe und Einfalt einkehren. [. . .]
Die Volksschule muß wieder eine Stätte schlichter, geordneter Arbeit werden, in der
religiöser Geist, echte Autorität, sinnvolles Leistungsstreben, Zusammenarbeit mit
5 Elternhaus und Kirche, der Geist des Verstehens und der Freude die Jugend zu edlem
Menschentum formt und die notwendigen Grundlagen für die Lebenstüchtigkeit
erworben werden.
(Bayerisches Staatsministerium für Unterricht und Kultus (1952), *Dokumente zur
Schulreform in Bayern*, Munich, p. 27)

Commentary

The opening sentence indicates an aversion to new methods, anticipating a
later CDU/CSU political slogan demanding 'no experiments'. The emphasis on
secondary virtues such as *Ruhe, Einfalt* and *Autorität* as well as on religion, are
reminiscent of the *Stiehlsche Regulative*, discussed in Chapter 2.

Vocabulary

Drang (m) = urge; aufzeigbar = demonstrable; Einfalt (f) = simplicity; Lebenstüchtigkeit (f) = fitness for life.

−6−

The Education System of the Federal Republic 1949–1989: The Reluctant Process of Modernization

Introduction

The ground rules in education were fairly well established by the time the Federal Republic came into being in 1949. Central government had little influence over education and was more concerned with creating an affluent society than with modernizing an education system which still seemed adequate to guarantee economic growth.

Research into the educational policies of the Federal Republic has all too often been restricted to comparisons with the GDR. Whilst such comparisons are perfectly justifiable and yield many interesting insights, with both systems sharing a common history, culture and language, they have occasionally led to generalizations or, by too great an emphasis on change, have depicted the West German education system in an unflattering light. While the socialist East saw education as essential to its comprehensive social reform programme, based on an ideological agenda, the West sought to re-establish a pre-fascist, mainstream capitalist society, cushioned from radical exploitation by its social-market economy. A return to the education policies of the Weimar period seemed both consistent and defensible, in line with the general conservative policy of 'no experiments'.[1] A comparison of the Federal Republic's education policy with Western capitalist models will certainly illustrate that, though somewhat old-fashioned, it did not appear to lag quite as far behind as comparisons with the GDR might suggest.

The first section of this chapter surveys the constitutional framework, emphasizing early developments, concentrating on the co-operation between federal and *Land* governments, and seeking to discover how far this framework helped or hindered the reform programme. A second section discusses the reform programme of the 1960s and early 1970s, exploring the question of whether these reforms were part of a wider, Western concept of reform and social modernization, originating in the United States, and to what extent the political constellation in Bonn at that time facilitated such a reform programme. In an attempt to produce an overall survey, the third section discusses reforms applied to individual sectors. Finally, the analysis covers the period from the mid-1970s up to German unification, years overshadowed by a post-modern philosophy, hostile to state control and social reform. Ecological and economic issues came to supplant education in public debate, while reform itself was often viewed through the sceptical eyes of an irrational, anti-Enlightenment age.

The Constitutional Framework – a Return to Weimar?

Chapter 5 has shown how those social forces, which survived the collapse of the Third Reich relatively unscathed, attempted, often at odds with the Allied powers, to pursue policies which sought to return to the political debate of the Weimar Republic and restore the educational elites of the Empire. The emerging education system, set up before the Federal Republic came into existence and therefore generally unresponsive to the democratic and social concerns of the *Grundgesetz* (Basic Law), bore all the hallmarks of an authoritarian system. Based on 'statist' principles of political culture, its teachers enjoyed civil-service status which, in the German tradition, gave them an unparalleled aura of authority. Its federalism, endorsed by the Allies in a bid to avoid the centralization which had existed under the Nazis, in effect delegated centralized control to the individual *Länder*, leaving virtually no autonomy to individual schools. Education at school level had, in fact, become more centralized than under the Weimar Republic, where some dialogue between educators and the public had been evident.[2] The new regional authorities showed little concern for social and educational developments, either in their own schools or in a broader context. Their isolationist attitude stems from the constitutional peculiarity which leaves education under the control of individual *Länder*:[3] it is important to note the marked contrast between the individual states, jealously guarding their autonomy, and the more progressive outward-looking federal government.

Compulsory schooling did not begin until after the age of six, with university entrance at nineteen after thirteen years of school, often further prolonged if educational difficulties necessitated repeating a school year, with military or community service still to come. University education remained faithful to the Humboldtian tradition, the study period often being extended beyond seven years. In financial terms, at least in the 1950s and 1960s, Germany appears to trail even more behind other countries, investing less money in education than almost any other industrialized nation.[4] A brief comparison with Western countries reveals that German children, even today, still tend to begin school later than average (USA at 5, Italy at 6, Spain at 6 and France at 6), that selection for secondary education, after four years, is more rigorous and operates earlier (USA after 6–9 years, Spain after 6 years, Italy and France after 5–6 years), that university studies begin relatively late, between 18–20 (USA at 17, Spain at 18–19, Italy at 19 and France at 18–19), and that students graduate between 27 and 29, significantly later than their peers (USA at 22, Spain, Italy and France at 24–5). In addition, most schools remain half-day schools with no school meal provision and only minimal supervision of homework – matters regarded as the responsibility of parents. In such a situation, it is easy to see that the newly established German democracy relied on an education system which, far from allowing the free development of individual personality, as Article 2 of the Basic Law prescribes, ensured the continuation of social divisiveness. This became particularly obvious with the restoration of the tripartite system which, following segregation at the age of ten, determined the whole of a person's future schooling and career. Statistical evidence for the 1940s and 1950s indicates that only some 11 per cent of a peer group entered the *Gymnasium*, with only some 2 per cent of these from a working-class background.[5] A brief analysis of the *Grundgesetz*, in so far as it concerns education, reveals that while stress is laid on individual rights (paragraph 7), at least as far as the rights of parents are concerned, the main emphasis of the law reflects the reactionary debate of the 1940s, paying particular attention to religious education and the right to attend private schools.

The few advantages which the emerging system offered did little to outweigh its weaknesses: it certainly provided stability, but the absence of harmonization across the Republic also created confusion and chaos. It was basically a fair system with little opportunity for corruption, except that it was intrinsically geared towards the middle and upper strata of society. Perhaps its strongest point was the high status conferred on education in general, despite the fact that funding remained far behind that of Germany's main competitors.

Private education, a hotly debated issue during the Weimar Republic,[6] continues to be of particular interest. Private schools, under strict state supervision, must guarantee equality of standards in education, teacher qualification and status. Above all, they must not select pupils on the basis of parental wealth. At elementary level, private schools are permitted only if they provide a special pedagogical input or represent a minority interest in terms of religion or ideology. Whilst the new law did not represent real progress from the position under the Weimar Republic, the ideological stance of these schools has changed. Private schools today pay greater attention to the individual pupil, often pioneering new teaching methods, particularly Waldorf Schools (Rudolf Steiner Schools), *Landerziehungsheime*, continuing the tradition of *Reformpädagogik*, and the *Odenwaldschule*, which was instrumental in promoting comprehensive education in Hesse.[7] Private education has set the pace in vocational training, the education of girls and the handicapped. A majority of private schools are, however, still church-maintained and allied to no particular reform movement. Low school fees cover only a small proportion of the running costs, with 90 per cent of the funding being state-subsidized.[8]

An issue of considerable importance was the liaison between individual *Länder* and their relationship to central government. Our discussion will concentrate on the earlier phase of such co-ordination, leading up to the actual reform period of the late 1960s. Compared with the position during the Weimar Republic or the Empire, the *Kulturhoheit* (cultural sovereignty) of the *Länder* was stronger after 1945, with the federal government being at best the guardian of religious freedom and special minority interests. As a result, the early 1950s saw a degree of diversity which bordered on chaos, so that children moving from one *Land* to another suffered a considerable upheaval, expressed in the maxim 'Vater versetzt, Sohn sitzengeblieben'[9] (Father moves, son repeats school year).

Early contacts between individual *Länder* were established, initially within individual occupation zones, later at inter-zonal level. A 1948 conference of German ministers of education, including, for the only time in the country's divided history, representatives from East and West Germany, could not even agree a common starting date for the school year, and heightened Cold War tension ended any further hopes of standardization between East and West. At the same time, greater rapprochement between Western zones became desirable and, in July 1948, the *Ständige Konferenz der Kultusminister* (KMK) (Standing Conference of Ministers of Education) was set up as a working party with the remit of co-ordinating matters of interregional importance.[10] It established its own secretariat in Bonn, a clear indication that it intended to liaise with a federal government which was yet to be set up. Individual *Land* governments were not legally committed to implement resolutions of the KMK and its constitution determined that decisions tended to be based on the lowest common denominator, with the result that its very nature was conservative. This becomes obvious if one observes its development over the decades: the KMK had a relatively strong position in day-to-day routine matters, but was overshadowed by other organizations when reform issues came to light.[11] Its achievements were mainly of an administrative nature: the *Düsseldorfer Abkommen* (Düsseldorf Agreement 1955), later modified by the *Hamburger Abkommen* (1964), resulted in the streamlining of organizational matters (e.g. start of the school year) and terminology but, even there, Bavaria gained special concessions. Furthermore, the KMK, hampered by the necessity for unanimity, tended to take the line of least resistance: reforms which seemed likely to threaten the tripartite system were held in abeyance,[12] selection at the end of primary education was restricted once more to the end of year four and the more progressive authorities of Hamburg, Bremen and Hesse were obliged to abandon their extended six-year primary schools.[13]

As a result of its passively conformist nature, the KMK was eventually downgraded in favour of a new, more radical committee with a wider remit: the *Deutsche Ausschuß für das Erziehungs- und Bildungswesen* (German Committee for Education and Training), set up in 1953 on the joint initiative of the KMK and the Federal Ministry of the Interior. Consisting of independent experts from a variety of backgrounds, it produced an outline plan in 1959, diagnosing problems with the position of education in the Federal Republic and warning against ignoring revolutionary international changes in society during the past fifty years.[14] Since its role was merely of an advisory nature and its general tone rather defensive, it failed to make a direct political impact, though it succeeded in initiating an educational debate, not least on the nature of the *Förderstufe*, the transitional two years between elementary and secondary education, and on the organization of the final stage of the *Gymnasium*.[15] A third element was the extension of the *Hauptschule* (non-academic secondary school) by one year, providing practical training for employment and creating an awareness of general social and economical structures. This latter reform is of interest in that it anticipated GDR plans for the introduction of the polytechnical school. These reform plans were opposed by the entrenched reactionary coalition between the Catholic Church and the *Philologenverband*, which vetoed any social and educational reform which undermined their dominant position as an education lobby in the parliamentary corridors of regional and federal power. The *Deutsche Ausschuß* was succeeded in 1965 by the *Deutsche Bildungsrat* (German Education Council), which also included representatives of different political parties. Its remit was much clearer than that of the *Ausschuß* and it worked in a climate of much greater urgency, since public debate on education was by now making headlines. The *Bildungsrat* contributed directly to the formation of the *Strukturplan* (plan for structural changes to the education system) and was indirectly involved in the establishment of a Federal Ministry for Education and Science.[16] Another committee, similarly organized but responsible for higher education and research, was the *Wissenschaftsrat* (Science Council), established in 1957 and still in existence. It brought about a rapid expansion in higher education, doubling its budget between 1960 and 1964. Another special committee, the *Bund-Länder-Kommission für Bildungsplanung* (federal and regional commission for educational planning), played a role in the development of structural renewal which will be examined later.

An examination of the federal nature of education in the FRG suggests that its constitutional framework was more of a bane than a blessing, in that it was instrumental in hindering the impetus towards reform and that the individual committees charged with co-ordinating or modernizing the system have been – variously – unsuccessful in the implementation of fundamental reforms. It is interesting to note in this context that the actual reform phase at the end of the 1960s received its momentum from the federal government. Three factors enabled these reforms to be implemented. Firstly, the emergence of the *Große Koalition* (Grand Coalition) in Bonn (1967), a consensus government, all but eliminated political tension between federal and regional administrations. Secondly, the Brandt government which followed in 1969 imparted a sense of great urgency to social and educational reform, expressed in Brandt's dictum 'Wir müssen mehr Demokratie wagen'[17] (We must dare to become more democratic). Thirdly, a change in the Basic Law (Art. 74) brought into being a new *Bundesministerium für Bildung und Wissenschaft* (Federal Ministry of Education and Science), allowing the federal government to have an input into education. However, the major impetus for reform was extra-parliamentary, reflecting widespread public unease with social and educational issues, mainly as a response to international developments.

The Implementation of Educational Reforms – the Road to Modernity

Initiatives by individual educationalists, sociologists and politicians were instrumental in raising public awareness of the state of education. However, their influence has been exaggerated: by the 1960s the many defects in the education system had already been diagnosed, but discussion had been confined to the relevant committees and had not yet entered the realms of public debate. During the mid-1960s, a few individual committee members became involved in publicizing these issues. Their contribution should be seen against a wider background of social and political developments, both at home and abroad, which had already prepared the ground.

Economic factors played the most important role in prioritizing education reforms; since the 1950s, US economists had been stressing the importance of education for improving economic output. Statistics were indicating a correlation between education funding and economic performance. Manpower research provided prognostications for future needs in science and in the burgeoning service industries. Friedrich Edding, the first German professor of *Bildungsökonomie* (economics of education), warned that these studies showed that highly populated industrial countries such as Germany and Japan should invest more heavily in education than their rivals, if they wished to remain competitive.[18] International organizations such as UNESCO and the OECD became alerted to the importance of education for economic growth. Such confidence in the economic function of education reflected the generally held Keynesian belief that economic growth could be guaranteed through careful planning. Increasing urbanization and changing employment patterns, such as the decline in agricultural workers (from 24.6 per cent in 1950 to 10.7 per cent in 1965),[19] made education the new priority. At the same time, the FRG seemed to be lagging behind its neighbours: forecasts for school leavers qualified to enter higher education suggested that the projected rise would only amount to 4 per cent, compared to 138 per cent in Sweden and 254 per cent in France.[20] Indeed, the number of students at the *Gymnasium* had begun to decline during the late 1950s, with many youngsters preferring to leave school and gain early entry to the employment market.[21]

Political factors were also important, particularly in the light of the East–West conflict. The Soviet Union's spectacular success with the Sputnik satellite appeared to put it ahead in the international technological race. The technological gap between the Federal Republic and the United States was also believed to be increasing.[22] Prior to the building of the Berlin Wall (1961), the large proportion of highly educated young GDR students fleeing to the West displayed an academic standard which suggested that the East German education system was outperforming that of West Germany. The Federal Republic's policy of integration with the West and closer European links also demanded increased resourcing for education, especially with the new policy of free movement of labour, closer co-operation in vocational education and a generally increased interest in education shown by the European Council of Ministers.[23] At its 100th session (1964) the KMK stated:

> Die Kultusminister und Senatoren stellen fest, daß die deutsche Kulturpolitik nach Abschluß der Periode des Wiederaufbaus nunmehr in einen Zeitabschnitt eingetreten ist, in welchem die zunehmende europäische Integration und die in allen Staaten gleichlautenden Bedürfnisse der modernen Industriegesellschaft verstärkt neue Impulse zur Weiterentwicklung der Schul- und Hochschulpolitik geben.[24]

> (The ministers and senators for education state that, after a period of rebuilding, German education policy has now reached a point at which, with increasing European integration and the identical needs of modern industrial societies, a new impetus needs to be given to the development of school and university policies.)

At his inaugural speech, Federal Chancellor Erhard placed education and research in a special category, maintaining that they were as important in his day as social questions had been a century earlier.[25]

Socio-cultural factors, too, raised general awareness of the need for new educational initiatives. The generation which had grown up during the affluent years of the 'Economic Miracle' began to distance itself from an obsession with ecomomic growth and consumerism. Turning instead towards more hedonistic values, they remained anxious, at the same time, to protect and further advance the political culture of democracy. They began to replace the 'sceptical generation'; we shall call them the 'protest generation'. They no longer unquestioningly accepted traditional German secondary values such as diligence, order, duty or punctiliousness, tending to associate such values with the 'authoritarian character'[26] which had aided Hitler's rise to power. Confidence in the traditional *Gymnasium* with its humanist canon and its claim to provide a general education gave way to an increasing interest in the sciences, social sciences and other 'relevant' subjects which contributed to the understanding of an ever more complex existence. A world-wide curricular reform movement pointed towards greater individualism, greater choice and a life-long process of learning.[27] A plethora of literary works, from Günter Grass's *Die Blechtrommel* (The Tin Drum) (1959), Rolf Hochhuth's *Der Stellvertreter* (The Representative) (1963) to Peter Weiss's *Die Ermittlung* (The Investigation) (1965), took as their subject the causes and consequences of National Socialism, intent on demonstrating that the 'Trauerarbeit'[28] had not yet begun in earnest.

The Eichmann trial in Jerusalem (1962) and the Auschwitz trials in Frankfurt (1963–5) contributed to this process of raising German awareness of national guilt and initiated a public debate, which cast a new light on the role of the Church, leading industrialists, military personnel and many other public figures, shattering the myth that nobody, apart from the Nazi hierarchy, had shared any knowledge of the Holocaust and other crimes against humanity. Adenauer's tendency to offer government posts to former Nazis, Kiesinger's Nazi past and a revised assessment of conservative opposition to Hitler all contributed to a growing alienation from the 'establishment'. This new atmosphere undermined confidence in the ecclesiastical and educational hierarchies, and since both had been associated with opposition to progressive education during the Weimar and the post-war periods, the stage was set for change. The sociologist Ralf Dahrendorf's observations on social modernity and the need to overcome rigid forms of conservatism prophetically anticipated a change in social awareness, a change associated with educational issues and foreshadowing the student protest of the late 1960s:

> We are moving here on the narrow line between stability and stagnation of political structures; and the question of how strong the forces of tradition are in German society has its meaning in relation to this issue. Stability is a fine thing to have; but if it degenerates into stagnation, [. . .] it would soon produce so much resistance that revolutionary upheavals would be imminent. [. . .] In Germany, it is still necessary to remind people that the road to modernity may be hard and painful for many, and in many respects; it means a departure from many an old love.[29]

The economic, political and socio-cultural factors were all aspects of a process of modernity that had reached the Federal Republic rather late, delayed by Hitler's rise to power and a post-war obsession with the 'Economic Miracle'. The need for educational planning, gathering momentum during the 1960s, had set the scene for a more comprehensive process of modernization: the demand for more education, based simply on economic considerations, was replaced by a more critical approach which sought to overcome social discrimination and reduce economic interference in education planning [Text 1]. An analysis of proposed reforms would indicate to what extent a process of democratization had been achieved. Willy Brandt's inaugural speech as Chancellor indicated his government's goal of a comprehensive democratization of society, acknowledging that the Republic was only just entering this process of democratization. The desire for emancipation which would turn this democratic system from a constitutional apparatus into a life form seemed near.[30] Educationalists praised Brandt's education programme as comparable to Humboldt's reform programme in Prussia,[31] a correct assessment in so far as the new government established a Ministry of Education and Science, thereby reducing the regional nature of educational planning. The assessment is wrong, however, in failing to recognize that this change was based on low central government funding and, more importantly, that Brandt's pronouncements failed to become political reality.

The public debate on education began in the spring of 1964 with a series of articles by Georg Picht in the weekly journal *Christ und Welt*, a far from revolutionary paper. Picht himself had been a leading member of the *Deutscher Ausschuß*; he was also director of an educational research institute, sponsored by the Protestant *Studiengemeinschaft*. The alarmist title of Picht's series, 'Die deutsche Bildungskatastrophe' (The German Educational Catastrophe) sought to establish a direct link between economic performance and education: without a highly qualified workforce, economic growth would grind to a halt, especially with the pre-fascist generation approaching retirement and the influx of highly qualified East German refugees now abruptly halted by the Berlin Wall. A potential teacher shortage would leave schoolchildren educationally disadvantaged and the Republic would sink to the economic level of countries like Ireland, Yugoslavia or Portugal:

> Die Zahl der Abiturienten bezeichnet das geistige Potential eines Volkes, und von dem geistigen Potential sind in der modernen Welt die Konkurrenzfähigkeit der Wirtschaft, die Höhe des Sozialproduktes und die politische Stellung abhängig.[32]

> (The number of university entrants reflects the intellectual potential of a nation, and in the modern world this intellectual potential determines economic competitiveness, levels of national productivity and political importance.)

Picht's thesis, based on the economics of education, suggested that whole sections of society had hitherto been excluded from higher education, these *Begabungs- reserven* (talent reserves) included women, children from rural areas, the working class and Catholics. Picht's warnings invoked a panic response: the media focus on his views implied that such opinions had never previously been expressed. Federal and *Land* parliaments met in special session to discuss the implications. Bavaria immediately set up a contingency programme to exploit educational reserves, distributing over half a million brochures under the title 'Aus Ihrem Kind soll etwas werden' (Your child shall make it).[33] Baden-Württemberg agreed to double the number of its *Abiturienten* and started a campaign 'Student aufs Land'

(Students into the country), dispatching education students into rural areas in order to persuade parents of the benefits of higher education for their children.

A reassessment of Picht's thesis would suggest that, though provocative, it was not altogether new, and his views on the exploitation of educational reserves were only partially vindicated. Whilst the number of women increased dramatically, but no more than in neighbouring countries, the number of children from rural or working-class backgrounds showed only a very modest increase. Picht's one-sided emphasis on the economic factor was immediately criticized by Dahrendorf, who introduced a more political note. His empirical studies on working-class children at German universities[34] led him to advocate shifting the emphasis of the debate to a more political level: he recognized that the educational deficiencies of certain social groups were determined not so much by financial factors as by the reluctance of parents to see their children abandon the conventional mould, be this a woman's role in the home or a working man's place in the factory. By formulating a citizen's right to education, Dahrendorf introduced a sociological angle which opened up a discussion on talent in general and one's right to foster this talent: schools should no longer select at an early age, thereby emphasizing sociological rather than psychological criteria.[35] There was a switch in emphasis from criticism of low productivity to criticism of deficiencies in social behaviour. The social segregation associated with German education, it was said, was essentially hindering the development of a liberal democracy. The debate at this modified level signalled a change from the conservative position, which left decisions on social change to the school,[36] to a wider debate on democracy suggesting that, as Habermas put it, the choice of accepting or rejecting educational opportunities must be left to the individual.[37] The debate was soon taken up by liberal politician Hildegard Hamm-Brücher whose party-political programme adopted Dahrendorf's formula 'Bildung ist Bürgerrecht' (Education is a citizen's right). She recognized that merely expanding education would not make Germany a more democratic country:

Die Erhöhung der Abiturientenquoten auf 9, 12 oder 15 Prozent löst unser Problem nicht – unser Problem heißt Identifizierung des Bildungssystems mit der demokratischen Staatsform und ihren gesellschaftspolitischen Voraussetzungen.[38]

(An increase of 9, 12 or 15 per cent in the number of school leavers with the *Abitur* does not solve our problem – our problem lies in identifying the education system with the democratic constitution and with its socio-political requirements.) [Text 2]

Reforms of Individual Institutions

The educational reforms initiated in the wake of this debate only partly fulfilled expectations. The *Deutscher Bildungsrat* (1965) was instructed to produce an educational blueprint; it published a *Strukturplan* in 1970, recommending changes in the structure of the education system. Though described as most progressive and all-embracing,[39] it was in fact a compromise, based on the recognition that replacing the tripartite system by a fully comprehensive one was not politically feasible. Despite its aim of *Chancengleichheit* (equality of opportunity), it cautiously stated that this must not be at the expense of 'Nivellierung der Anforderungen'[40] (levelling-out of standards). Although recognizing the problem of regional, social or individual discrimination, but remaining averse to abolishing the tripartite system outright, it attempted to introduce some form of comprehensive education, in that different age levels would be defined by terms applied across the board to all school types. Compulsory schooling would end at the age of eighteen and the tertiary sector would cover various forms of higher education. The most controversial decision was the introduction of an *Orientierungsstufe* (orientation stage), a revised form of the *Förderstufe*, already foreshadowed in the *Rahmenplan* (frame-work structure). This stage would apply to years five and six and facilitate the changeover from the primary to the secondary sector. It was, in fact, designed as a two-year comprehensive stage for all schools in the secondary sector, with a common curriculum, so that, on its completion, pupils could be assigned to the appropriate school. Even so, some of the more conservative states did not fully enter into the spirit of the reform and preferred to set up the *Orientierungsstufe* in existing secondary schools, thereby minimizing the opportunity for change. A school-leaving certificate was to be awarded in all schools at the end of Secondary Sector One (*Abitur I*). This would be based on assessment in nine common core subjects, including German, mathematics, science, a foreign language and civics. For Secondary Sector Two (*Abitur II*), greater flexibility was envisaged, again based on the core and option principle, guaranteeing an element of traditional German *Allgemeinbildung*, but taking into account the need for specialization, in the light of future studies. Again, barriers between academic and vocational education were to be broken down and an enhanced status conferred on new schools with a vocational element, the specialized *Gymnasium*, the *Fachoberschule* (technical secondary school) and the *Gesamtschule*. Teacher training was to be standardized with all teachers obtaining a university qualification.[41] The *Bildungsbericht* (1970), a federal government report, endorsed the recommendations of the *Struktur-plan*, but also included valuable information on the Republic's low educational performance on the international league table. Whilst there had been some increase in funding and in the number of higher certificates awarded, the curriculum itself had changed very little. One critic noted: 'despite all the efforts there still prevails the traditional picture of a highly selective school system based on the idea of grading down all the pupils who can't cope with the standards set by historically evolved curricula and inflexible teaching methods'.[42]

The *Bildungsgesamtplan* (1973) (comprehensive education plan), the final reform phase, was an attempt to implement the *Strukturplan* and was the work of the *Bund-Länder-Kommission für Bildungsplanung*, a joint committee of federal and regional governments, responsible for educational planning up to 1985. By the time of the plan's publication, it had been considerably watered down, not only because of compromises necessary to accommodate different political groups, but also because reforming zeal had begun to wane. Serious disagreement had arisen on the nature of comprehensive education. The federal government and six progressive *Länder* were in favour of implementing an integrated *Gesamtschule*, very much on the British model. The five more conservative *Länder* agreed to introduce comprehensive education on an experimental basis, but were unwilling to develop integrated schools. Instead, they opted for a co-operative model which would, in essence, be based on the existing tripartite system.[43] Similar divisions applied to the introduction of the *Orientierungsstufe*. Given the history of the education system, it was only to be expected that the more conservative parties would again win the day, consigning the more progressive plans to oblivion.

Vocational training was set up according to Kerschensteiner's principles[44] and became compulsory for those leaving school at sixteen. The dual system, with apprentice training partly in school and partly at work, was much acclaimed, and in the early 1980s comparisons with Britain seemed to suggest that this aspect of education was much superior in Germany and contributed to her prosperity. During the 1960s, however, certain weaknesses had begun to appear: insufficient training places were available, especially during periods of economic stagnation. Standards of workplace training needed to be raised and the rights of apprentices improved. Training courses at college were often too traditional and specialized, not looking towards the requirements of a modern industrialized society. This resulted in 80 per cent of apprentices opting to change their career on finishing their training.[45] Reforms in vocational education led to curricular changes, the most prominent being the introduction of a general foundation course, covering a wide range of related skills. Basic legal training, civics and commercial German were integrated into the curriculum and the teaching skills of the master craftsmen at the workplace were improved. As a result, the general standard in maths and technical core subjects is significantly higher in Germany than in Britain.[46] David Phillips, in his comparison of vocational training in both countries, concludes: 'in 1981 in West Germany 92 per cent of sixteen-year-olds, 89 per cent of seventeen-year-olds, and 72 per cent of eighteen-year-olds were participating in some kind of education and training; in the UK the corresponding figures were 84 per cent, 60 per cent, and 42 per cent'.[47]

University reforms were perhaps the most problematic within the general reform movement. Seen within the overall perspective of this study, it is not surprising that a clash of interests should develop between modernist progressive forces and the traditionally reactionary mandarin establishment. The student movement of 1968 played a major role in this development, despite the fact that the basic ideas for reform had been conceived earlier. The whole issue is highly controversial and cannot be developed in detail here. Neo-conservatives such as Hermann Lübbe considered the notion that higher education reforms had been triggered by the student movement to be a myth.[48] As far as the actual reform plans were concerned, Lübbe is right, but he fails to see that the major input of the student movement was a demand for change in the university ethos, to espouse democracy and co-determination, to develop a new curriculum and new teaching methods, and to open up the ivory tower to the changing needs of a modern, democratic society. The *Wissenschaftsrat* (Science Council) had expanded higher education in the 1960s, but in failing to tackle organizational and curricular reforms, the seeds of student unrest had been sown.

In their attempts to reinterpret the student movement, neo-conservative historians such as Klaus Hildebrand could justifiably be accused of distorting the course of events. The students' provocative actions, in agitprop theatre style, such as unfolding a banner at a pompous academic celebration in Hamburg, proclaiming 'Unter den Talaren Muff von 1000 Jahren'[49] (Underneath the gowns lurks the musty smell of a thousand years), are denigrated as evil and squalid. Hildebrand criticizes the protest generation for not adhering to traditional German values, seemingly unaware of any relationship to Germany's fateful *Sonderweg* which had led to Auschwitz. He defames the student movement as totalitarian, and comparisons with the Nazi Youth Movement abound.[50] These sentiments echo an outburst by Habermas who, in an angry confrontation with Rudi Dutschke, criticized the students for a leftish form of fascism. Habermas, however, also repeatedly recognized the compensatory function of their protest and their attempt to create the political awareness necessary for a democratic way of life.[51] Hildebrand and others associated with the new right would not accept such an interpretation. They brand the student protest as 'anti-Western',[52] but fail to see that the movement itself is steeped in Western tradition.

Incidents at the Free University of Berlin in 1965 are generally recognized to mark the beginning of the student unrest. They can be seen as symptomatic of the general climate and of the need for reform. The catalyst was a student invitation to several eminent speakers from different political backgrounds for a round-table discussion to mark the twentieth anniversary of the end of the Second World War. The university *Rektor*, supported by all the deans and a vast majority of professors, vetoed the invitation to a left-wing participant and also sought to prevent the involvement of Karl Jaspers. The student organizers, together with some 3,000 sympathizers, adopted the motto of the Berkeley Free Speech Movement: 'to hear any person speak in any open area on campus at any time on any subject'.[53] The incident reflected the tense and generally authoritarian climate prevalent at all West German universities. In this case, the situation was pointed up by the fact that, although the Free University had been founded as a bulwark against Communist dictatorship,[54] German students were still educated as subjects of the state, not as free citizens. A grass-roots protest movement was the only means of initiating a wide-ranging debate on university reform. Whatever its later excesses, the student movement was guided initially by the desire to democratize the university, to abolish the autocratic structure of the *Ordinarienuniversität*, in which full-time professors had sole decision-making rights, and to introduce a spirit of accountability which would accept students as partners in the process of learning. Students not only demanded participation for themselves and the non-professorial staff in university decision-making processes, but also advocated the abolition of the rigid faculty structure, to be replaced by a more dynamic division into sections which would allow for innovative interdisciplinary studies and greater individual or group initiatives. Anglo-American practices were advocated, with new teaching posts to be advertised and a more open examination process.[55] These demands were initially accepted; the KMK agreed to the introduction of new *Fachbereiche* (Sections) with a more democratic structure. In some regions the *Gruppenuniversität* was founded, based on democratic participation involving one-third each of professors, non-professorial staff and students. The concept of academic freedom was redefined 'nicht mehr nur negativ als Abschirmung individueller Gelehrsamkeit gegen interessierte Einwirkung von außen [. . . sondern] auch im Sinne von Teilhaberrechten'[56] (not only in a negative sense as the protection of individual scholarship against outside interests [. . . but] also in the sense of partnership rights) and in response to social and political needs. The majority of universities were opposed to this new spirit, believing that they could not function under such conditions and that the future of scholarship itself was being jeopardized.

Society and Education in a Post-Modern Climate

The various reform projects were gathering momentum at a time of change in the intellectual climate. The student protest had run its course and was succeeded by an isolated, extreme left-wing terrorist movement, provoking a hysterical over-reaction within society. Ecological and economic issues were gaining priority over social ones; Dennis Meadows's book *Limits of Growth* (1972) can be seen as symbolic of a change in outlook, suggesting a more sceptical attitude towards growth and progress, especially with regard to the destruction of non-renewable natural resources. The oil crisis, caused by the Yom Kippur War (1973), had cast a shadow on the economic future of industrialized society. In general, this new climate rejected modernity and instead adopted key concepts of post-modernism, a movement which had developed out of the philosophical and linguistic disciplines of post-structuralism.

This intellectual change was registered in the Federal Republic at a session of the *Bayrische Akademie der schönen Künste* in the autumn of 1974, where the term *Tendenzwende* (tendency change) was coined.[57] The participants at this session diagnosed a new intellectual movement, away from left-wing, neo-Marxist ideologies and their emancipatory claims. The new age supported free-market, individualistic programmes, culminating in demands for less state intervention and a return to both private and national values, thereby anticipating the policies of the 1980s epitomized by Margaret Thatcher's Britain, Ronald Reagan's America and Helmut Kohl's Germany. Anti-intellectual tendencies began to emerge. Kurt Sontheimer, one-time champion of freedom and democracy at Berlin's Free University, produced a highly controversial book, *Das Elend unserer Intellektuellen*, a title recalling Marx's own *Misère de la Philosophie* (1847). Sontheimer accused the intellectual left of being obsessed with social theory at the expense of common sense and of advocating an emancipatory understanding of democracy as a social process, with self-determination as the major issue.[58] Rejecting the major tenets of the Critical Theory and, in particular, Habermas's theory of legitimation, a concept which can be traced back to Rousseau's *Contrat Social*, Sontheimer sided with the conservative Richard Löwenthal and with Karl Popper's 'piecemeal engineering'.[59] The post-modern tendency of rejecting all normative values has since been attacked by Habermas as 'neue Unübersichtlichkeit' (new obscurity), symptomatic of a general crisis in Western civilization.[60] The general scepticism towards normative values and moral judgements was shared by Dahrendorf, who also employed the term *Elend* when pronouncing the demise of social democracy. Dahrendorf believes that social democratic intellectuals underestimated the vitality of the open, pluralist society and, in overestimating the revolutionary potential of the industrial proletariat, they failed to recognize the advent of a new service industry which was of a generally conservative nature. He declares administrative bureaucracy, especially the domination of the civil service, to be at an end and welcomes an age of entrepreneurs, of private initiative and less reliance on the state.[61]

We shall restrict ourselves here to those aspects of the intellectual scene which had an impact on social and educational matters.[62] The introduction of the *Radikalenerlaß* (the Radicals Decree) by the Brandt government (1972), in administrative terms a mere streamlining of existing laws concerning public sector employees, soon developed into a weapon against radical students seeking state employment and against young academics critical of the current state of democracy in the Federal Republic. The law demanded of public sector employees that they demonstrate a positive attitude towards the Republic's democratic Constitution, and was frequently interpreted by judges in such a way that any left-wing association was sufficient reason for being excluded from state employment. Such an interpretation led to widespread injustice, inducing furious attacks from German writers and other public figures and in the longer term leading to political abstention.[63]

The *Hochschulrahmengesetz* (Framework Law for Higher Education) was another example of reformist measures cut back in favour of traditional conservatism. It sought to rationalize the different forms of higher education, supporting the concept of a *Gesamthochschule* (comprehensive university), and also tried to introduce some norms, regulating the length of study for individual courses (*Regelstudienzeit*). Support for *Gesamthochschulen* was half-hearted, finally resulting in the establishment of eleven such institutions with only a handful offering an integrated programme. Any attempt at a reduction of the study period failed altogether and still awaits a resolution, based on a comprehensive restructuring of study programmes. The clause reintroducing the *Ordinarienuniversität*, however, was successful in re-establishing the absolute authority of university professors.[64] All matters relative to teaching, research and appointments once again required the majority decision of full-time university professors. This reversal of the previous reform measures has an interesting history. To counter the successful demands by students and non-professorial staff for greater participation, professors at Berlin's Free University founded the *Notgemeinschaft für eine freie Universität* (Emergency Committee for a Free University) (1969), expanded in 1970 into the *Bund Freiheit der Wissenschaft* (Federation for Scholastic Freedom) with members throughout the Federal Republic. Its aim was the restoration of the old university order, allegedly in the interests of greater efficiency and academic freedom.[65] Soon other issues favouring emancipatory trends in education were attacked: the concept of *Chancengleichheit* (equality of opportunity) should be replaced by *Chancengerechtigkeit* (right of opportunity), restricting university access to an educational elite. Neoconservative, even right-wing professors set the agenda, amongst them Hans Mayer, later Education Secretary for Bavaria, Richard Löwenthal, Ernst Nolte, the leading revisionist in the Historians' Debate, and the neo-conservative philosopher Hermann Lübbe, former secretary of state for North Rhine-Westphalia. The student movement was described as escapist, with strong Marxist tendencies, whose attempt to infiltrate educational establishments had to be stopped.[66] Members of the *Bund* were opposed to any form of *Gruppenuniversität* and openly supported the CDU/CSU, then in opposition. In 1973 they succeeded in their attempt to persuade the Constitutional Court that the parity of students, assistants and professors in matters of teaching and research was unconstitutional, in that it restricted the academic freedom of long-term university employees.[67] Universities have since fallen back into deep crisis with students increasingly unable to identify with their studies and with the general culture of academia [Text 3].

Other proponents of this counter-reform movement attacked the whole concept of emancipation in pedagogics. All too aware of recent terrorism, they condemned this type of education as anti-democratic, leading to the tyranny of the child over the adult. Emancipation pedagogics was held responsible for increasing youth crime, the collapse of family values and lack of respect for state and Church.[68] Neoconservative, anti-emancipatory elements advocated the abolition of many of the reforms of the 1960s and 1970s, in favour of a return to small village schools, an end to the *Orientierungsstufe* experiment and a revival of class teaching under a single form teacher. An *Antipädagogik* (counter-pedagogics) movement developed, sceptical of all kinds of scientifically assessed education, questioning the concept of life-long learning. In view of overcrowded universities and a poor employment outlook for academics, the concept of higher education itself became suspect: *Wozu noch studieren?*[69] takes a cynical view of university studies, reflecting a growing opinion among *Gymnasium* pupils that it is better to learn a trade or take a skills-based short course than to devote five or six years to university studies. The notions of self-fulfilment and intellectual curiosity seem to have given way to a more functional approach, and some 40 per cent of *Abiturienten* now become apprentices. According to the educationalist Udo Müllges, the fashionable type of emancipatory pedagogics is flawed, since it ignores anthropological and moral factors. He is particularly critical of the Frankfurt School and its claim of 'Systemüberwindung' (overthrowing the existing system).[70] Emancipation, in Müllges's opinion, should remain within the given social and political order. The most hysterical onslaughts against emancipation pedagogics appeared in the *Frankfurter Allgemeine Zeitung*, where it was attacked as a combination of psychoanalysis and Marxism, ideologically indebted to the Critical Theory of the Frankfurt School.[71] A return to the German tradition and to practical education is advocated; schools must embrace an acceptance of authority and of traditional social values. A closer study of such articles reveals them all to be part of a new anti-intellectual movement, directed against the chief postulates of the Enlightenment. They are not only opposed to the Critical Theory, but also to major tenets of *Reformpädagogik*, and are anxious to absorb the child as quickly as possible into an adult world where secondary virtues such as industriousness, a sense of duty and responsibility have again become priorities, at the expense of the development of a self-reflective, critical mind and of personal fulfilment.

Education and reform in the Federal Republic seem to have come full circle: neo-conservative politicians and educators appear to be reverting to the reactionary concepts of the post-war period, to the tripartite school system and elitism. Universities seem unable or unwilling to adjust to the needs of a modern, democratic and industrialized society. Fear of academic unemployment discourages students from completing their studies, despite statistical evidence that unemployment among academics is clearly lower than average.[72] And yet, we have to be careful not to present a one-sided, negative picture. While criticism of the often too utopian and abstract manifestations of emancipation pedagogics is obviously necessary, it should aim to achieve some kind of synthesis between emancipatory objectives and social and economic realities, without neglecting the practical side of the teaching process. Returning to these issues in Chapter 8, we can ask to what extent the unification process has developed a wider understanding of, and shed new light on, the complexities of education and society.

Notes

1. 'Keine Experimente' was the title of a 1957 CDU election programme.
2. H. Becker (1989), 'Bildungspolitik', in W. Benz (ed.), *Die Geschichte der Bundesrepublik Deutschland*, Frankfurt/M., vol. 1, p. 338.
3. The so-called *Kulturhoheit*, laid down in Paragraph 30 of the Basic Law.
4. L. Jochimsen (1971), *Hinterhöfe der Nation. Die deutsche Grundschulmisere*, Reinbek b. Hamburg, p. 21.
5. A. Hearnden (1974), *Education in the two Germanies*, Oxford, p. 81.
6. Cf. Chapter 3, p. 55.
7. C. Führ (1989), *Schools and Institutions of Higher Education in the Federal Republic of Germany*, Bonn, pp. 134–9.
8. Ibid., p. 136.
9. L. von Friedeburg (1992), *Bildungsreform in Deutschland. Geschichte und gesellschaftlicher Widerspruch*, Frankfurt/M., p. 319.
10. Cf. J. Raschert (1980), 'Bildungspolitik im kooperativen Föderalismus. Die Entwicklung der länderübergreifenden Planung und Koordination des Bildungswesens der Bundesrepublik Deutschland', in Max-Planck-Institut für Bildungsforschung (ed.), *Bildung in der Bundesrepublik Deutschland*, Stuttgart, vol. 1, esp. pp. 117–25.
11. Ibid., pp. 114 and 117.
12. L. Froese (ed.) (1969), *Bildungspolitik und Bildungsreform*, Munich, p. 310.
13. Hearnden, *Education in the Two Germanies*, Oxford 1974, p. 68.
14. *Rahmenplan zur Umgestaltung und Vereinheitlichung des allgemeinbildenden öffentlichen Schulwesens*, in B. Michael and H. H. Schepp (eds) (1993), *Die Schule in Staat und Gesellschaft. Dokumente zur deutschen Schulgeschichte im 19. und 20. Jahrhundert*, Frankfurt/M., p. 413.
15. For the purposes of this study the terms *Förderstufe* and *Orientierungsstufe* are taken as synonymous. For a general description cf. S. Robinson and J. C. Kuhlmann, 'Two Decades of Non-reform in West German Education', reprinted in D. Phillips (ed.), *Education in Germany, Tradition and Reform in Historical Context*, London and New York, p. 23, also mentioned in the *Bildungsgesamtplan* in O. Anweiler, H. J. Fuchs et al. (eds) (1992), *Bildungspolitik in Deutschland 1945–1990*, Opladen, pp. 151f.
16. Raschert, 'Bildungspolitik', pp. 165–88.
17. I. Willharm (ed.) (1985), *Deutsche Geschichte 1962–1983*, vol. 2, Frankfurt/M., p. 27.
18. F. Edding (1959), 'Der Aufwand für Bildungseinrichtungen im internationalen Vergleich', *september-gesellschaft*, Heft 2, pp. 23f.
19. J. Naumann, 'Entwicklungstendenzen des Bildungswesens der Bundesrepublik

Deutschland im Rahmen wirtschaftlicher und demokratischer Veränderungen', in Max-Planck-Institut (ed.), *Bildung*, p. 30.

20. F. Edding (1963), *Ökonomie des Bildungswesens. Lehren und Lernen als Haushalt und als Investition*, Freiburg, p. 362.

21. Friedeburg, *Bildungsreform*, p. 347.

22. Naumann, 'Entwicklungstendenzen', p. 38.

23. Arbeitsgruppe Bildungsbericht am Max-Planck-Institut für Bildungsforschung (ed.) (1994), *Das Bildungswesen in der Bundesrepublik Deutschland*, Reinbek b. Hamburg, pp. 154f.

24. Quoted from Becker, 'Bildungspolitik', p. 332.

25. K. Hildebrand (1984), *Geschichte der Bundesrepublik Deutschland. Von Erhard zur großen Koalition 1963–1969*, Stuttgart, p. 46.

26. T. W. Adorno (1973), *Studien zum autoritären Charakter*, Frankfurt/M.

27. Becker, 'Bildungspolitik', p. 340.

28. A term used by Alexander and Margarete Mitscherlich (1967) in *Die Unfähigkeit zu trauern. Grundlagen kollektiven Verhaltens*, Munich.

29. R. Dahrendorf (1979), *Society and Democracy in Germany*, Westport, Conn., pp. 111f.

30. J. Habermas (1971), *Kultur und Kritik*, Frankfurt/M., p. 49.

31. K. Hurrelmann (1975), *Erziehungssystem und Gesellschaft*, Reinbek b. Hamburg, p. 60.

32. G. Picht (1965), *Die deutsche Bildungskatastrophe*, Munich, p. 17.

33. Quoted from Friedeburg, *Bildungsreform*, p. 352.

34. R. Dahrendorf (1965), *Arbeiterkinder an deutschen Universitäten*, Tübingen.

35. R. Dahrendorf (1965), *Bildung ist Bürgerrecht*, Bramsche and Osnabrück. Cf. also W. Klafki (1963), *Studien zur Bildungstheorie und Didaktik*, Weinheim; H. Hentig (1968), *Systemzwang und Selbstbestimmung. Über die Bedingungen der Gesamtschule in der Industriegesellschaft*, Stuttgart.

36. H. Schelsky (1963), *Anpassung oder Widerstand? Soziologische Bedenken zur Schulreform*, Heidelberg.

37. J. Habermas (1961), 'Pädagogischer "Optimismus" vor Gericht einer pessimistischen Anthropologie', in *Neue Sammlung*, vol. 1, p. 4.

38. H. Hamm-Brücher (1967), *Aufbruch ins Jahr 2000 oder Erziehung im technischen Zeitalter*, Reinbek b. Hamburg, p. 147.

39. Attributed to Hans Leussink, Federal Minister of Education and quoted from A. Hearnden (1976), *Education, Culture and Politics in West Germany*, Oxford, p. 67.

40. Deutscher Bildungsrat (ed.) (1970), *Strukturplan für das Bildungswesen*, Bonn, p. 30.

41. Cf. Arbeitsgruppe (ed.), *Bildungswesen*, pp. 218–22.

42. P. Seidl (1972), 'Comprehensive Education in West Germany and Austria', *Forum*, vol. 15, no. 1, p. 22.
43. Raschert, 'Bildungspolitik', pp. 136–47.
44. Cf. Chapter 2, pp. 32–4.
45. R. Crusius, W. Lempert and M. Wilke (eds) (1974), *Berufsausbildung – Reformpolitik in der Sackgasse? Alternativprogramm für eine Strukturreform*, Reinbek b. Hamburg, p. 8.
46. D. Phillips, 'Lessons from Germany? The Case of German Secondary Schools', in Phillips (ed.), *Education*, p. 65.
47. Ibid., pp. 74f.
48. H. Lübbe (1991), *Freiheit statt Emanzipationszwang*, Zurich, p. 112.
49. Hildebrand, *Geschichte*, p. 379.
50. Ibid., pp. 429, 432.
51. J. Habermas (1969), *Protestbewegung und Hochschulreform*, Frankfurt/M., pp. 14ff, 34ff.
52. Hildebrand, *Geschichte*, p. 429.
53. J. F. Tent (1988), *Freie Universität Berlin, 1948–1988. Eine deutsche Hochschule im Zeitgeschehen*, Berlin, p. 313.
54. Cf. Chapter 5, pp. 101f.
55. Friedeburg, *Bildungsreform*, pp. 384–6.
56. Habermas, *Protestbewegung*, p. 203.
57. C. Graf Podwelis (ed.) (1975), *Tendenzwende? Zur geistigen Situation der Bundesrepublik*, Stuttgart.
58. K. Sontheimer (1976), *Das Elend unserer Intellektuellen*, Hamburg, pp. 272, 200, 204.
59. Ibid., pp. 217, 271, 268.
60. J. Habermas (1985), *Die neue Unübersichtlichkeit, kleine politische Schriften 5*, Frankfurt/M., p. 143.
61. R. Dahrendorf (1987), 'Das Elend der Sozialdemokratie', *Merkur*, vol. 41, pp. 1028–30, 1035.
62. For a more comprehensive debate cf. H. J. Hahn (1996), '"Es geht nicht um Literatur". Some Observations on the 1990 *Literaturstreit* and its recent anti-intellectual implications', *German Life and Letters*, vol. 50, pp. 65–81.
63. Cf. F. Duve, H. Böll and K. Staeck (eds) (1977), *Briefe zur Verteidigung der Republik*, Reinbek b. Hamburg.
64. U. Schlicht (1980), *Vom Burschenschaftler bis zum Sponti. Studentische Opposition gestern und heute*, Berlin, pp. 103f.
65. Ibid., pp. 97f.
66. Ibid., pp. 99f.
67. Ibid., p. 102.

68. H. Glaser (1989), *Kulturgeschichte der Bundesrepublik Deutschland. Zwischen Protest und Anpassung*, vol. 3, Munich, p. 161.
69. W. Harenberg (ed.) (1985), *Wozu noch studieren?*, Spiegel-Buch No. 64, Reinbek b. Hamburg.
70. U. Müllges (1996), *Erziehung und Bildung. Analysen ihrer Theorie und Wirklichkeit*, Frankfurt/M., p. 55.
71. Jürgen Oelkers (1994), 'Zur Erziehung verurteilt. Nach fünfundzwanzig Jahren: Die Folgen der emanzipatorischen Pädagogik', reprinted in *Bildung und Wissenschaft*, Nr. 4, p. 13.
72. Statistisches Bundesamt (ed.) (1987), *Statistisches Jahrbuch für die Bundesrepublik Deutschland*, Stuttgart, p. 111: unemployment rate for graduates: 3.9 per cent, compared to 50.8 per cent for people with no qualifications.

TEXTUAL STUDIES

1. Hellmut Becker, 'Demokratisierung von Bildung'

Was heißt Demokratisierung von Bildung? Das heißt, bezogen auf die Bundesrepublik, Förderung statt Auslese und Ersatz eines vertikal gegliederten Bildungswesens durch ein horizontal gegliedertes, das heißt Abbau der Schranken zwischen den drei Formen der Schule, Erleichterung der Übergänge, Überwindung der schichtenspezifischen
5 Frühauswahl durch Ausbau der Kindergärten und der vorschulischen Einrichtungen, das heißt in der Sprache der Schulsysteme Orientierungsstufe im 5. und 6. Schuljahr, das heißt Gesamtschule, das heißt aber auch wissenschaftsorientiertes Lernen für alle, Überwindung der harten Trennung zwischen allgemeinem und beruflichem Lernen, zwischen Theorie und Praxis, das heißt Abbau eines schichtenspezi-
10 fischen Zensuren- und Examenssystem, das heißt tiefgreifende Veränderung des Bildungssystems vom frühen Lernen bis in die ständige Weiterbildung das ganze Leben hindurch.

(Hellmut Becker, 'Bildungspolitik', in W. Benz (ed.) (1989), *Die Geschichte der Bundesrepublik Deutschland*, Frankfurt/M., vol. 1, pp. 330f)

Commentary

(numbers in parenthesis refer to line numbers in the text)

Written in a rhetorical, emotional style, the passage states the various deficiencies of democracy, as far as the education system is concerned. It summarizes the major arguments for educational reform, especially during the late 1960s. The first seven lines highlight contrasts: those between the selection and support of children from different backgrounds (3–5), between a school system that separates children according to educational standards and one that separates them by age groups (6), between the tripartite system and one which allows for transfer (6f), between selection by social background and pre-school education, helping the less advantaged members of society. The passage then formulates certain goals which were not met: the nation-wide introduction of the *Orientierungsstufe* (6) which would have facilitated transfer between different schools, the comprehensive school (7), greater emphasis on academic subjects in the curriculum (7f), the merging of academic and vocational skills (8), the demand for continuing education (11f).

Vocabulary

Förderung (f) = support, sponsoring; Abbau der Schranken = dismantling of barriers; Erleichterung (f) = relief; schichtenspezifisch = with reference to social strata; Überwindung (f) = the overcoming of; tiefgreifend = far-reaching.

2. Hildegard Hamm-Brücher, 'Gedanken über Schülermitbestimmung'

> [. . .] Dafür haben junge Engländer und Franzosen statt des vagen und vieldeutigen Begriffes der 'democratization' den konkreteren und konkretisierbareren der 'partici-pation' geprägt – einen Begriff, den ich im folgenden deshalb bevorzugen werde, weil sich mit seiner Hilfe anschaulicher und eindeutiger beschreiben läßt, worauf es in der
> 5 Schule so entscheidend ankommt: auf die Abkehr von der verordneten und deshalb mit Passivität beantworteten SMV, die als 'Feigenblatt' für mehr oder weniger autoritäre Schulordnungen empfunden wird, und auf die Hinwendung zu einem offenen, emanzipatorischen Prinzip engagierter Teilhaberschaft.
> (Hildegard Hamm-Brücher (1970), *Über das Wagnis von Demokratie und Erziehung*, 2nd edn, Frankfurt/M., p. 18)

Commentary

'Schülermitverwaltung' (SMV) refers to the participation of pupils in the running of their school. The concept can be traced back to turn of the century *Reform-pädagogik*, where it was employed by some educators in the sense referred to by the author. SMV was practised in a very formal manner during the 1950s and 1960s; it never included genuine participation, but instead gave pupils some token representation. The passage must be judged within the context of emancipatory education.

Vocabulary

konkretisierbar = definitive; anschaulich = vividly; Feigenblatt (f) = figleaf;
Teilhaberschaft (f) = participation.

3. Georg Heinzen and Uwe Koch, 'Abschied von der Uni'

Mit der Zeit einigten sich alle Beteiligten an der Uni stillschweigend, über den Ernst
der Lage hinwegzusehen. Wir waren rücksichtsvoll genug, uns nicht gegenseitig nach
unseren Plänen zu fragen, wie die Patienten eines Lungensanatoriums, die wohl wissen,
daß es schlecht um sie steht. Wir saßen in einem Kurswagen ohne Ziel, der schon
5 lange abgekoppelt war, und das Prüfungsamt und die Professoren rüttelten von außen
an dem Waggon, damit wir drinnen glauben konnten, es ginge noch weiter. Allein die
verantwortungsbewußte Studentenvertretung ging mit mahnenden Flugblättern durch
die Mensa und störte die Studenten beim Verdrängen. [. . .]
Früher teilten sie [die Assistenten] sich zu dritt ein Zimmer, nun teilten sie sich zu
10 zweit eine Stelle. Früher schrieben sie mit Kreide draußen auf die Tür: 'Bin Kaffee
trinken, komme gleich wieder.' Nun hängten sie einen maschinegeschriebenen Aushang
auf: 'Während der vorlesungsfreien Zeit findet meine Sprechstunde zweiwöchentlich
zur gewohnten Zeit statt.' Irgendwann hatten sie zwischen geliehenen Gummibäumen
ihre Antrittsvorlesung gehalten, waren Privatdozent geworden und saßen nun, einige
15 Jahre später, immer noch auf einer Assistentenstelle. In traurigen Seminaren verteilten
sie Kopiertes und stellten Fragen, die niemand beantworten mochte. Und sie spürten
wohl manchmal wie wir Studenten: Da stimmte etwas nicht mehr. Die Behauptungen,
unter denen der Universitätsbetrieb veranstaltet wurde, trafen nicht mehr zu.
(Georg Heinzen and Uwe Koch (1985), *Von der Nutzlosigkeit erwachsen zu werden*,
Reinbek b. Hamburg, pp. 87 and 91)

Commentary
(numbers in parenthesis refer to line numbers in the text)

A satirical text, reflecting on the changes in university life. The reference to a
sanatorium (3) raises echoes of Thomas Mann's *Zauberberg* (Magic Mountain)
and flirtation with sickness and death. The image of the railway carriage in the
sidings (4f), shaken by professors and state examiners so that its passengers think
that it is still in motion, is typical of the tenor of the whole passage: the teachers
have created a make-believe situation, the students play along with them, but have
no illusions about the true state of affairs. Student representatives alone are still
'verantwortungsbewußt' (7) in a world where responsibilities have long been
abandoned. The act of 'Verdrängen' (8) (repression) is reminiscent of other such
acts, i.e. that of repressing the Nazi past. Assistants have to share jobs (10), the
informally scrawled messages of the past (10) have been replaced by official, rather

pompous jargon. The reference to the 'Antrittsvorlesung' (14) (inaugural lecture) has lost its meaning, since these assistants will never be launched on a professorial career, but will languish in the poorly paid uncertainty of an assistant-professorship (15).

Vocabulary

rücksichtsvoll = considerate; abgekoppelt = disconnected; rütteln = to shake; Flugblatt (n) = leaflet; Mensa (f) = refectory; maschinegeschriebener Aushang = typed notice; vorlesungsfreie Zeit = lecture-free period; Gummibaum (m) = rubber plant; Privatdozent (m) = extraordinary professor.

Education in the Former GDR: Socialist Education in Theory and Practice

Introduction

Various comments made in Chapter 6 apply equally here, in that we are presented with the situation in reverse, whereby research into education in the GDR all too often resolved itself into a comparison with the FRG. Any account or discussion of the system inevitably contained a great deal of ideology, even propaganda, and analysis of its nature often proved partisan and one-sided. With the collapse of the GDR, every aspect of its workings and institutions again came under the microscope of ideological analysis, making a reasoned assessment even more difficult.

On re-reading official reports or studies on East Germany's education system, it is difficult to overlook the often hollow tone of socialist self-satisfaction or the anti-Western venom, expressed in comparisons of socialist achievement with perceived capitalist failure. Such biased accounts present an unclear picture and all too easily lead to over-simplification.[1] The history and structure of the GDR education system have been analysed by many West German and British scholars, particularly in the monographs of Anweiler and Waterkamp.[2] However, discussion here will focus less on the structural and historical facets of the system, including instead some actual class-room material, an approach which adds a new dimension to the debate on the GDR's education system and, at the same time, redresses the balance of some previous, all too partisan, accounts.

The Basic Principles of the Socialist Education System

Any study of the development of the socialist education system as practised in the GDR must begin with the ideological aims which such a system is designed to fulfil. The introduction of reforms in the Soviet Zone, prior to their systematic incorporation into a framework of socialist pedagogics, has been covered in Chapter 5. Central to this socialist education ideology was the 'allseitige Entwicklung der sozialistischen Persönlichkeit'[3] (all-round development of the socialist personality), an aim which could be achieved only by a dialectic process defining the socialist personality as both factor and goal in such a development. This all-round development differs from Western concepts of individualism, in its claim to have obliterated any form of egoism by its total dedication to the socialist society. Playing a pivotal role in forming this all-round socialist personality is a socialist education system which promotes collective work experience as an essential precondition for such development, integrated as it is into the world of labour and anchored in a totalitarian, scientifically based concept of man. Margot Honecker, then Secretary of Education, defined scientific education as the 'Herausbildung politischer und moralischer Persönlichkeitsqualitäten [. . .] in dem sich mit Hilfe des Kollektivs die Individualität jedes einzelnen Schülers sinnvoll entwickelt und alle Fähigkeiten und Begabungen einschließt'[4] (development of political and moral personal qualities, so that pupils' individuality can, with the help of the collective, be developed sensibly, incorporating all their abilities and talents). By comparison, Western capitalist education concepts are seen to atomize knowledge, in an attempt to prevent any overview of the production process which would expose a monopolistic system of exploitation.[5] The socialist education system works to oppose the capitalist, static form of society to which individuals are forced to adapt and to replace it by a dynamically changing concept of society in which individuals are enabled to perfect themselves.

Socialism, itself developing according to scientific laws, is part and parcel of the new scientific age. Dialectic Materialism demands a comprehensive understanding of the scientific process. In Leninist terms, scientific-technological development is the ultimate achievement of human striving:

> Die Arbeiterklasse ist objektiv, infolge ihrer historischen Mission, an der wissenschaftlichen Erkenntnis der Welt, an der Aufdeckung der wissenschaftlichen Wahrheit interessiert. Die Parteinahme für die Arbeiterklasse und ihre Ideologie ist demzufolge gleichbedeutend mit der Parteinahme für die wissenschaftliche Wahrheit, für die Nutzung dieser wissenschaftlichen Wahrheit im Interesse des gesellschaftlichen Fortschritts, des Sozialismus.[6]

> (The working class, because of its historic mission, has an objective interest in the discovery of scientific truth in order to arrive at a scientific comprehension of the world. The commitment to the working class and its ideology is therefore synonymous with commitment to scientific truth, to the utilization of this scientific truth in the interests of social progress, of socialism.)

This quotation expresses a missionary zeal in the quest for scientific truth intrinsically linked to the ideology of socialism. Seeming to confine individuals within their own social function, it defines labour as man's *raison d'être*, in the Marxist sense of self-determination.

Even a superficial acquaintance with the various stages of educational development in the GDR reveals this teleological, apparently scientific progression towards a socialist education system. Yet, from a socialist perspective, the system was actually designed to avoid any such *Einformung* (uniformity) which would retain a rigid social system, intent on producing 'useful' citizens. While the ideological superstructure has a rather mechanistic tone, unappealing to most Western-trained teachers, certain elements and some routine teaching practices offer insights which have an attraction even to Western pedagogues. This analysis will concentrate on the principles of *Allgemeinbildung* (general education) and the concept of punishment.

Allgemeinbildung is defined, in contrast to the Humboldtian, Western tradition, as education for the whole of society, enabling everyone to participate in the scientific-technological revolution. As a result, general education presupposes a comprehensive concept and places greater emphasis on the natural sciences, mathematics, technology and economics.[7] Above all, it seeks to integrate school and work in order to obviate the divorce between theory and practice and remove the division of labour. The traditional Humboldtian concept is seen as progressive but utopian, no longer relevant in a modern, scientific age, and its distinction between classical *Bildung* and vocationally defined *Ausbildung*, between universal elementary education for the masses and elitist academic education for the few, is rejected.[8]

A case study at Lichterfelde indicates how individual efforts not only helped overcome various social inequalities that still existed between privileged and less privileged children, but how the system also provided opportunities, unheard of in the Federal Republic, for pupils to prepare homework or take up sports and games. The Lichterfelde experiment also introduced meaningful democracy into schools, allowing children to influence their school environment, be it the state of the classroom, the organization of games or other similar activities.[9]

Punishment in schools is seen not so much as a disciplinary measure, but as an attempt to reintegrate pupils into the school and work environment. The socialist concept of punishment, not as an exercise in violence, but as a form of education, is designed to lead individuals back to self-determination and a better understanding of their role in relationship to society. While some ideas were gleaned from *Reformpädagogik*, notably in the psychological field, the socialist concept of punishment rejected bourgeois concern over individual expression and concentrated on rehabilitating individuals and successfully developing their all-round socialist personality. Indeed, according to the Soviet pedagogue Makarenko, punishment provided a means of re-entering the collective, of being accepted once more into the socialist community of workers.[10]

Whilst such measures appear an acceptable method of correction, the practical 'exegesis' of socialist theory sometimes reveals an essentially traditional German element in education. A case in point is the 'modernization' of *Struwwelpeter*, the children's classic from the 1840s, where discipline consisted entirely of punishing offences against a narrow bourgeois moral code. The socialist version follows a similar pattern: children are subject to illness, accident or social ostracism if they transgress the socialist code. The notion of rehabilitation is entirely absent [Text 1].

A major cause of concern among West German critics of the GDR system was the total absorption of the individual by the state. A popular school introduction to Marxism-Leninism uses Brecht's *Die Maßnahme* (The Measure Taken), one of his *Lehrstücke* (propagandist teaching plays) designed to indoctrinate workers into Marxism, advocating the complete erasure of individualism and total immersion into the Party.[11] Although any rational observer would admit that such commitment is in itself no worse than the egoistical Western obsession with self, the practical integration of young children into the GDR system almost from birth is chillingly reminiscent of National Socialist *Gleichschaltung* (political co-ordination). The state undoubtedly made generous provision for nursery schools and day-care centres, freeing women to pursue careers, but at the same time incorporating infants, only a few months old, into the socialist system. No matter how often reasoned argument draws some distinction between a totalitarian system based on doctrines of race and leadership and one which seeks to liberate the working class from capitalist diktat, the organizational parallels are just too compelling.

An interesting example of official propaganda and centralized involvement in socialist education was the *Jugendweihe*, introduced in 1954 as the formal initiation of a young person into the socialist system. In a ceremony reminiscent of the confirmation service in West Germany, participants received a book designed as a socialist, 'scientific' alternative to the Bible, with an introduction by the head of state. The high moral tone of many exhortations is understandable, given the revolutionary fervour of a socialist system working towards its Communist ideal and under threat from imperialism. Nevertheless, constant pressure to shoulder responsibility from an early age must have inflicted some strain on youngsters and may help to explain why, in the latter phase of the GDR's life, such exhortations were treated with scepticism and regarded as hypocritical. The socialist propaganda became so crude, the scientific indoctrination so one-sided,[12] that it is hardly surprising that many young people opted for privacy, for fantasy lifestyles, Western rock music and blue jeans,[13] rather than pursue the unrelenting struggle for a better world in which every human activity was subordinated to collective progress.

The History of the GDR's Socialist Education System

The GDR's education system evolved in five stages, with major ideological developments during the first two decades and a more pragmatic, less revolutionary pace during the second half of its life. We have already seen[14] how the Soviet Sector used the Potsdam Agreement to implement a system closely modelled on socialist principles. During the transition period prior to the founding of the GDR (1949), an 'anti-fascist' school system emerged, based on comprehensive principles, with strict separation of school and church, abolition of private education and increased educational provision in rural areas.

With the establishment of the GDR, a second stage began, officially designated as the 'transition to socialist development of the school system'[15] but described by those outside the establishment as 'Sovietization',[16] referring to the adoption, in the early 1950s, of many Soviet concepts into the GDR's pedagogical system. The Constitution formulated the principle of the 'all-round development of the socialist personality' (paragraph 39) and introduced a system of positive discrimination in favour of the children of workers and peasants. In 1949, special *Arbeiter- und Bauernfakultäten* (workers' and peasants' faculties) were established to correct a perceived imbalance in secondary and higher education and with the aim of developing a 'new intelligentsia that felt itself firmly allied with the working class'.[17] The concept of *Reformpädagogik* was rejected in favour of an overall Marxist-Leninist approach to education, initially introduced at school level. By 1952, this applied also at universities, with compulsory instruction in Marxism-Leninism and considerable emphasis on Russian language and literature, in addition to sports and the practical application of individual subjects to the social and economic needs of the state.[18] Education in general was further integrated into society by the involvement of parents and youth organizations in the shaping of a new 'revolutionary' system. Parents were encouraged to contribute, through personal example, to the development of a socialist work ethos and Parents' Advisory Councils and seminars introduced parents to the new ideology, where their own role within the family was clarified.[19] Educational standards, particularly in working-class areas, began to rise and by 1955 nearly half of all pupils in secondary schools came from a working-class background.[20] Discussions were held on the introduction of polytechnical education and individual projects were set up. In the GDR, the one-teacher village school educating pupils from six to sixteen in one classroom had been virtually abolished, in marked contrast to the Federal Republic.

The years 1959–65 marked a third decisive stage, beginning with the *Gesetz über die sozialistische Entwicklung des Schulwesens* (Law on the Socialist Develop- ment of the School System) which introduced the *Zehnklassige allgemeinbildende polytechnische Oberschule* (ten-year general polytechnical school). Some analysts also distinguish an intermediate stage beginning in 1956,[21] and there is some merit in this point of view: in February 1956, Khrushchev's dramatic break with Stalinism resulted in a period of some uncertainty, often described as an ideological thaw. This period culminated in the Hungarian uprising and, following the Soviet invasion, a new freeze developed. Some instability was also experienced in the GDR, which saw the dismissal of the Republic's second most senior leader, Karl Schirdewan, and a group of dissidents around him. In terms of the education debate, the incident is referred to as revisionism and 'a brake on the socialist advance' in an attempt to gain 'concessions from the imperialist forces'.[22] The 'revisionists' had favoured a degree of selection after six school years and the retention of different types of secondary education, in essence a system not substantially different from that in the West.[23]

In the wake of these revisionist moves, socialist dogma was reinforced in a renewed effort to integrate the whole of the education system into the country's scientific and economic ideology and to incorporate Soviet policy on polytechnical education. By December 1958, the Soviet Union had introduced an 'act for the strengthening of the link between school and life and for the further development of the education system in the USSR',[24] while the GDR had already initiated the *Unterrichtstag in der Produktion* (Work Experience Day). Obviously designed to develop greater socialist awareness in all pupils and heralding a major departure from all previous forms of education, trial runs of the *Unterrichtstag* had been carefully organized in specially selected middle schools. The child's individual, personal development was subordinated to complete integration into society. The development of the imagination by play was subordinated to the requirements of the workplace, while the scientific-technological claims of Marxism-Leninism replaced what remained of the traditionally humanist education system. Such a revolution in pedagogics obviously called for further changes in curricular design, in vocational training, in industrial and agricultural production methods, leading to a take-over by ideologues of the traditional academic elites.

The overall effect of these changes is difficult to assess, but should be regarded as part of a more general wide-ranging process of modernization. The change-over spelt the end of the German mandarin tradition and ensured support for the scientific and economic requirements of a technological age. It afforded much greater equality of opportunity for all those groups identified in the Federal Republic as 'educational reserves'. And yet, a closer study of the *Unterrichtstag* and of claims made for it would suggest that the process of 'Sovietization' had been carried too far: the priority given to agriculture and heavy industry was more in tune with Communist practice in the 1920s and 1930s than with requirements of the 1960s, such as a prestigious new space research programme. In fact, the whole concept seemed more in keeping with the needs of a newly evolving industrialized society than with a comparatively modern developed state such as East Germany, and subsequent policies would attempt to correct this anachronism. In pedagogical terms, the *Unterrichtstag* was an attempt to close the gap between industrial and agricultural workers and schools. The Day was intended to impart a basic knowledge of organization and economics, of socialist production methods in agriculture and industry and of practical metalwork, woodwork and construction. The development of the all-round socialist personality called for work experience relevant to the stage of intellectual maturity of the individual pupil. Because the *Unterrichtstag* was introduced for pupils in the age group thirteen to eighteen, the logistical implications were considerable: one day per week had to be set aside for the training of some 450,000 children, foremen in industry had to have their educational skills enhanced and teachers needed instruction in the basic skills which their pupils had to acquire. Christa Wolf's *Der geteilte Himmel* (The Divided Sky) gives a vivid description of a teacher's industrial experience, although not of the *Unterrichtstag* itself.

It would be misleading to concentrate on this development in isolation, as it was designed as an integral part of polytechnical education. A new subject, *Einführung in die sozialistische Produktion in Industrie und Landwirtschaft* (Introduction to Socialist Production Methods in Industry and Agriculture), introduced in September 1958, devoted two lessons per week to economics, technology and Marxist-Leninist ideology. This innovation helped to alleviate the dislocation generated by local and seasonal aspects of the *Unterrichtstag* and which had been criticized by many pedagogues. In order to develop a scientific world-view, an increasingly methodical approach was needed:

> Ein wissenschaftliches Weltbild [. . .] setzt sich nicht zusammen aus Zufallskomplexen, die die örtlichen Bedingungen bescheren. [. . .] Das Weltbild, das gewonnen wird, ist zerstückelt. Es fehlt ihm die Schau von oben, die die einzelnen Erscheinungen system-atisch in das Ganze einordnet. Der so erzogene Mensch vermag bestenfalls auf einzelne Erscheinungen zu reagieren. Er ist reaktiv. Was wir aber im Sozialismus brauchen, ist der aktive Mensch, der sich der Wissenschaft bedient, um die Welt zu verändern.[25]

> (A scientific world-view [. . .] cannot be constructed from accidentally created complexes, as local conditions present them. [. . .] It lacks an overview which can systematically incorporate individual phenomena into the overall system. A person educated in this way can at best react to individual phenomena. He is reactive. However, socialism needs proactive people, people who employ science in order to change the world.)

The decisive, final step in the implementation of polytechnical education was the introduction of the *Zehnklassige, allgemeinbildende polytechnische Oberschule* (Ten-Year General Polytechnical School). It replaced the eight-year *Grundschule* (elementary school) and, by 1964, became cumpulsory for all pupils.[26] Vocational training, taught on two days per week, formed an integral part of every child's education. The proportion of time spent on natural sciences was increased and a Marxist-Leninist bias was given to all subjects. A greater awareness of Soviet thought and culture was encouraged. The new school was generally referred to as the *Oberschule* and effectively replaced most other types of school. Some special schools, mainly for exceptionally gifted children in the arts, sciences, mathematics, Russian and sports, were already in existence and others were established. The *Erweiterte Oberschule* (Extended Secondary School) was the exception which never fitted happily into the comprehensive system: pupils entered this type of school after eight years at the polytechnical school and, during a further four years, they received sufficient academic training to enable them to follow a university course. Admission criteria were based on academic performance, political and ideological commitment and social background. Working-class children were favoured, though overall figures suggest that the proportion of children from an academic background was proportionally higher.[27] Every effort was made to integrate these academically orientated pupils into the socialist workforce. Experience with students from workers' and peasants' faculties was used to produce an academic elite fully in accord with the rest of society. By 1960 this type of school was also offering a vocational qualification, enabling its pupils to become *Facharbeiter* (skilled workers) by following a shortened apprenticeship course. At the same time, school leavers from the polytechnical school could prepare for university studies during their apprenticeships. There were two types of university entry qualification (*Abitur*): awarded either at the end of twelve school years (plus an additional vocational year) at the *Erweiterte Oberschule* or after ten years at the polytechnical school and three further years of apprenticeship. The latter, described as a *Berufsausbildung mit Abitur*, was a qualification designed particularly for those wishing to study technological subjects.

By 1965, a fourth step in educational development had been reached, beginning with the *Gesetz über das einheitliche sozialistische Bildungssystem* (Law on the Integrated Socialist Education System). In comparison with previous phases, however, this was little more than a period of consolidation. With the polytechnical school established, a streamlining of the rest of the system was the next logical step. The *Erweiterte Oberschule*, now reduced to two years, became partially reintegrated into the polytechnical school (figure 9). New curricula and textbooks were developed, teacher training was reformed and university education standardized by a change which limited courses to four years, based on a broad syllabus and with the opportunity for further periods of specialization and training later in life. A *Grundstudium* (foundation study course) prepared for the *Fachstudium* (specialist course), culminating in the award of a diploma. In addition, the study period had to include a vocational element, equipping students for specific work within the socialist system, and students were encouraged to follow academic studies directly relevant to their work experience. Marxism-Leninism was a compulsory element, normally included in the foundation course. Research was usually restricted to the practical or vocational application of the subject studied, most other forms of research being delegated to academies. The old faculties were transformed into sections, allegedly in order to foster interdisciplinary projects, but primarily in order to involve universities more closely with the rest of the education system and with industry. In general, more practical needs were dealt with during this phase, needs which were also apparent in the West, where they still remain to be fully addressed.

Class

			Berufsschule	
13			*Berufsschule*	
12	*Erweiterte Oberschule* Extended Secondary School	*Berufsschule* Vocational Training	*mit Abitur* Vocational Training with *Abitur*	
11				
10	10-class general upper school			*Spezialschulen*
9	*Zehnklassige allgemeinbildende*			Special Schools
8	(upper level)			
7	*polytechnische Oberschule*			
6				
5	(middle level)			
4				
3				
2	(lower level)			
1				

Figure 9 The GDR education system (late 1960s). The first ten school years were taught in a comprehensive manner, an element of differentiation being introduced only in the last two to three years.

A final reform stage coincided with Honecker's accession to the leadership in 1971, but this change at the top was less significant than a series of other developments: the GDR became more closely involved in a programme of 'world-socialism',[28] especially after the Prague Spring and the elimination of the Dubcek government (1968), when a closer alignment with Soviet Communism seemed advisable, not least in order to subdue voices of dissent within the GDR. An element of fluctuation is nevertheless detectable in GDR policy: whilst the system was becoming more pragmatic and following the less ideological route of 'real existierender Sozialismus' (actually existing socialism), the mid-1970s saw it celebrate the ultimate achievement of Communist education. The reasons for this apparent inconsistency lie outside education policy. The new Five-Year Plan of 1971 aimed to raise living standards and increase the availability of consumer goods. The material differences between the GDR and the Federal Republic had to be reduced, so that the GDR could present a credible image on the international stage, with entry into the United Nations and UNESCO. Its growing international profile, however, necessitated a clearer ideological division from the West. The scientific foundation of socialism, based on steady progress towards Communism, should be seen to be bearing fruit. Taking advantage of weaknesses in the West German education system, the GDR sought to promote her own system as exemplary. There was also evidence of increasing co-operation with COMECON, involving regular conferences on all aspects of education. The Berlin *Akademie der pädagogischen*

Wissenschaften (Academy of Education) took a lead at these conferences, representing ideological stability within the Eastern bloc.

The most important changes affected higher education, where the effect of economic policy was strongest. Earlier expansion of higher education had resulted in a shortage of skilled workers and the new Five-Year Plan sought to reduce the number of university students, with a concomitant increase in skilled workers. The academic year 1972/3 saw a fall of over 10 per cent in university places and, despite a modest increase in the 1980s,[29] the percentage of students did not exceed 12 per cent[30] of an age group, compared to over 22 per cent in the FRG.[31] Changes in polytechnical education were only minor. Emphasis was given to an even greater input from parents and state enterprise into education in order to increase course efficiency and produce a higher standard of proficiency. This encouraged *Prozentgläubigkeit*[32] (obsession with percentages); teachers and schools were rewarded for high marks and the resulting inflation frequently led to a reduction in overall standards. In 1980 a new subject, *Wehrunterricht* (military defence training), was introduced for the final two years of the *Oberschule*. This development occurred at the height of the peace movement in the West. Young people in the GDR, too, were becoming increasingly attracted to peace movement activities, notably those organized by the Protestant Church under the banner 'swords into ploughshares', which were eventually to assume greater independence and form the nucleus of the 1989 'revolution'.[33] In December 1981, East and West German writers, meeting in East Berlin to discuss disarmament and peace, coined the slogan 'Frieden schaffen ohne Waffen' (peace works without weapons).[34] Unofficial peace seminars and workshops, only loosely associated with the Church, began to spring up in many GDR cities and soon attracted punks, greens and gays, in short all those who wished to protest against the repressively centrist regime [Text 2].

Another important change in education policy reflected the increasing emphasis on key technologies, notably micro-electronics and bio-technology, as the guarantee of future economic growth. Micro-electronics entered the school curriculum as part of *Einführung in die sozialistische Produktion*, accounting for up to 60 per cent of the subject by the mid-1980s.[35] Personal computers and pocket calculators, introduced in vocational training, also became increasingly common in *Oberschulen* at a time when they were still the exception in the FRG.

The sum of all these changes had a major impact on the routine functioning of education. A dichotomy arose between, on the one hand, socialist dogma with its emphasis on increasing individual involvement in the socialist process and, on the other, an obvious divergence from traditional socialist production methods. The introduction of information technology inevitably involved a growing internationalization and a need for greater individual specialization. The economic necessity for greater individual efficiency further strengthened these tendencies. The suppression, over several decades, of individuality and personal expression began to give way. Authoritarian attitudes in schools, together with traditional training methods in some areas, were no longer tolerated. Vague promises of more consumer choice further stimulated a latent dissatisfaction, sporadic at first, but widespread by the late 1980s, manifesting itself in criticism of the system and an opting-out of society altogether [Text 3].

Leading pedagogues and politicians recognized the danger signs and attempted to stem the tide. Margot Honecker demanded that teachers respond positively to the increasing maturity and critical awareness of the younger generation.[36] Individual achievements were rewarded, especially in science and technology. Talented young people increasingly gained access to university on their own merit; unconventional thinking within a discipline was promoted and politicians were coming to recognize that society could not afford to sacrifice even one individual talent.[37] In 1983 'facultative lessons' were introduced in the the last two years of the *Oberschule*, allowing students to specialize in particular subjects, a change designed to maximize individual talent and to increase personal responsibility. Such developments, however, created some official anxiety over this deviation from 'objectivism' and growing disillusionment with socialist ideology. In a corrective move, parents and youth organizations were exhorted to intensify the 'allseitige Bildung und die kommunistische Erziehung der Kinder und Jugendlichen'[38] (comprehensive education and Communist upbringing of children and young people). The concept of democratic centralism was tied even more to the dogma of Marxism-Leninism and the revised school directive of 1979 compelled headteachers to adhere strictly to the decisions of the Socialist Unity Party. Teachers, the socialist teachers union, parents' councils and youth organizations all contributed towards reinforcing this ideological line, preventing any form of personal initiative being taken by schools.

This final stage in the GDR's education policy acknowledged growing unease with socialist dogma and the centralist administration. The need to allow individual imagination a freer rein and the yearning for some degree of personal privacy could no longer be dismissed as bourgeois or capitalist. Whatever the reasons for the collapse of socialism, and there are certainly divergent factors which contributed to its downfall, the suppression of individuality was a major feature, despite the fact that the GDR education system as a whole was marked by considerable innovation, fulfilled many modernist criteria and advanced educational debate in many different spheres.

An Evaluation of Some GDR Textbooks

So far this analysis has been based on the evolution of the GDR education policy and its structure. Its development within a closed political system may have resulted in a lack of balance and over-emphasis on ideological issues, while perhaps obscuring some of its achievements in day-to-day teaching and syllabus design.

This section will examine some GDR textbooks in use from the late 1950s to the 1980s, especially in those subjects with a sociological or humanist content, where an overall picture of GDR education and, in particular, its specific ideological bias can be discerned. Textbooks on German literature, English, history and related subjects have been assessed, but with no scientific validity claim, since the sample is not sufficiently representative. This analysis, restricted to individual school books and limited in scope, should still offer some insight into school-life in the GDR.

German Studies

As a general background, most of the teaching was undertaken collectively by staff in specific subject-rooms. The *Lichterfeld Oberschule* subject-room, introduced in 1965, contained large notice-boards and blackboards, the former displaying posters with standard German grammar rules. Special multicoloured markers were used to underline or highlight individual topics. Among the many learning and teaching aids available for independent work by the pupils were handbooks on spelling, grammar, histories of literature and anthologies.[39] Each room was also equipped with a tape-recorder and slide-projector. The very existence and resourcing of such subject-rooms compared favourably with West German schools. It also indicated a fair amount of time available for private study. Teaching was based on the scientific theory of Marxism-Leninism,[40] in order to convey its validity within nature and society. Tuition had to be 'parteilich' (partisan):

> Die politisch-ideologische Erziehung ist ein dialektischer Prozeß des Zusammenwirkens von Erziehung und Selbsterziehung, von pädagogischer Führung und Selbsttätigkeit der Schüler. Es muß bei allen an der Erziehung Beteiligten Klarheit darüber geschaffen werden, daß die politisch-ideologische Erziehung nur gemeinsam mit der Jugend, nur durch ihre aktive Einbeziehung in den Prozeß der sozialistischen Bewußtseinsentwicklung erfolgreich durchgeführt werden kann.[41]

> (Political-ideological education is a dialectic process of the alliance between education and self-tuition, between pedagogical leadership and the autonomous activity of pupils. All participants in education must be made aware that political and ideological education can be successfully carried out only in partnership with young people, by their active integration into the process of the development of socialist awareness.)

An analysis of textbooks is based on *Lesebuch Klasse 7* (Class 7 German Reader) and on three volumes of *Aus deutscher Dichtung* (Anthology of German literature). The *Lesebuch*,[42] published in 1985, was intended for thirteen-year-olds. Its approximately 200 pages fall into three major sections: the Old High German and medieval period, the 'bourgeois-humanist heritage' and twentieth-century socialist literature.

All three sections include examples from outside the German-speaking world and, specifically, from Russian literature. The early section concentrates on Germanic tradition and folklore, with a significant absence of Christian texts. (Excerpts from the *Nibelungenlied* concentrate on the Siegfried element.) The inclusion of Aeschylus' *Prometheus Bound* may be seen as a parallel to Genesis and the expulsion from Paradise. Whilst most of the anthology is restricted to the text, the Georgian story by Rustaweli contains editorial comment [Text 4]. Four non-German authors are included among nineteen in the bourgeois-humanist section. Most of the pieces selected are fairly simple, but the Hans Sachs play is the original version and fairly demanding for this age range. The majority of the texts are parables or ballads and the very few introductory passages are designed to aid comprehension. The last section is obviously intended to strengthen GDR identity: of the thirty-four authors represented, only five are non-Germans, whereas twenty-two are contemporary GDR citizens. Many of the texts are pure propaganda, celebrating Communist heroism in the face of imperialism or fascism. The pattern is predictable: a disadvantaged childhood brings the hero/heroine into contact with Communists and a triumphant victory is achieved after great sacrifices, even death, in the name of Communism. Many of the stories are highly sentimental, despite their claim to be 'Wunder der Wirklichkeit' (miracles of reality) (L. 147). One of the more contemporary stories takes John Lennon as its subject: Lennon is hailed as a fighter for peace and ecology and the author is somewhat critical that the GDR does not include him in Meyer's *Enzyklopädie* (L. 216). Three textbooks on German literature, *Aus deutscher Dichtung*[43] dating from 1958–60, cover the last three years of the *Oberschule*: they offer an extremely high standard of specialist knowledge, dealing with a wide and complex selection of German literature from its earliest beginnings to the end of the nineteenth century. The last five of its twenty-nine sections introduce socialist literature, with virtually all the texts by German authors, presented chronologically from 1850 up to the end of the Second World War. The final section covers GDR literature right up to the contemporary scene. Practically all the texts are of a literary nature, but some assume a more philosophical or political function, e.g. the Communist Manifesto and speeches by Grotewohl and Ulbricht. A meaningful comparison between the three 1950s textbooks and the 1985 *Lesebuch* is problematic, since they are written for different age groups and school types. Whilst the ideological tenor of the *Lesebuch* is much stronger and sometimes almost crude in its anti-capitalist polemics, it seems, nevertheless, to fulfil an important function in defining GDR identity.

English

English was the second or even third foreign language after Russian. Our analysis is based on just one book for thirteen-year-olds,[44] the same age group targeted by the German reader. Written for pupils who are learning English in their third year, it emphasizes grammatical accuracy, sometimes at the expense of the communicative approach. Of particular interest here is the image of Britain it seeks to convey. A comparison with a West German reader from the same period and for the same age group would highlight major differences: while the West German texts emphasize tourist attractions and the day-to-day life of ordinary families, illustrated by attractive photographs, this textbook describes Britain from the point of view of working-class families in Birmingham, Liverpool and Glasgow. The Black Country, Scotland, Wales and London are represented as major industrial regions; Scottish farmers are seen in a struggle against property-owning landlords. In contrast to the restrictions on free movement for GDR citizens, several sections describe visits by British schoolchildren to the GDR. References abound to disadvantaged working mothers, housing problems, unemployment and poverty in Britain. Many of the characters featured belong to trade unions, take part 'in the workers' fight for their jobs'(E. 33) and look to the Communist Party for support. By comparison, the GDR is presented as a modern high-tech country with a contented and secure work force (E. 66). The Communist Party, the peace movement and CND are seen to co-operate in a struggle for peace and a fight for jobs (E. 75). While traditional cultural features are not much in evidence, sections cover the Tower of London, the Beatles in Liverpool, Robert Burns in Scotland and attempts to revive the Welsh language at the Eisteddfod. There is some mention of sport, mainly confined to football and athletics. Facts contained in the textbook are certainly accurate, but create an impression of a society in the final phases of late capitalism and witnessing the great liberation movement of its working classes.

History

An outsider would expect this subject to have a specifically socialist flavour, but upon closer study the topic is found to have been entirely subsumed by Marxism-Leninism. A guide to socialist education states that history has to be scientific in the Marxist sense and an instrument of socialist propaganda:

> Der Unterricht in Geschichte und Staatsbürgerkunde stattet die Schüler mit bedeutungsvollen Erkenntnissen über die sozialistischen Produktionsverhältnisse in der DDR und ihre Überlegenheit gegenüber den kapitalistischen Produktionsverhältnissen in Westdeutschland aus.[45]

> (Lessons in history and civics equip pupils with significant insights into the socialist production processes of the GDR and their superiority to the capitalist production methods in West Germany.)

History teaching had become entirely functional, designed to instil in pupils a respect for the working class and to educate them in a commitment to any form of work that was of service to society.[46] The syllabus was designed in a holistic fashion: each year's lessons were devised to make pupils aware of the 'inhaltlich-ideologische Linienführung' (ideological line inherent in the subject) (M. 53). History was taught from Class 5 (age eleven) onwards, the first four years dedicated to *Heimatkunde*, a subject relating history to geography and biology and taught with specific regard to the school's own environment. The historical aspect covered the working class in its long fight against exploitation, with close reference to events in the Soviet Union and the GDR. The actual history course began in Class 5 with an introduction to prehistoric primitive society and its later formation into a class-based society in Babylon, Athens and Rome, with particular emphasis on slavery. Class 6 followed the decline of the Roman Empire, and feudalism as it developed first in Byzantium, then in the Arab caliphates and finally in Europe. A focal issue was the growth of a European bourgeoisie, city life and particularism. The syllabus ended with an introduction to various European peasant uprisings, the Hussites, humanism, the German Reformation and the Peasants' War.

Space does not permit a detailed account of the syllabus in years seven to ten: the rise of imperialism and capitalism were central themes, as manifested in the French Revolution and the Industrial Revolution, the Communist Manifesto and the 1848 Revolutions, and the Paris Commune. Twentieth-century topics concentrated on the First World War and its position within European imperialism, the Russian October 1917 Revolution and its international significance, Germany's November 1918 Revolution, the fight against imperialism and fascism as a joint struggle of international and German proletarian forces, the development of a 'socialist world order' after 1945, the establishment of the GDR as an anti-fascist bulwark, and the simultaneous decline of imperialism and advance of socialism. Class 10 concluded with the conflict between aggressive capitalist imperialism, as embodied in the FRG, and the strengthening of socialism in an attempt to keep the peace in Europe. Classes 11 and 12 at the *Erweiterte Oberschule* were devoted to case studies, where such topics as the German working-class movement in particular and international movements from the Paris Commune to today were the subject of in-depth examination.

Even non-specialists will recognize that the systematic development of history, from primitive social structures to contemporary socialist working-class society, was comparable to the Hegelian theory of the unfolding of the objective spirit in today's world, except that the 'objective spirit' was replaced by the Communist ideal. History became a one-way street, devoid of detours or even cul-de-sacs, with the ubiquitous presence of socialist doctrine inhibiting any critical awareness or methodological, disinterested analysis. Whilst it will have become obvious that the GDR pupils acquired an impressive amount of knowledge, the actual means by which this was achieved militated against independence of mind and methodological pluralism.

Conclusion

Many readers may well be critical of the approach taken in this chapter, either because several findings are rather negative and sceptical in tone or because of its defence of major aspects of the system, despite many shortcomings which recent investigations have brought to light. There is no doubt, however, that initial attempts to modernize a discredited German system were genuine and promising. The new pattern that emerged did abolish the tripartite structure with its largely socially based selection, eradicated the mandarin tradition at university level and succeeded in reconciling the world of learning with that of labour. The system's shortcomings, however, also seemed to stem from that same ideology which had so successfully overcome the bourgeois tradition. By wedding the new education programme to a system which was at best holistic, at worst based on an outdated, romanticized understanding of a socialist order supported by the working classes it was, by its very nature, doomed to fail. This working-class ethos, itself historically defined and probably outdated by the time it was so rigorously applied, inevitably clashed with the reality of the advanced technological society of the 1970s and 1980s. The teleological understanding of history evident in the history textbooks also applied to a Marxist-Leninist ideology so restricted in its concept of the all-round socialist personality that it could not accommodate individual imagination and creativity. This became obvious in the early invectives against teachers who had sought to apply aspects of *Reformpädagogik*, but it was also present in a sometimes idiosyncratic insistence on petit-bourgeois values and secondary virtues such as neatness, order and discipline. From the mid-1960s, education seemed divided between a progressive teaching system with a well-developed school democracy, whose curriculum was open to the concerns of a modern industrial society, and a heavy-handed party administration, intent on binding students and pupils ever closer to the state, by means of the *Jugendweihe*, *Wehrunterricht* or party propaganda. The final days of the GDR witnessed a growing dissatisfaction amongst young people, displayed either through an openly unpolitical attitude or by escape into an idealistic fantasy world. Since few of these disaffected elements identified with the West, the charge of massive Western infiltration seems untenable.

Many of these observations have been reflected in the comments on textbooks. The over-centralized system, in offering less and less freedom for individual experiment, encouraged stereotypical responses. An unrealistic, exaggerated view of Germany's past credited the industrial proletariat with an importance that flew in the face of unbiased historical evidence. Chapter 8 will assess the extent to which the best of the GDR's education system could have been adopted by the enlarged FRG and how East German society adjusted to a changed lifestyle.

Notes

1. As an example cf. K.-H. Günther and G. Uhlig (1973), *History of the Schools in the German Democratic Republic 1945 to 1968*, Berlin.
2. O. Anweiler (1988), *Schulpolitik und Schulsystem in der DDR*, Opladen; D. Waterkamp (1987), *Handbuch zum Bildungswesen der DDR*, Berlin.
3. G. Neuner (1973), *Zur Theorie der sozialistischen Allgemeinbildung*, Berlin, p. 15.
4. M. Honecker (1965), 'Referat auf der Konferenz der Lehrer und pädagogischen Wissenschaftler', *Deutsche Lehrerzeitung*, No. 23, Beilage, p. 5.
5. Neuner, *Zur Theorie*, p. 19.
6. Based on W. I. Lenin (1959), *Werke*, vol. 31, Berlin, p. 272. Quoted from Neuner, *Zur Theorie*, p. 231.
7. Neuner, *Zur Theorie*, p. 146f. For a systematic overview cf. ibid., p. 164.
8. *Verfassung der DDR* (1968), article 25.4. Also: Staatsverlag der DDR (1965), 'Gesetz über das einheitliche sozialistische Bildungssystem', *Unser Bildungssystem – wichtiger Schritt auf dem Wege zur gebildeten Nation*, Berlin.
9. E. Lange, G. Perner and J. Polzin (1966), *Sozialistische Erziehung in der Schulpraxis. Erfahrungen der Oberschulen Lichterfelde und Ehrenberg bei der planmäßigen Bewußtseinsentwicklung der Schüler*, Berlin, p. 62f.
10. A. S. Makarenko (1952), *Ausgewählte pädagogische Schriften*, Berlin, p. 257. Quoted from I. Berg (1961), *Zur Theorie der Strafe in der sozialistischen Schule*, Berlin, p. 25.
11. H. Hümmler (1967), *Die Partei, ABC des Marxismus Leninismus*, Berlin, p. 63.
12. A. Kosing et al. (1954), *Weltall Erde Mensch. Ein Sammelwerk zur Entwicklungsgeschichte von Natur und Gesellschaft*, Berlin.
13. A good illustration of the yearning for alternative lifestyles is given in U. Plenzdorf (1973), *Die neuen Leiden des jungen W.*, Rostock.
14. Chapter 5, pp. 96f.
15. Günther and Uhlig, *History*, p. 63.
16. Anweiler, *Schulpolitik*, p. 60.
17. Günther and Uhlig, *History*, p. 73.

18. H. J. Hahn (1990), 'Kahlschlag und Dschungel in der deutschen Germanistik nach 1945', *German Life and Letters*, vol. 43, p. 259.
19. Lange, Perner and Polzin, *Sozialistische Erziehung*, pp. 78f.
20. *Geschichte der Erziehung* (1957), Berlin, p. 477. Quoted from Günther and Uhlig, *History*, p. 81.
21. Günther and Uhlig, *History*, p. 91.
22. Ibid., p. 97.
23. A. Hearnden (1974), *Education in the Two Germanies*, Oxford, p. 110.
24. Günther and Uhlig, *History*, p. 119.
25. W. Reischock (1958), 'Systematik und Leben', *Deutsche Lehrerzeitung*, no. 42.
26. Thesen des Zentralkomitees der SED (1960), H. Klein (1974), *Bildung in der DDR, Grundlagen, Entwicklungen, Probleme*, Reinbek b. Hamburg, p. 76.
27. Hearnden, *Education in the Two Germanies*, p. 253, appendix vi.
28. Anweiler, *Schulpolitik*, p. 107.
29. From a high point of 160,967 in 1972 to 153,558 in 1973, 127,473 in 1978 to 130,097 in 1983.
30. Anweiler, *Schulpolitik*, p. 110.
31. Figure calculated from dates extracted from Statistisches Bundesamt (ed.) (1986), *Statistische Jahrbuch für die Bundesrepublik Deutschland*, Stuttgart, pp. 356f.
32. Anweiler, *Schulpolitik*, p. 113.
33. J. Sandford (1992), 'The Peace Movement and the Church in the Honecker Years', in G. J. Glaeßner and I. Wallace (eds), *The German Revolution of 1989*, Oxford, pp. 124–43.
34. H. Bussiek (1984), *Die real existierende DDR. Neue Notizen aus der unbekannten deutschen Republik*, Frankfurt/M., p. 201.
35. Anweiler, *Schulpolitik*, p. 120.
36. Ibid., p. 110.
37. G. Kröber (1980), 'Wissenschaftlich-technische Revolution und Bildungswesen', *Pädagogik*, vol. 35, p. 670.
38. Elternbeiratsverordnung, 15. 11. 1966, quoted from Anweiler, *Schulpolitik*, p. 142.
39. Lange, Perner and Polzin, *Sozialistische Erziehung*, p. 30.
40. W. Ulbricht (1966), *Probleme des Perspektivplanes bis 1970*, Berlin, p. 90, quoted from Lange, Perner and Polzin, *Sozialistische Erziehung*, p. 11.
41. Ulbricht, *Probleme*, p. 91.
42. W. Freitag (ed.) (1985), *Lesebuch Klasse 7*, Berlin. Subsequent references will be given as L. plus page number in parenthesis in the text.
43. Autorenkollektiv (eds) (1958), *Aus deutscher Dichtung*, vols. 1–3, Berlin.

44. M. Meinhardt et al. (eds) (1980), *English for You*, vol. 3, Berlin. Subsequent references will be given as E. plus page number in parenthesis in the text.

45. Lange, Perner and Polzin, *Sozialistische Erziehung*, p. 33.

46. B. Gentner, R. Kruppa et al. (eds) (1975), *Methodik Geschichtsunterricht*, Berlin, p. 26. Subsequent references will be given as M. plus page number in the text.

TEXTUAL STUDIES

1. 'Die Geschichte vom Kaputtmacher Siegfried'

Siegfried war ein Satansbraten,
tat nur immer böse Taten,
bog die Kleiderhaken krumm,
kippte Tintenfässer um,
5   schlug mit Beil und Schraubenschlüssel
Glas kaputt und Suppenschüssel,
stutzte Omas Wäscheleine,
riß dem Kaspar aus die Beine,
schwärzte Muttis Puderdose,
10 schnitt sich Löcher in die Hose.
Nichts ließ Siegfried ungeschoren,
immer mußte er nur bohren,
klecksen, sägen, zerren, zupfen
und zerreißen und zerrupfen.

15 'Was soll werden?' sprach der Vater.
Doch da fand sich ein Berater!
'Siegfried', sagte Kaufmann Pelle,
'ist ein ruppiger Geselle.
Da ist nur noch eins zu machen:
20 Kauft dem Bub kaputte Sachen,
dann vergeht ihm bald das Scherzen,
und er nimmt es sich zu Herzen!'

Siegfrieds Vater war sehr froh,
und er sprach: 'Das mach ich so!'
25 Und die Eltern, hübsch zu zwein,
kauften Murks für Siegfried ein.

Ging nun Siegfried aus dem Haus,
sah er ganz erbärmlich aus!
Ganz kaputt und ganz verbogen
30   war der Knabe angezogen.
Was er trug und mit sich nahm,
war kaputter Trödelkram,
und es ging von Mund zu Mund:
Siegfried ist ein Vagabund.
35   Benno, Eberhard, Irene
und sogar die Magdalene,
die nur selten Späße macht,
haben sich kaputtgelacht.
(H. Stengel and K. Schrader (1973), *So ein Struwwelpeter*, Berlin)

Commentary

The story is modelled on the 'Victorian' *Struwwelpeter*, published by the physician Heinrich Hoffmann in 1847. It is a strange concoction of old-fashioned authoritarian pedagogics and socialist methods, as Makarenko might have taught them. However, far from being reintegrated into society, the boy becomes further estranged by being made the laughing-stock of his peer group. It is punishment by public humiliation with little thought of correcting the social misfit.

Vocabulary

Satansbraten (m) = devil of a boy; Tintenfaß (n) = inkstand; Beil (n)= axe; Schraubenschlüssel (m) = spanner; Puderdose (f) = powder-box; ungeschoren = untouched; Berater (m) = adviser; ruppig = unkempt; Murks (m) = rubbish; verbogen = twisted; Trödelkram (m) = trash; kaputtgelacht = laughed themselves silly.

2. Berlin *Friedensseminar*, July 1983

Welche Fortschritte die DDR-Friedensbewegung in nur einem Jahr gemacht hat, zeigte sich bei der zweiten Friedenswerkstatt in Ost-Berlin. Motto: 'Sprich mal frei'. Für zehn Stunden blühte da an der Erlöserkirche auf dem abgelegenen Kirchengrundstück am S-Bahnhof Rummelsburg eine politische Kultur auf, von der die 3000 Teilnehmer
5   im Alltag nur träumen konnten.

    Mehr Besucher, mehr Gruppenstände waren aufgebaut, offenere Diskussionen fanden statt. Die neue Basisbewegung stellte sich in ihrer ganzen Breite dar, die Palette reichte weit über das Friedensthema hinaus. Umweltschützer meldeten sich ebenso zu Wort wie Schwulen- und Frauengruppen. Am Ökostand etwa informierten Grüne aus

10 Mecklenburg über den geplanten Bau der Schweriner Autobahn. Probleme, über die sich die Ost-Berliner Szene, ebenso wie die Angereisten aus der Provinz, erstmals öffentlich informieren konnte.

(W. Büscher and P. Wensierski (1984), *Nullbock auf DDR. Aussteigerjugend im anderen Deutschland*, Reinbeck b. Hamburg, p. 140)

Commentary

The passage describes the general atmosphere at this second unofficial peace meeting: the ten-hour-long 'teach-in' under the motto 'speak freely' was typical of the political culture which existed in the underground movement and continued during the final collapse of the GDR. Fringe groups, as in other Western countries, discussed issues of specific interest to them and sought contact with other groups. In another part of the text an official of the GDR-CDU is met with ridicule for his statement that the GDR is peaceful even in its internal policy. A member of the feminist peace group won applause for her assurance that she and her friends were not *agents provocateurs*.

Vocabulary

Kirchengrundstück (n) = church premises; Gruppenstand (m) = stall; Basisbewegung (f) = grass-roots movement; Umweltschützer (m) = environmentalist; Schwuler (m) = gay person; Ökostand (m) = ecology stall; Angereiste (m/f) = visitor.

3. Gabriele Kachold, 'an die 40jährigen' (1982/3)

das ist das gedicht einer 30jährigen, ohne strophe, ohne vers, ohne reim, ohne maß, damit ist schon alles gesagt oder vieles, wir sind die zu spät gekommenen, ein klein wenig zu spät für eure ordnung, um eintritt zu finden dazu, zutritt in den raum der geregelten abläufe. ihr hattet noch zeit, euch einzurichten, in das land, in das leben, in
5 die zeit, ihr seid die generation, die jene andere generation in die welt setzte. [. . .]
  wir haben nichts, wir können nichts, wir wollen nichts, wir brauchen nichts. wir sind roh, ungebildet, ungepflegt, unkultiviert. wir halten uns nicht an eure abmachungen, eure gesetze besitzt ihr ohne uns, ihr habt uns nicht gefragt, ihr habt immer für uns mitgeredet, ihr habt eure worte für unsere worte gehalten, eure wahrheit
10 für unsere wahrheit.

(G. Kachold (1990), *zügellos*, Frankfurt/M., pp. 79f)

Commentary

Gabriele Kachold was born in 1953. She studied German and art history, was expelled from university and imprisoned, but became a freelance author in 1980.

She belongs to the group of writers loosely associated with the *Prenzlauer Berg*. This poem describes the protest of her fringe group against the over-regulated GDR, but with no suggestion that the FRG might offer any improvement. The poem is anarchist in nature and does not observe stylistic conventions. It contains no positive socialist message; elsewhere the poem suggests: 'wir haben keine zukunft, wir haben keinen platz, wir haben keine hoffnung, wir haben kein ziel.' Openly hedonistic, this generation of 'nachgeborene' (a Brecht reference) suggests in its last lines: 'aber übersehen könnt ihr uns nicht, überleben könnt ihr uns nicht, vernichten könnt ihr uns nicht und: vergessen könnt ihr uns nicht. denn wir sind euch eine andere form von hoffnung.'

Vocabulary

Strophe (f) = stanza; die zu spät Gekommenen = the late arrivals; geregelte Abläufe = regulated sequence of events; in die Welt setzen = to give birth to; Abmachung (f) = arrangement.

4. 'Die beste Hoffnung ist die Tat'

Der Dichter [Rustaweli] selbst gehört zum Dienstadel, dessen Vertreter nicht durch Herkunft, sondern um bestimmter Verdienste willen zu Landbesitz und Adelsrang gekommen waren. [. . .] 'Das Böse ist vergänglich, nur das Gute ist von Dauer', sagt Rustaweli. Aber ein Mensch allein richtet wenig aus. 'Wer nicht Freunde sucht auf
5 Erden, ist sich selbst der ärgste Feind.' Erst das Bündnis der Tapferen sichert den Erfolg. Tariel, Awtandil und Fridon, Männer aus verschiedenen Völkern, vereinigen sich, um Unrecht aus der Welt zu schaffen. Unmögliches wird möglich, weil sie gemeinsam vorgehen und weil sie einander lieben und achten. Am Stahl ihres Freundschaftsbundes schlagen sich räuberische Feinde die Stirn blutig.
(W. Freitag et al. (eds) (1985), *Lesebuch Klasse 7*, Berlin, pp. 52f)

Commentary

This commentary on a Georgian text from about 1200 is given a socialist interpretation, suggesting that evil can be eradicated by a just society and that an individual will achieve nothing without joining a group of the like-minded. This emphasis on action within a group is so strong that it could easily have been used to describe a fascist system.

Vocabulary

Dienstadel (m) = ministerial nobleman; richtet . . . aus = achieves; Bündnis (n) = alliance; Freunschaftsbund (m) = friendship bond.

—8—

Trends in Education and Society since Unification

Introduction

The initial exuberance generated by the collapse of the Berlin Wall met with a sceptical, even negative response from most intellectuals in East and West and has since been superseded by the image of the 'Mauer im Kopf' (wall in the head), signalling a widespread disillusionment or even hostility towards the actual unification process, amongst people on both sides. In addition, many critical foreign commentators voice fears of the advent of a Fourth Reich[1] or cynically view unification as a process of colonization, although any detailed discussion of the revolutionary process should dispose of the widespread myth that the revolution was initiated by West German capitalism. Nevertheless, the painful procedure of growing together has gone ahead; differences between 'Ossis' and 'Wessis', though still noticeable in political culture and social attitude, have lessened.

The Effects of the 1989 'Revolution' on the German Education System

The events of the autumn of 1989 are commonly referred to as the 'peaceful revolution', a description which renders the term 'revolution' somewhat redundant. If judged against other such upheavals, either historical or in contemporary Eastern Europe, certain peculiarities come to light. This revolution led only partially to the anticipated political and social emancipation, as the newly emerging elite soon surrendered its autonomy and sought *Beitritt* (accession) to its dominant Western neighbour. The revolutionary potential was inexorably subsumed within the Federal Republic's established order. Underlining this feature was the fact that a large number of the 'revolutionaries' had already embraced West Germany and toppled the system, not by climbing barricades, but by fleeing the country, thus sapping the regime of its workforce: by 9 November, when the Wall came down, more than a quarter of a million people, 1.5 per cent of the whole population, had already fled to West Germany.[2] A further peculiarity concerns the activists in this 'revolution'. Although many intellectuals, artists and church leaders voiced dissent and inspired the masses, their revolutionary appeal was not as potent as that of West German television and their impact on the course of events was infinitely less than Gorbachev's political vision or the economic collapse of COMECON.

These, by now familiar, observations are nevertheless important for a closer understanding of the changes that affected the GDR's education system and for correcting some of the myths which have developed since 1989. Particularly interesting was the position of the GDR's universities, where an unmistakable air of inertia was evident, in marked contrast to student involvement in the revolutions in Poland, Bulgaria, Romania and Czechoslovakia, or in Western unrest in 1968. Earlier dissent had been promoted by individual university teachers and some students, too, voiced opposition,[3] many subsequently joining semi-official organizations such as *Neues Forum* and the Protestant Church-backed *Demokratischer Aufbruch* and *Demokratie Jetzt*. At the same time, a majority of students vehemently opposed unification[4] and earlier statistical surveys suggest that the 'regime socialization policies achieved some measure of success in disseminating supportive political attitudes'[5] among the student body, even if this support fell away during the Republic's end-phase. Estimates of student participation in the Leipzig Monday protests suggest that 20 per cent of students took part in at least five marches,[6] a figure which seems low in comparison to the student role in other East European countries. This lack of commitment was largely explained by the students' privileged position in society: students and professors, rigorously selected in accordance with the country's Marxist-Leninist ideology, saw their future as dependent on the preservation of the status quo. Insiders seem to confirm this observation: 'Es war deshalb kein Wunder, daß die ostdeutschen Hochschulen nur wenig zur politischen Wende des Herbstes '89 beitrugen. Die Erneuerungskräfte innerhalb der Hochschulen standen auf sehr schwachen Füßen.'[7] (It was therefore no wonder that East German universities contributed little to the changes of autumn '89. The rejuvenating forces within the universities had no foundation.) Other contributary factors reinforced this state of affairs: universities were largely restricted to teaching, with research hived off to academies. The dominant cadre principle was marked by the lack of a political culture which might have fostered public debate; the large proportion of students in science and technology, university organization by *Sektion* (section) rather than interdisciplinary faculty and a strong vocational orientation towards industry all served to produce a subaltern dimension, alien to any form of open opposition.

In contrast to the apparent political quietism at university level, dissatisfaction with the Honecker regime in general was rife. It organized itself, once the old system had begun to lose its grip. A closer study of the events of autumn 1989 will reveal some of the classical patterns of a revolution.[8] Tentative revolutionary moves at universities demanded true socialism, followed by calls for free debate, for *Basisdemokratie* (grass-roots democracy), leading to pressure for a new political elite and a new social order. Several of the dissenting elements mentioned in Chapter 7[9] began to organize: rock musicians, women's groups, peace movements and, most prominently of all, the Protestant Church. One of the first official manifestos came from a group of rock musicians. Disturbed by the exodus of many GDR citizens and the stubborn silence of the regime, they declared their support for *Basisdemokratie* and its 'millionenfache Aktivierung von Individualität' (the individual activity of millions), but warned, at the same time, of the rise of right-wing nationalism. Their aim was socialism within an independent GDR:

> Es geht nicht um 'Reformen, die den Sozialismus abschaffen', sondern um Reformen, die ihn weiterhin in diesem Land möglich machen. Denn jene momentane Haltung gegenüber den existierenden Widersprüchen gefährdet ihn.[10]

> (The issue is not 'reforms which will abolish socialism', but reforms which will allow it to carry on in this country. For it is threatened by the current attitude towards existing contradictions.)

A month later the Leipzig demonstrations attracted some 120,000 people, representing the largest mass movement since 1953. Artists were in the forefront: after each performance at the Dresden State Theatre, actors read a short declaration, accusing the government of incompetence and cataloguing their demands for the classical freedoms of information, thought, movement and political participation, to which they added the self-imposed responsibilities of exposing official lies and redefining socialism.[11] Egon Krenz's new government, offering concessions and admitting its estrangement from the people,[12] was a further classical aspect of wavering authority in times of revolution. Krenz's speech of 3 November included the pledge of a change in policy, a general amnesty and new travel laws. A first mention was made of educational reforms, promising a renewal of society, but otherwise lacking in substance.[13]

These aspects of revolutionary activity seem to have had much in common with events in other COMECON countries. Influence from the Federal Republic at this stage was still minimal; one British observer even goes so far as to suggest that 'this East German rising was not contemplated in Bonn's Deutschlandpolitik'.[14] Indeed, Helmut Kohl repeatedly emphasized throughout October and November that a continuation of the evolutionary change was the only sensible policy. Whilst praising the political involvement of a people so long suppressed within the country's maligned *Nischengesellschaft* (niche society), he supported the GDR's democratic awakening, but in the spirit of rapprochement rather than political union:

> Was wir tun können, ist vor allem, daß wir sie ermutigen und in der Hoffnung bestärken, daß sich auch in der DDR ein Prozeß demokratischer Veränderungen in absehbarer Zeit

vollziehen wird. [. . .] Die Bundesrepublik wird alles in ihren Kräften stehende tun, um den Prozeß einer Öffnung in der DDR zum Wohle unserer Landsleute zu unterstützen. Sie bleibt deshalb entschlossen, in ihrer bisherigen Politik der praktischen Zusammenarbeit mit der DDR im Interesse der Menschen auf beiden Seiten fortzufahren.[15]

(What we can do in particular is to encourage them and to strengthen their hope that, even in the foreseeable future of the GDR, a process of democratic change will take place. [. . .] The Federal Republic will do everything in its power to support the process of opening up the GDR for the benefit of its citizens. It therefore remains determined to continue its prevailing policy of practical co-operation with the GDR, in the interest of people on both sides.)

Even in his 'Ten Points Programme' of 29 November, Kohl limited himself to envisaging a confederate structure between the two German states, though this was ultimately to lead to unification. His speech concluded with the observation that there was no definitive answer to the many difficult questions which the situation posed.[16] Hans Modrow's speech at the special party conference of the SED is approving of Kohl's proposal for a confederation,[17] and concrete plans for unification were not considered until after the elections of March 1990.

The majority of intellectuals in both German states were opposed to unification. Many leading GDR intellectuals, amongst them Christa Wolf, Stephan Heym and Volker Braun, published the plea 'Für unser Land', in which the possibility of unification was rejected in favour of a new socialism, in solidarity with other socialist countries.[18] Günter Grass, too, was opposed to German unification, fearing a revival of German nationalism and a destabilization of Europe.[19] In general, however, younger intellectuals in the West showed considerably less interest in unification, while the pleas of their former compatriots were rejected by exiled GDR intellectuals, who regarded them as arrogant and lacking in political realism.[20]

Within the world of education, first reactions to the political events began in October, when some 500 students and staff at the Humboldt University, expressing sympathy with *Neues Forum*, demanded electoral reform and structural changes to university education, particularly the abolition of the foundation course in Marxism-Leninism, the official history course on the GDR and the system of democratic centralism.[21] In September, *Neues Forum* had already demanded a greater degree of openness and pluralism in education. Whilst endorsing the preschool education system, guaranteeing the equality of opportunity, they demanded an education free of ideology, with far greater democratic involvement at parental and general grass-roots level and, above all, greater emphasis on individuality, in order to foster more responsibility and participation. This programme amounted to a compromise rather than a break with the existing system, synonymous with the stance of individual writers such as Christa Wolf, advocating a less dogmatic form of socialism [Text 1]. A resolution by the *Sektion Pädagogik* at Leipzig University criticized the 'encrusted' stagnation of the system, but rejected any departure from socialist principles.[22] Other university resolutions emphasized the need for socialist renewal, for greater university independence from the demands of industry and state, for greater individualism in study patterns and syllabuses, and for ideological pluralism, offering students a more meaningful, modern understanding of Marxism-Leninism.[23] The general tenor of such declarations favoured the free development of individuality, equal opportunity, increased parental representation and more emphasis on humanistic traditions – in the Humboldtian, rather than the socialist, sense of the word [Text 2]. The polytechnical school was criticized for exaggerated uniformity, an excessively ideological syllabus, particularly in civics, history and German literature, the predominance of Russian as first foreign language and for an insufficiently structured *Abitur* which failed to prepare students for a modern university career.[24] Any form of ideological or religious involvement in education was rejected.

A special SED party programme agreed to all these demands, but made no further concessions or positive suggestions for change. Under Hans Modrow's new government and with the removal of the SED as the leading political party (December 1989), opportunities for inter-German discussions had improved. In January 1990 the first meeting was held between the West German Education Minister and his East German counterpart and an inter-German working party on the co-ordination of educational matters was established. The West German Conference of University Vice-Chancellors and the Standing Conference of Ministers for Education soon met with GDR authorities to discuss specific problems: help was promised for the reorganization of GDR universities and material assistance granted, with mutual recognition of study programmes. The March 1990 elections saw the formation of a new government under Lothar de Maizière and the actual end of the revolution. Immediately, a detailed paper on education, *Thesen zur Bildungsreform*, the work of a group of scholars from the *Akademie der Pädagogischen Wissenschaften* (academy of pedagogical studies), was published and, prior to unification, became the decisive discussion paper for reforms. It postulated a fundamental change in education policy and a radical overhaul of education practices in the GDR, insisting, at the same time, on the 'positive Aufhebung des Bewahrenswerten, das mit der Bildungsreform in der DDR in den Prozeß der Einigung Deutschlands einzubringen ist.'[25] (positive preservation of all those aspects worth keeping which, together with the education reform in the GDR, are to be incorporated into a process of German unification.) In line with previous reform plans, the emphasis was on individuality, greater parental involvement, increased focus on humanist and general ethical education, and more concentration on scholarly achievement. Aspects of particular interest, not least because they include specific elements which were to be preserved in an all-German education system, were: the principle of life-long learning, the integration of crèche facilities into the education system, the retention of polytechnical education, albeit in a modernized form with special emphasis on ecological issues, a ten- to twelve-year period of general schooling, vocational education geared to the principles of a free-market economy and the opportunity of university education for everyone with the necessary qualifications.

Developments towards an All-German Education System

The new CDU-dominated *Allianz für Deutschland* coalition, elected in March 1990, ensured that the German Democratic Republic would become integrated into the larger, economically powerful Federal Republic. The Unification Treaty of October 1990 clearly established this reality, acknowledging GDR law only in cases where it was in agreement with the Basic or European Law.[26] Among the many crucial changes that were to affect GDR citizens, education was a minor component. In his inaugural speech, de Maizière described education in terms of a catastrophic heritage,[27] with suggestions for modernization reading like a blueprint of the FRG constitutional model: a new framework for higher education was promised, education in general would fall under the impending sovereignty of new *Länder*. In May an inter-German commission on education was established, responsible for overseeing all transition arrangements.[28] By the time of the October elections in the five new *Länder*, all major educational principles had been agreed, virtually every case involving the imposition of existing FRG law; only a handful of issues remained to be resolved by the *Länder* within a designated period of nine months.

Curricular changes had already taken place, with West German schoolbooks replacing East German texts in those subjects where ideological content was unacceptable. The new education laws enacted in almost all the new *Länder* by July 1991 were surprisingly diverse in even basic structures, leading to a situation reminiscent of the 'Schulchaos' during the formative years of the FRG. This was the more unexpected as the Unification Treaty had established clear guidelines, based on the Hamburg Agreement and previous decisions by the Standing Conference of Ministers for Education.[29] Without going into a detailed survey of school structures in the new *Länder*,[30] it is obvious that the ensuing diversity reflected the political make-up of individual *Land* governments, further influenced by the specific West German partner *Land* involved in implementing the particular structure.[31] Opinions on the various degrees of conservatism differ; from a structural point of view and compared with Western models, the Thuringian school system appears most conservative: elementary education up to the age of ten, with selection to a thinly disguised tripartite system and no orientation stage. This reflects the fact that Thuringia had the strongest CDU representation in its October elections (45.5 per cent) and had opted for Bavaria as partner state. By contrast, Brandenburg, where the SPD polled strongly, chose Berlin as its partner. As a result, its system continues primary education through to the age of twelve, retains comprehensive schools as its main type, with entry to the *Gymnasium* only at the age of sixteen (figure 10).

School Structure in the New *Länder*
Thuringia
School Year

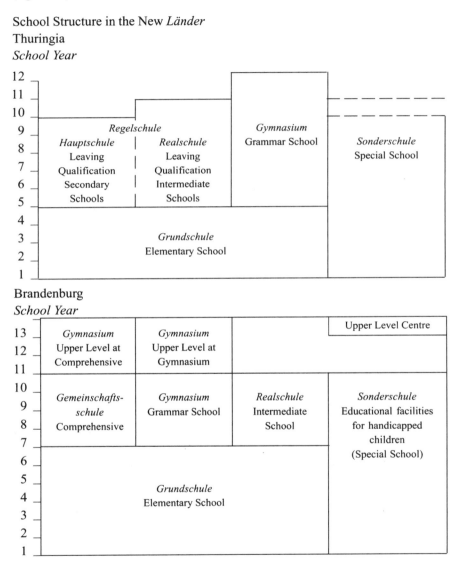

Brandenburg
School Year

Figure 10 The education systems in Thuringia and Brandenburg-Vorpommern after unification. The Thuringian school system follows the more conservative Bavarian model with strict selection at the age of ten and three clearly differentiated types of school, leading to different forms of qualification. The Brandenburg-Vorpommern system was modelled after the West Berlin system, extending uniform elementary schooling up to the age of twelve and retaining major elements of the polytechnical school.

Whilst most teachers seem to favour the new systems, parents appear less enthusiastic, with only 45 per cent in favour of the transformation.[32] Such evidence is obviously of limited use in judging the success of the actual change. Financial and organizational difficulties may have influenced parental opinion. The West's political culture, too, with the opportunities of a pluralist, free-market social democracy, has not yet been fully appreciated. Many former East Germans still tend to indulge in a sentimental 'Ostalgie', adopting a 'Trabi-Trotz-Kultur'[33] (truculent Trabi mentality) and failing to accept that the grass-roots movements of the autumn of 1989 could not have prevented unification or coped with its various economic and social complexities. Subsequent cuts in education provision, especially in nursery education and in the availability of industrial training places,[34] have done nothing to dispel a general disillusionment, while a severe fall in the birth-rate, of between 35 to 65 per cent,[35] has had a very negative impact on schools provision, felt mostly in elementary education and the more rural areas.

A particularly controversial measure was that of *Abwicklung*, literally translated: 'winding down', of academies and those specific university subjects tainted by Marxist-Leninist ideology. Schools were also affected, though generally only at the most senior staff level. The process of *Abwicklung*, which led to staff redundancies or transfer to other institutions, was criticized not only in the new *Länder*, but also condemned in much of the academic world. The British *Times Higher Educational Supplement*, on the side of those who were adversely affected, described it as a 'purge' of former GDR universities by West German academics and writers in league with the CDU.[36] In reality, events unfolded much more gradually, were less dramatic and were generally a good deal fairer than had first been suspected. Existing posts were usually dissolved and subsequently redefined. Incumbents were permitted to reapply and a majority were reappointed. A number of initial and somewhat hysterical reactions to the process of *Abwicklung* demonstrated a lack of objectivity. It has, however, by now been accepted that steps leading to unification were, on the whole, taken too quickly and that the opportunity of adapting the more progressive features of the GDR system to the Western model was lost. However, three angles in particular need to be examined.

Firstly, the close links between industry and higher education made it virtually impossible to transform the former and leave the latter intact. Some 75 per cent of all GDR research was funded by state industry,[37] centred almost exclusively on East Berlin's *Akademie der Wissenschaften*. With the rapid collapse of COMECON, this type of research was doomed and, to meet Western industrial demands, a complete transformation of research patterns was necessary. Moreover, the dominant status of the *Akademie* under the GDR had sapped universities of serious research potential, relegating them to teaching institutions which were unable to compete with their more advantaged counterparts in the West. The impact of the longstanding migration of their students and academics to West Germany cannot be played down and to this day there is spare university capacity in the new *Länder*.

Secondly, a continuation of ideologically determined disciplines within a Western pluralist society was not possible. University teachers employed on foundation courses in Marxism-Leninism had to be redeployed or, if unsuitably qualified, made redundant. Many of these posts were of a political nature, rewarding party loyalty at the expense of academic standards. A similar pattern applied to sections teaching Russian or Soviet literature or subjects relating specifically to the study of socialist economic systems.[38] Failure to address these ideological changes would have consigned an entire generation of students to an obsolete labour market, unemployable in the capitalist system.

The third consideration militating against any retention of the old system was the legacy of academic corruption. This was particularly relevant at senior level, where academics had often ended the careers of students or junior colleagues on the grounds of reading 'forbidden literature' or being involved in political protest. Extra-institutional, even international, committees were an essential element in preventing any possibility of 'alte Seilschaften' (party cliques) assisting each other to regain former positions. A much-publicized case was that of Humboldt University, whose combative *Rektor* Heinrich Fink, professor of theology, was appointed after the *Wende*, but later discredited and forced to resign.[39] Former high-ranking SED officials such as Kurt Hager, GDR Secretary for Science and Culture, were appointed to chairs and nearly half of the dissolved section of Marxism-Leninism were reappointed.[40] A member of the *Bund Freiheit der Wissenschaft* (Federation for the Freedom of Scholarship) highlighted the complexity of appointment procedures, stating that it had been unable to transform the corrupt relationships and involvements of individuals with the GDR party and state apparatus into a situation which could be understood by the people involved as justice, in a politically moral sense.[41]

A closer study of the process of *Abwicklung* would suggest that extra-university measures were necessary to prevent further corruption and to stem the migration of promising younger academics to the West. Appointment committees consisted of representatives of the university in question, new *Land* representatives and experts from West German or other German-speaking universities. The reform programme at university level was financed jointly by the federal and the new *Länder* governments in a ratio of 74:26;[42] research programmes outside the university sector were financed entirely by the federal government. Since staffing levels between West and East German universities differed by a ratio of 1:4, the number of posts in the East was drastically reduced. A further difficulty was the future of 2,000 research staff from the academies, many of whom could not be integrated into the university sector because of their previous ideological background. The development of new posts was based on the following principles:

1 Some 200 chairs were created for West German academics, specifically in the more contentious subjects of law, economics, teacher training and, to a lesser extent, philosophy, politics, languages and social sciences.[43] This move was widely criticized as an attempt by West German universities to exploit the situation and dispose of second-rate staff or to manoeuvre their own protégés into privileged positions. Whilst it is difficult to substantiate such claims, the new posts proved useful in reducing corruption and creating valuable links with Western universities. By 1993 East German universities were employing some 1,200 West German academics, compared to 5,000 'home-grown' teachers.

2 In order to raise the academic profile, leading former GDR academics were given financial inducements to encourage them to remain in post.

3 Younger academics were sponsored to pursue post-doctoral degrees or to spend sabbaticals at Western universities.

Several far-reaching changes affected the institutional structure of higher education. Some institutions were amalgamated, others newly created and yet others changed their status to *Fachhochschule*, an institution not known in the GDR. Today the new *Länder* have thirteen universities with new foundations in Erfurt, Potsdam and Frankfurt/Oder, twelve academies specializing in art or music and twenty-one *Fachhochschulen*. Overall capacity has increased to approximately 150,000 study-places, anticipating a continuation of the sharp increase of some 15 per cent in student numbers.

It is still too early to attempt a definitive assessment of the integration process as far as education is concerned. After the March 1990 elections, moves towards unification had become irreversible and, whatever the well-founded reservations of intellectuals and opposition parties, nothing could slow down the momentum. The main agents of change by this stage were the federal government and its various agencies. Bureaucratic measures to ease and simplify the transition took precedence over a more objective assessment of possibilities for reform. The Hamburg Agreement and the *Hochschulrahmenrecht* (University Framework Law), neither of them progressive forward-looking measures, were used to coerce the GDR education system into line with Western patterns. It was historically most unfortunate that unification coincided with a period in which the reform impetus in education, not very vigorous even at its height, had succumbed to a post-modern new conservatism [Text 3].

The Present State of Education in Germany (Figure 11)

In the new Germany, as in many other Western countries, public opinion has diagnosed a crisis in education. It is difficult to assess the reality of this crisis, or to what extent the end of the millennium, the post-modern condition or the break-

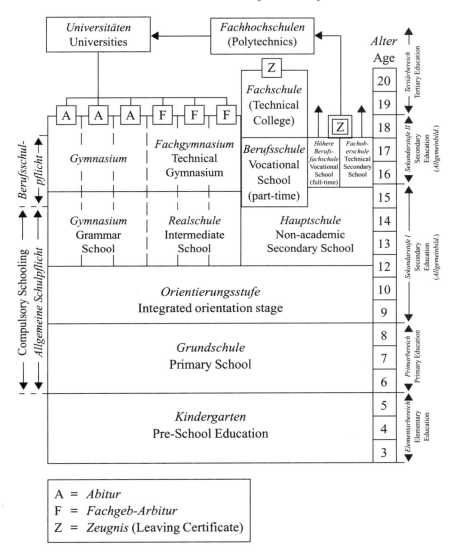

A	=	*Abitur*
F	=	*Fachgeb-Arbitur*
Z	=	*Zeugnis* (Leaving Certificate)

Figure 11 The FRG education system today. This general overview indicates that selection at the age of ten is cushioned by a two-year 'comprehensive stage', with a variety of paths leading on to higher education.

up of Eastern Europe with a diversion of attention from the Cold War to internal problems may have contributed to public awareness of an apparent educational malaise. Furthermore, a survey of education history would demonstrate that education systems have frequently experienced a 'crisis', from Humboldt's early assessment via the 1840s, through to the end of the nineteenth century, right up to our own times. Indeed, important new impulses have generally emerged from these crises and the conclusion can be drawn that a perceived crisis is necessary for the rejuvenation of any system.

The general symptoms of today's crisis can be easily recounted: an increasingly aggressive younger generation, the rise of fundamentalism and concomitant intolerance towards minority ethnic or religious groups, the loss of a common canon of values, the impact of new technologies, particularly the new media, on schooling. Such ills, by no means confined to Germany, afflict much of the Western world. In general, the perceived education crisis must be blamed on a society which has not only become sceptical of state control but which regards personal success and happiness more highly than social involvement. As a result, politicians change their priorities, giving precedence to a different agenda, such as the fight against crime, transport strategies, youth unemployment and other high-profile issues.[44] An often sensational, mostly unsympathetic press compounds this perceived crisis, accusing teachers of incompetence and laziness.[45] This final section will attempt to discuss some of these problems and will relate them to the traditionally German framework of education.

There are some specifically German problems, indicative of a system still rigidly adhering to antiquated structures and dessicated traditions, such as the domination of a strong state sector, with teachers part of the civil service, often more reluctant to embrace change than those in less bureaucratic systems. The vast majority of German teachers at all levels are *Beamte* (civil servants). As such, they enter employment via government examinations, and are expected to serve the state and accept the basic tenets of the Constitution, gaining the benefits of life-long tenure and a generous pension. With education under the control of *Land* authorities, teachers seldom move beyond their own region, so that a certain insularity becomes unavoidable. As *Beamte*, almost without exception, have to be German nationals, a further exclusivity is ensured and foreign entry to the profession is almost impossible. Whilst the position of civil servant bestows unparalleled status and security on teachers, it also restricts them to a more narrowly legalistic outlook than is the case in other countries, producing less personal initiative and enterprise. The *Beamte* status of teachers has been a topic of public debate in Germany for some time, particularly since unification, but teachers' organizations are fighting hard to preserve their privileged position.[46]

A recent example of German defensiveness in education policy is the 1992 government response to a European Community memorandum on higher education.[47] Although generally supportive of EU integration policies, the general tenor of the response is cautious, jealously guarding the German position. Reminiscent of many British reactions to EU proposals, the 'subsidiarity principle' is frequently invoked, demanding the strictest adherence to cultural autonomy for member states. German interests in Central and Eastern European higher education are emphasized, indicating some desire to return to a Central European German *Mittellage* (middle position) in cultural and economic affairs, but with no overt political implications.[48] Anxious about the German position in *Geistes- und Kulturwissenschaften*, the German response is critical of the memorandum's functional dimension. Legal objections are frequently raised, reflecting a narrow interpretation of the German Constitution. The promotion of European languages in addition to the native language is supported, especially as a tool of instruction at universities, yet Germany is as yet apparently unable to administer the European Credit Transfer System (ECTS). Constantly seeking to defend German language and culture against the ubiquitous advance of English as the *lingua franca*, the document reveals an underlying fear of an Anglo-American cultural hegemony. Whilst many Germanists would recognize a cause for concern, some echoes of the cultural hysteria of the mandarin position of the 1890s are evident.

Seeking a solution to the wider problem of the educational malaise, many pedagogues are returning to *Reformpädagogik*, particularly in the new *Länder*, which have seen a marked increase in Waldorf and Montessori Schools and where the *Reformpädagogik* tradition had continued clandestinely within the Marxist-Leninist system. The salient fact which tends to get overlooked is that most of these reformist innovators owed their success to personal charisma rather than theory. The former Bielefeld professor of education, Hartmut von Hentig, offers a wide-ranging critique of today's schools, intent on integrating the school into a democratic civil society.[49] Only such a society, he maintains, will overcome the existing crisis of values, uphold our Western civilization, and guarantee a free and peaceful existence in a society unaffected by the worst excesses of social injustice. He advocates a return to the philosophy of Rousseau's *Emile* and the *Contrat Social*, to a society which inculcates in its members a sense of responsibility and a respect for public order, values all but lost in a world of merciless competition and economic rationalization. Hentig's vision contains aspects of *Reformpädagogik*, in particular the concept of the *Landerziehungsheim* and the all-day school.[50] Some of his suggestions have been put to the test abroad in schools such as the Magnet Schools in Los Angeles or the more progressive British comprehensives. Some argue that Hentig's reformist zeal bears fruit only in schools with the advantage of middle-class or academic environments.[51] Examples from the field of *Reformpädagogik* would suggest, however, that experiments in socially deprived areas can be similarly successful. Several of Hentig's proposals seem to offer a way forward: a school's integration into its local environment, a return to smaller schools with a more personal management style, the greater involvement of the local community in the life of the school.

Counter-arguments on the political right by 'educationalists' such as Konrad Adam, Karlheinz Weissmann and Botho Strauß border on the fatalistic or hysterical, castigating the 1968 generation for current social and pedagogical problems and rejecting the principles of the Enlightenment. Their arguments exhibit irrationalism and are directed against a 'widerwärtige Vergesellschaftung'[52] (nauseating socialization). Other conditions which conflict with Hentig's school environment as 'Lebens- und Erfolgsraum' (successful living space) are more difficult to counter. Today's media society, an excess of consumerism, an exaggerated careerism, targeting children from an ever younger age group, all threaten the enlightened and democratic tenets of civil society. The impact of television and computers on schools is particularly problematic. The need for computer-literacy in today's high-tech society is obvious and the endeavours of government and industry to introduce computers into every school[53] are necessary, if the *Standort Deutschland* (Germany's industrial position) is to be preserved. However, few can deny that children today are more influenced by the image on the TV screen than the teacher in the class-room. Comparative studies of East and West German pupils seem to indicate that the latter's lifestyles often exclude conventional play, conversation skills or group activities, so vital for normal socialization.[54] Furthermore, computers have shifted the balance in education from the acquisition and digestion of knowledge to its mere accumulation. This is a particularly relevant aspect for the German tradition, which has always encouraged a more individualistic, problem-related approach to knowledge, knowledge as personal experience, as opposed to the positivistic accumulation of facts.

At school level, primary education seems comparatively free of problems.[55] There has been considerable fluctuation in recruitment, brought about by changes in the birth-rate, with a sharp drop in most of the new *Länder* and, in the old, a predicted increase of 20 per cent by the end of the century. A new addition to the curriculum is media studies, while traditional *Heimatkunde* (local history and geography) has been adapted to include lessons on multi-ethnicity and tolerance.[56] More emphasis is given to the study of standard German, particularly in its written form, in response to the fact that on average some 10 per cent of pupils learn German as a foreign language, rising to more than 50 per cent in large conurbations. Changing work patterns and the break-up of family structures have brought new priorities: longer opening hours for schools, the desirability of school-meal provision, closer co-operation with parents and with religious organizations, and greater awareness of the problems of mentally or physically handicapped children.

Secondary education has seen a dramatic increase in *Gymnasium* pupils, mainly at the expense of the *Hauptschule*. The latter's 'death' is proclaimed:[57] the Saarland and three of the new *Länder* will no longer run *Hauptschulen*, amalgamating them with *Realschulen* as *Regelschulen* or *Sekundarschulen*. While this may lead to problems in some rural areas where *Hauptschulen* remain popular, there are many advantages: selection will be less rigid, the tripartite system will no longer dominate and the new schools will concentrate more on skills-orientated education, with enhanced employment prospects for the pupils. On the other hand, the *Gymnasium* has become a victim of its own success, chosen by those who wish to improve their children's social and professional chances, regardless of its traditional academic ethos. As a result, the *Abitur* has lost esteem and apparently no longer guarantees automatic entry to university.[58] However, an analysis of social patterns indicates that only 11 per cent of working-class children attend the *Gymnasium*, while the percentage of children of civil servants remains at 50 per cent. The percentage of working-class university students has remained virtually constant at 5 per cent.[59] Among the recognized *Begabungsreserven*, only Catholics and women seem to have gained ground, with women now equally as successful as men in passing the *Abitur*.

Despite much criticism, the plurality and opportunity for choice offered by the German system must be acknowledged, notably in comparison with the British model, where shortcomings in comprehensive education frequently make headlines and where choice is even more dependent on income and social status. The German combination of choice and flexibility, affording access to higher qualifications by many different pathways in the education process, would seem to hold more promise than a system where pupils with varying talents remain confined to the same class-room.

German universities in particular have been criticized for not meeting the demands of today's mass higher education. Student drop-out rates are unacceptably high, the period spent studying for a first qualification disproportionately long, with teachers traditionally not required to exhibit any aptitude for teaching. This situation is already changing with new appointments having to demonstrate their teaching expertise.[60] While some of the attacks on an outdated university concept seem justifiable, other onslaughts are unfair or insincere. In comparison to a 70 per cent rise in the number of students entering higher education over the past twenty years, staffing has increased by only 7 per cent.[61] OECD statistics reveal that Germany is bottom of the league of industrialized countries in its funding of universities, spending just 5 per cent of its domestic product compared to an average of 6.1 per cent.[62] These figures need to be fully digested before proceeeding to any serious criticism of university professors withdrawing from teaching, responding unsympathetically to student needs or retreating into the realms of lucrative research contracts.[63] Such attacks, although not without foundation, fail to recognize the complexity of a situation to which there is no easy answer: can any teacher establish personal contacts with students, when attendance figures at seminars are in the hundreds, accommodation so overcrowded that overflow facilities in corridors or adjoining rooms are necessary? Should the hallowed combination of tuition and research be abandoned, leaving research to the Max Planck Institutes and emulating a system which, in the GDR, had demonstrated that universities suffer from a lack of research?

And yet, German universities remain less flexible, more reactive than their British and American counterparts. The *Wissenschaftsrat*, charged with reforming higher education, has a more passive and constrained role, reflecting a self-interest absent from the remit of an independent adviser such as Sir Ron Dearing, charged with reforming the British system. Little progress has been made in the establishment of centres of excellence such as the *Graduiertenkolleg* (graduate college), while the dual-track system, introduced with the establishment of *Fachhochschulen*, offers a clear alternative only in some skill-based areas such as business studies and engineering.

There is some evidence that German universities are abandoning state support in favour of a more entrepreneurial approach. A number of reforms have been implemented: control of universities is no longer solely in the hands of the elected *Rektor*, responsible for an enterprise of some 40,000 people. Nevertheless, universities still need greater independence from government bodies, becoming accountable for salaries, material programmes and general resourcing, as is the case with their Anglo-American counterparts. However, if such measures are seen exclusively as *Effizienzsteigerung* (efficiency increases), their success will be limited; didactic and cultural considerations ought to remain the priority. Whether the current climate of cutbacks in public funding is an appropriate time for greater independence from the state is open to question. The 'reforms' in Baden-Württemberg are a case in point. The *Bildungsguthaben*, awarded to students at the beginning of their study period, is similar in approach to the experimental voucher system adopted in the British nursery school sector. The award covers a maximum study period of seven years, after which students have to pay heavy fines. In addition, students must pay matriculation charges, offending against the principle of free education as laid down in the Basic Law. The *Land* has negotiated a *Solidarpakt* with each university, giving much greater freedom in funding and administration, but at the expense of any increase in income.[64]

One of the most serious issues is the length of university study (figure 12). Compared with international norms, German students perform badly, though on average their final qualification is considerably higher than that of their British or American peers. Moreover, it is often forgotten that 60 per cent of German students have industrial or vocational experience, one third having completed vocational training. Such a pattern also illustrates an important aspect of life-long learning and the acquisition of transferable skills.[65] Politicians seem determined to reduce study periods by regulation (*Regelstudienzeit*), involving penalty clauses, without structuring degree courses to accommodate such regulation. A much more rigorous reform is necessary: universities must introduce undergraduate studies, leading to a Bachelor qualification, and the economy must recognize the valuable contribution which such graduates can make to the ranks of lower and middle management. A greater international or at least European dimension is required; a European Credit

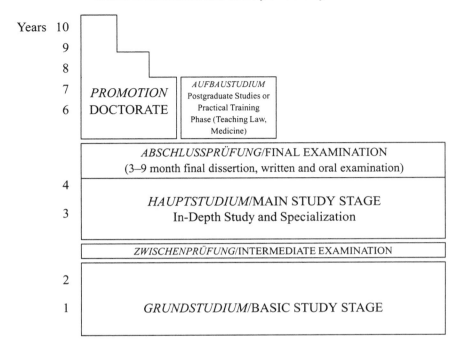

Figure 12 University study pattern. The diagram presents an over-simplified picture of university studies. German universities nowadays generally offer a basic study period, often leading to an internal examination which precedes the main study period. The first generally recognized qualification is the MA (Magister Artium) or, in subjects preparing for entry to the civil service, the *Staatsexamen*.

Transfer System (ECTS) is essential if students are to be encouraged to gain international experience by spending part of their study period abroad. Whilst some success has been achieved in removing the mandarin professor from his precious pedestal, greater efforts are still needed to democratize universities. An environment must be provided in which professors are obliged to fulfil their teaching and research contracts and be more accessible to their students, while differences between professors and other university teachers (*akademischer Mittelbau*) must be reduced. Some of these measures will inevitably undermine the hallowed Humboldtian tradition in favour of more structured study programmes, with increased student support and guidance. Many German 'reformers' admire the Anglo-American system of course evaluation and staff appraisal, with little regard to the disadvantages of practices which result in over-simplification or distortion, in extreme instances threatening academic freedom by a pursuit of short-term objectives. German universities must be wary of the threat of the 'Verschulung der Universität' (school-type university curricula); a distinction between the traditional university and the *Fachhochschule* must be maintained.

Established in 1968, the *Fachhochschulen* offer a limited alternative to the traditional university pattern. Their professors, primarily teachers with industrial experience, pursue research of an applied nature, geared towards the needs of industry and commerce. *Fachhochschulen*, catering predominantly for engineering and business studies, have a skills-based and vocational orientation and fill an important gap in German higher education. They provide their students with a highly structured four-year study course and an internationally recognized qualification with a drop-out rate of about 10 per cent. (Comparable figures for universities indicate approximately six years of study and a drop-out rate of nearly 30 per cent.[66]) *Fachhochschulen* enjoy great popularity, apparently justifying their funding by measurable results. However, such a conclusion fails to recognize that their applied research relies on basic and theoretical research carried out at universities. Moreover, the pursuit of knowledge is not a matter of simple conversion into immediate success and the still manageable size of *Fachhochschulen* facilitates an efficient delivery of their objectives.

The various recent debates illustrate a degree of unanimity, though reforms are unlikely to prove excessive:[67] university fees are enjoying little popularity, but greater competition among universities is seen as positive, provided this involves enhanced financial freedom. Increased choice on the part of students and universities in application procedures is welcome, although entrance examinations to replace the *Abitur* seem less desirable. The separation of research and teaching is unlikely, even if some teaching at the lower level falls to staff with little research experience. The greatest problem is the indifference of a society in which a serious irrational distrust exists towards the image of universities as instruments of progress. This is an international problem, particularly acute in Western Europe, where progress is often considered less important than issues which impinge on daily life or on vocal minority interests. Universities have lost some of their prestige in the eyes of the general public. This is not necessarily to be deplored; a less elevated, more flexible university, better integrated into society, may well sit more easily within a modern, pluralist and industrialized Germany and lead it towards a greater understanding of democracy.

Notes

1. R. Scruton, 'Don't Trust the Germans', *Sunday Telegraph*, 21 June 1989.
2. E. and W. R. Baumann (1990), 'Die friedliche Revolution in der DDR', in H. Kobert and A. Rasch (eds), *Der Fischer Weltalmanach, Sonderband DDR*, Frankfurt/M., p. 142.

3. G. Johannes and U. Schwarz (eds) (1978), *DDR. Das Manifest der Opposition, eine Dokumentation*, Munich.

4. "'Frohe Botschaft, Stalin lebt'", *Der Spiegel*, 19 February 1990, p. 143.

5. H. Krisch (1992), 'Changes in Political Culture and the Transformation of the GDR 1989–1990', in G. J. Glaeßner and I. Wallace (eds), *The German Revolution of 1989*, Oxford, p. 90.

6. Ibid., p. 96.

7. F. Hähle (1993), 'Situation der Hochschulen und Hochschulpolitik in den neuen Bundesländern', in H. Hammer (ed.), *Bundesvertretung Akademischer Mittelbau, die Hochschulen im vereinigten Deutschland*, Aachen, p. 16.

8. Some may choose to speak of a counter-revolution; in both cases, however, the pattern remains the same.

9. Cf. Chapter 7, pp. 145f.

10. DDR Rockmusiker et al., "'Wenn wir nichts unternehmen, arbeitet die Zeit gegen uns'", *taz DDR Journal zur Novemberrevolution* [August to December 1989], p. 14.

11. Aus der Erklärung des Ensembles des Staatsschauspiel Dresdens, "'Wir haben ein Recht . . .'", *taz DDR Journal*, p. 45.

12. 'Krenz an die Bürger der DDR', *taz DDR Journal*, p. 53.

13. E. Krenz (3 November 1989), 'Hörfunk- und Fernsehansprache des Generalsekretärs des ZK der SED und Vorsitzenden des Staatsrates der DDR', in *Der Fischer Weltalmanach, Sonderband DDR*, Frankfurt/M. 1990, col. 320.

14. T. Garton Ash (1990), 'Germany Unbound', *New York Review of Books*, 22 November, p. 11.

15. H. Kohl (8 November 1989), 'Bericht der Bundesregierung zur Lage der Nation im geteilten Deutschland', *Fischer Weltalmanach*, col. 323.

16. H. Kohl (28 November 1989), 'Zehn Punkte Programm zur Überwindung der Teilung Deutschlands und Europas', *Fischer Weltalmanach*, col. 342.

17. *Neues Deutschland*, 8 December 1989.

18. *Neues Deutschland*, 28 November 1989.

19. G. Grass, 'Der Zug ist abgefahren – aber wohin?', *taz DDR Journal* Nr. 2 [January to March 1990], pp. 114f.

20. M. Maron, 'Die Schriftsteller und das Volk', *Der Spiegel*, 12 December 1990, pp. 68–70.

21. H. W. Fuchs and L. R. Reuter (eds) (1995), *Bildungspolitik seit der Wende. Dokumente zum Umbau des ostdeutschen Bildungssystems*, Opladen, pp. 80f.

22. Ibid., p. 86.

23. Ibid., pp. 123–6.

24. Ibid., pp. 18f.

25. Ibid., pp. 137f.

26. *Einigungsvertrag*, Artikel 9, in I. von Münch (ed.) (1990), *Die Verträge zur Einheit Deutschlands*, Munich, p. 47.

27. Fuchs and Reuter (eds), *Bildungspolitik*, p. 16.

28. E. Neather (1995), 'Education in the New Germany', in D. Lewis and J. R. McKenzie (eds), *The New Germany, Social, Political and Cultural Challenges of Unification*, Exeter, pp. 156f.

29. *Einigungsvertrag*, Artikel 37,4.

30. Cf. C. Führ (1992), *On the Education System in the Five New Länder of the Federal Republic of Germany*, Bonn.

31. Neather, 'Education in the New Germany', p. 163.

32. Ibid., p. 168.

33. H. J. Hahn (1993), 'Ossis, Wessis and Germans, an Inner-German Perception of National Characteristics', *Journal of Area Studies*, no. 2, p. 123.

34. Fuchs and Reuter (eds), *Bildungspolitik*, pp. 27, 35.

35. Neather, 'Education in the New Germany', p. 167.

36. P. Chamberlayne, 'A Purge of What's Left in East-Germany', *Times Higher Educational Supplement*, 11 January 1991, p. 10. Cf. also J. Matthews, 'From Frying Pan to Fire', *Education*, 25 May 1990, p. 515.

37. *German University Affairs*, 6 July 1990, p. 2.

38. S. Schattenfroh (1993), 'Die schwierige Erneuerung', *Bildung und Wissenschaft*, Nr. 3/4, p. 16.

39. Cf. Minutes of the *Humboldt Universität*'s Senate via *Internet*, Vorlage 185/93.

40. '"Laßt die Studenten selber denken", Interview mit Heinrich Fink', *Der Spiegel*, 21 January 1991, p. 74.

41. Schattenfroh, 'Die schwierige Erneuerung', p. 16.

42. Bundesminister für Bildung und Wissenschaft, 'Erneuerungsprogramm für Hochschule und Forschung', *Bildung, Wissenschaft, Aktuell*, Nr. 7/91, p. 16.

43. Ibid., pp. 2f.

44. H. Korte (1995), 'Zur Lage der Universitäten in Deutschland', *German Monitor*, no. 34, p. 135.

45. '"Die sind satt und festgefahren"', *Der Spiegel*, 14 June 1993, pp. 34–44.

46. P. Glotz, 'Sieben Zauberer für die Uni', *Die Zeit*, 26 April 1996, p. 35.

47. Bundesminister für Bildung und Wissenschaft, Ständige Konferenz der Kultusminister der Länder (eds), *Stellungnahme der Bundesrepublik Deutschland zum 'Memorandum zur Hochschulpolitik der Europäischen Gemeinschaft'*, 17 November 1992.

48. Cf. M. Zimmer (1997), 'Return of the *Mittellage*? The Discourse of the Centre in German Foreign Policy', *German Politics*, vol. 6, pp. 23–39.

49. H. von Hentig (1993), *Die Schule neu denken*, Munich, pp. 265–79.

50. Ibid., p. 237.

51. Akademie für Bildungsreform, *Tübinger Modell* and *Bielefelder Laborschule*, quoted in Hentig, *Schule neu denken*, pp. 240f.

52. B. Strauß, 'Anschwellender Bocksgesang', *Der Spiegel*, 8 February 1993, p. 204.

53. 'Schulen ans Netz – die Welt ins Klassenzimmer', *Bildung und Wissenschaft*, Nr. 2 (1996), pp. 13f; *GermNews* 4 November 1996.

54. M. L. Moeller and H. J. Maaz (1991), *Die Einheit beginnt zu zweit. Ein deutsch–deutsches Zwiegespräch*, Berlin, pp. 35f, 64, 75.

55. C. Führ (1995), 'Fünfundsiebzig Jahre deutsche Grundschule', *Bildung und Wissenschaft*, Nr. 3, p. 4.

56. Ibid., p. 6.

57. 'Schlechter Ruf', *Der Spiegel*, 29 January 1996, p. 64; S. Etzold, 'Die Hauptschule. Ein Nachruf', *Die Zeit*, 2 February 1996, p. 46.

58. Gewerkschaft Erziehung und Wissenschaft [1992], 'Bildung verwirklichen – Positionen und Perspektiven gewerkschaftlicher Bildungspolitik', in B. Michael and H. H. Schepp (eds) (1993), *Die Schule in Staat und Gesellschaft. Dokumente zur deutschen Schulgeschichte im 19. und 20. Jahrhundert*, Frankfurt/ M., p. 540.

59. Ibid., p. 538.

60. H. Horstkotte (1995), 'Universitäten sollen effizienter werden', *Bildung und Wissenschaft*, Nr. 3, p. 22.

61. M. Tidick (1996), '"Ich fühle mich betrogen"', *Die Zeit*, 24 May, p. 30.

62. M. Gardner (1995), 'Germany Lacks Competitive Edge', *Times Higher Educational Supplement*, 2 June, p. 11.

63. 'Das Chaos an den Hochschulen', *Der Spiegel*, 2 November 1992; 'Apathie im Hörsaal', *Der Spiegel*, 15 June 1996.

64. S. Etzold (1997), 'Nulldiät statt Reformkost', *Die Zeit*, 14 March, p. 49.

65. P. Glotz and M. Daxner (1996), 'Sieben Zauberer für die Uni', *Die Zeit*, 26 April, p. 35.

66. C. Bode (1996), *Kommentierte Graphiken zum deutschen Hochschul- und Forschungssystem*, Munich, pp. 10, 15.

67. 'Falsch programmiert: der neue Bildungsnotstand', *Zweites Deutsches Fernsehen*, 5 December 1996.

TEXTUAL STUDIES

1. 'Christa Wolf über vierzig Jahre Sozialismus in der DDR'

[. . .] Diese Losung [von den Siegern der Geschichte] [. . .] hat dazu beigetragen, das Verstehen zwischen den Generationen in unserem Land zu erschweren. Eine kleine Gruppe von Antifaschisten, die das Land regierte, hat ihr Siegesbewußtsein zu

irgendeinem nicht genau zu bestimmenden Zeitpunkt aus pragmatischen Gründen auf
5 die ganze Bevölkerung übertragen. Die 'Sieger der Geschichte' hörten auf, sich mit
ihrer *wirklichen* Vergangenheit, der der Mitläufer, der verführten, der Gläubigen in
der Zeit des Nationalsozialismus auseinanderzusetzen. Ihren Kindern erzählten sie
meistens wenig oder nichts von ihrer eigenen Kindheit und Jugend. Ihr untergründig
schlechtes Gewissen machte sie ungeeignet, sich den stalinistischen Strukturen und
10 Denkweisen zu widersetzen, die lange Zeit als Prüfstein für 'Parteilichkeit' und
'Linientreue' galten und bis heute nicht radikal und öffentlich aufgegeben wurden.
Die Kinder dieser Eltern, nun schon ganz und gar 'Kinder der DDR', selbstunsicher,
entmündigt, häufig in ihrer Würde verletzt, wenig geübt, sich in Konflikten zu
behaupten, gegen unerträgliche Zumutungen Widerstand zu leisten, konnten wiederum
15 *ihren* Kindern nicht genug Rückhalt geben, ihnen nicht das Kreuz stärken, ihnen außer
dem Drang nach guten Zensuren, keine Werte vermitteln, an denen sie sich hätten
orientieren können.
(Christa Wolf, '"Das haben wir nicht gelernt"', *taz DDR Journal zur Novemberrevolution* [August to December 1989], p. 22)

Commentary

(numbers in parenthesis refer to line numbers in the text)

Wolf discusses the generation conflict between those anti-fascist socialists who
had a leading role in the establishment of the GDR, contrasting them with the many
who simply adjusted to the new situation and educated their children in the spirit
of political correctness. The 'Sieger der Geschichte' (5) was a term used for
socialists who, according to Marxist-Leninist propaganda, had been victorious not
only over fascism, but also over capitalism. 'Mitläufer' (6) refers to those Nazi
members who accepted Nazi policies without being implicated themselves in actual
Nazi crimes. 'Parteilichkeit' und 'Linientreue' (10f) refer to the discipline expected
of members of the Communist Party which, though different from its fascist rivals,
could be perverted by members who lack strength of character and personal
judgement.

Vocabulary

Losung (f) = motto; Siegesbewußtsein (n) = confidence of victory; ausein-
andersetzen = to deal with; untergründig = subversively; Prüfstein (m) = touchstone;
entmündigt = disenfranchised; Rückhalt (m) = backing; das Kreuz stärken = to
stiffen someone's backbone; Zensur (f) = school report.

2. 'Freiheit für Individuum und Gemeinschaften in einer erneuerten Gesellschaft'

Wir streben eine gesellschaftliche Struktur des Zusammenlebens und des gemeinsamen Handelns der Bürger und Bürgerinnen an, in der der freien Initiative so viel wie möglich Raum bleibt und nur so viel staatliche Regelung wie nötig besteht. Diese bemißt sich an der Schutzbedürftigkeit der Schwächeren. Unser Ziel ist eine ökologisch orientierte
5 Sozialgemeinschaft, die durch demokratisches Miteinander aller Mitglieder getragen wird. [. . .]
Bei der Schulbildung setzen wir uns ein für:
Die Bildungs- und Erziehungsarbeit in allen Einrichtungen muß unabhängig sein von jeglicher Ideologisierung. Das bedeutet: Organisationen, Parteien, Kirchen und
10 Militär sind räumlich und inhaltlich von der Schule zu trennen.
In der Neugestaltung orientieren wir uns auf:
Größeres Gewicht von humanistischem und geistig-kulturellem Bildungsgut;
Umwelterziehung, Gesellschaftskunde, Friedenserziehung und ein breiteres Angebot an Wahlfächern (z.B. Sprachen);
15 stärkere Entwicklung der musischen, kreativen und spielerischen Möglichkeiten der Kinder;
flexibel an regionale und aktuelle Besonderheiten angepaßte Pläne (Rahmenpläne und Auswahlstoffe).
('Aus dem Programm des Demokratischen Aufbruch' [1989], in H. W. Fuchs and L. R. Reuter (eds) (1995), *Bildungspolitik seit der Wende. Dokumente zum Umbau des ostdeutschen Bildungssystems*, Opladen, pp. 93f)

Commentary
(numbers in parenthesis refer to line numbers in the text)

The passage illustrates the political mood in the autumn of 1989: whilst more individual freedom and independence from the state is demanded (2f), some idealized socialist principles are still adhered to (3) and strong emphasis is given to ecology issues (4), reflecting the political outlook of dissenting groups in the final phase of the GDR. The education policies reflect this: individual freedom and independence, even from the churches and other pro-democracy organizations (8f).

Vocabulary

Schutzbedürftigkeit (f) = need for protection; Bildungsgut (n) = cultural heritage; Auswahlstoff (m) = material for selection.

3. 'Über die Versäumnisse bei der Einigung'

Drei Jahre später ist die Chance nicht nur verpaßt, es ist vielmehr deutlich, daß es sie
ernstlich nie gegeben hat. [. . .] Die allgemeine Entwicklung begünstigt die falsche
Bildungspolitik, die falsche pädagogische Philosophie. Weil die Pädagogik keine
eigene politische Kraft entfaltet, weil man der sozialistischen Gesinnungs- und
5 Betreuungsschule entrinnen will, [. . .] weil die Eltern ihrem Kind einen guten Startplatz
im Wettlauf um die drastisch verknappten und veränderten Arbeitsplätze zu sichern
suchen, weil es also ein Abitur haben soll und man dafür Gymnasien braucht, bekommt
man in den neuen Ländern – statt der Schule mit der Möglichkeit und dem Mut zur
Erziehung – eine Karriereanstalt; [. . .] 'Kollektiv' und 'Autorität' sind verschwunden,
10 aber 'Gemeinschaft' und 'Autonomie' können sich wegen der zuerst genannten
Umstände nicht einstellen. Und so geben sich die neuen Bundesländer just die Schule
nicht, die sie am meisten brauchen und die, weil sie sie haben könnten, nun auch den
alten Bundesländern abgeht als Beispiel für einen geordneten Wandel 'aus dem Geist',
als Widerlegung der permanenten Anpassung durch Maßnahmen zur Rettung von
15 Maßnahmen zur Rettung von Maßnahmen.
(H. von Hentig (1993), *Die Schule neu denken*, Munich, pp. 16f)

Commentary

The author blames the new *Länder* for the failure to bring about a fundamental
change in education. With the desire to escape from political diktat and the perceived
need for a competitive system, the opportunity was lost to replace the detested
concepts of collectivity and authority with a truly autonomous school community.
The passage can either be read as an example of somewhat harsh criticism by
'Wessis' of the GDR system, or as an indication that, with the demise of socialism,
the chance for genuine reform and modernization was missed.

Vocabulary

verknappt = cut back; Karriereanstalt (f) = career establishment; just = precisely;
Widerlegung (f) = refutation.

Select Bibliography

Anweiler, O. (1988), *Schulpolitik und Schulsystem in der DDR*, Opladen: Leske and Budrich.

——, Fuchs, H. J. et al. (eds) (1992), *Bildungspolitik in Deutschland 1945–1990*, Opladen: Leske and Budrich.

Arbeitsgruppe Bildungsbericht am Max-Planck-Institut für Bildungsforschung (ed.) (1994), *Das Bildungswesen in der Bundesrepublik Deutschland*, Reinbek b. Hamburg: Rowohlt.

Baumgart, P. (ed.) (1980), *Bildungspolitik in Preußen zur Zeit des Kaiserreichs*, Stuttgart: Klett-Cotta.

Benz, W. (ed.) (1989), *Die Geschichte der Bundesrepublik Deutschland*, vols 1–4, Frankfurt/M.: Fischer.

Berg, C. (ed.) (1991), *Handbuch der deutschen Bildungsgeschichte*, Munich: Beck.

Blankertz, H. (1982), *Die Geschichte der Pädagogik von der Aufklärung bis zur Gegenwart*, Wetzlar: Büchse der Pandorra.

Bollenbeck, G. (1994), *Bildung und Kultur. Glanz und Elend eines deutschen Deutungsmusters*, 2nd edn, Frankfurt/M.: Insel.

Bruford, W. H. (1975), *The German Tradition of Self-Cultivation. 'Bildung' from Humboldt to Thomas Mann*, Cambridge: Cambridge University Press.

Bussiek, H. (1984), *Die real existierende DDR. Neue Notizen aus der unbekannten deutschen Republik*, Frankfurt/M.: Fischer.

Dahrendorf, R. (1979), *Society and Democracy in Germany*, Westport, Conn.: Greenwood Press.

Dithmar, R. (ed.) (1989), *Schule und Unterrichtsfächer im Dritten Reich*, Neuwied: Luchterhand.

Edding, F. (1963), *Ökonomie des Bildungswesens. Lehren und Lernen als Haushalt und als Investition*, Freiburg.

Elias, N. (1992), *Studien über die Deutschen, Machtkämpfe und Habitusentwicklung im 19. und 20. Jahrhundert*, Frankfurt/M.: Suhrkamp. In English translation as: (1995) *The Germans*, Oxford: Blackwell.

Fest, J. (1982), *Hitler*, Harmondsworth: Penguin.

Flessau, K.I. (1977), *Schule der Diktatur*, Munich: Ehrenwirth.

Flitner, A. (ed.) (1965), *Deutsches Geistesleben und Nationalismus. Eine Vortragsreihe der Universität Tübingen*, Tübingen: Niemeyer.

Friedeburg, L. von (1992), *Bildungsreform in Deutschland. Geschichte und gesellschaftlicher Widerspruch*, Frankfurt/M.: Suhrkamp.

Fuchs, H. W. and Reuter, L. R. (eds) (1995), *Bildungspolitik seit der Wende. Dokumente zum Umbau des ostdeutschen Bildungssystems*, Opladen: Leske and Budrich.

Führ, C. (1972), *Zur Schulpolitik der Weimarer Republik*, 2nd edn, Weinheim: J. Beltz.

——, (1989), *Schools and Institutions of Higher Education in the Federal Republic of Germany*, Bonn: Inter Nationes.

——, (1992), *On the Education System in the Five New Länder of the Federal Republic of Germany*, Bonn: Inter Nationes.

Füssl, K.H. (1994), *Die Umerziehung der Deutschen. Jugend und Schule unter den Siegermächten des Zweiten Weltkriegs 1945–1955*, Paderborn: Schoeningh.

Glaeßner, G.J. and Wallace, I. (eds), *The German Revolution of 1989*, Oxford: Berg.

Glaser, H. (1989), *Die Kulturgeschichte der Bundesrepublik Deutschland*, vols 1–3, Frankfurt/M.: Fischer.

Glöckner, E. (1976), *Schulreform im preußischen Imperialismus*, Glashütten/ Taunus: Topos.

Günther, K.-H. and Uhlig, G. (1973), *History of the Schools in the German Democratic Republic 1945 to 1968*, Berlin: Volk and Wissen.

Habermas, J. (1969), *Protestbewegung und Hochschulreform*, Frankfurt/M.: Suhrkamp.

——, (1971), *Kultur und Kritik*, Frankfurt/M.: Suhrkamp.

——, (1985), *Die neue Unübersichtlichkeit, kleine politische Schriften 5*, Frankfurt/ M.: Suhrkamp.

Hahn, H. J. (1995), *German Thought and Culture. From the Holy Roman Empire to the Present Day*, Manchester: Manchester University Press.

Hamm-Brücher, H. (1967), *Aufbruch ins Jahr 2000 oder Erziehung im technischen Zeitalter*, Reinbek b. Hamburg: Rowohlt.

Hartmann, K., Nyssen, F. and Waldeyer, H. (eds), *Schule und Staat im 18. und 19. Jahrhundert*, Frankfurt/M.: Suhrkamp.

Hearnden, A. (1974), *Education in the Two Germanies*, Oxford: Blackwell.

——, (1976), *Education, Culture and Politics in West Germany*, Oxford: Pergamon Press.

——, (ed.) (1978), *The British in Germany. Educational Reconstruction after 1945*, London: H. Hamilton.

Heinemann, M. (ed.) (1981), *Umerziehung und Wiederaufbau. Die Bildungspolitik der Besatzungsmächte in Deutschland und Österreich*, Stuttgart: Klett-Cotta.

Hentig, H. von (1968), *Systemzwang und Selbstbestimmung. Über die Bedingungen der Gesamtschule in der Industriegesellschaft*, Stuttgart: Klett.

——, (1993), *Die Schule neu denken*, Munich: Hanser.

Herf, J. (1984), *Reactionary Modernism. Technology, Culture and Politics in Weimar and the Third Reich*, Cambridge: Cambridge University Press.

Herrlitz, H.-G. et al. (1993), *Deutsche Schulgeschichte von 1800 bis zur Gegenwart*, Weinheim and Munich: Juventa.

Humboldt, W. von (1960), *Schriften zur Anthropologie und Geschichte, Werke in 5 Bänden*, A. Flitner and K. Giel (eds), Stuttgart: Cotta.

Hurrelmann, K. (1975), *Erziehungssystem und Gesellschaft*, Reinbek b. Hamburg: Rowohlt.

Jarausch, K.H. (1982), *Students, Society, and Politics in Imperial Germany. The Rise of Academic Illiberalism*, Princeton: Princeton University Press.

——, (1984), *Deutsche Studenten 1800–1970*, Frankfurt/M.: Suhrkamp.

Jaspers, K. (1923), *Die Idee der Universität*, 1st edn, Berlin; 2nd edn (1946), Berlin and Heidelberg: Springer Verlag.

Jochimsen, L. (1971), *Hinterhöfe der Nation. Die deutsche Grundschulmisere*, Reinbek b. Hamburg: Rowohlt.

Kerschensteiner, G. (1967), *Der Begriff der Arbeitsschule*, 17th edn, Oldenburg: Teubner.

Kershaw, I. (1993), *The Nazi Dictatorship, Problems and Perspectives of Interpretation*, 3rd edn, London: E. Arnold.

Klafki, W. (1963), *Studien zur Bildungstheorie und Didaktik*, Weinheim: Beitz.

Klein, H. (1974), *Bildung in der DDR, Grundlagen, Entwicklungen, Probleme*, Reinbek b. Hamburg: Rowohlt.

Kobert, H. and Rasch, A. (eds) (1990), *Der Fischer Weltalmanach, Sonderband DDR*, Frankfurt/M.: Fischer.

Kocka, J. (ed.) (1987), *Bürger und Bürgerlichkeit im 19. Jahrhundert*, Göttingen: Vandenhoeck and Ruprecht.

Koebner, T. et al. (eds) (1985), *'Mit uns zieht die neue Zeit'. Der Mythos Jugend*, Frankfurt/M.: Suhrkamp.

Kraul, M. (1984), *Das deutsche Gymnasium 1780–1980*, Frankfurt/M.: Suhrkamp.

Laqueur, W. (1984), *Young Germany, a History of the German Youth Movement*, 2nd edn, New Brunswick and London: Transaction Books.

Lewis, D. and McKenzie, J.R. (eds) (1995), *The New Germany, Social, Political and Cultural Challenges of Unification*, Exeter: University of Exeter Press.

Max-Planck-Institut für Bildungsforschung (ed.), *Bildung in der Bundesrepublik Deutschland*, vol. 1, Stuttgart: Metzler.

Michael, B. and Schepp, H. H. (eds) (1974), *Politik und Schule von der Französischen Revolution bis zur Gegenwart. Eine Quellensammlung zum Verhältnis von Gesellschaft, Schule und Staat im 19. und 20. Jahrhundert*, 2 vols, Frankfurt/M.: Schmidt.

—— (1993), *Die Schule in Staat und Gesellschaft. Dokumente zur deutschen*

Schulgeschichte im 19. und 20. Jahrhundert, Frankfurt/M.: Schmidt.

Mitscherlich, A. and M. (1967), *Die Unfähigkeit zu trauern. Grundlagen kollektiven Verhaltens*, Munich: Piper.

Münch, I. von (ed.) (1990), *Die Verträge zur Einheit Deutschlands*, Munich: dtv.

Neuner, G. (1973), *Zur Theorie der sozialistischen Allgemeinbildung*, Berlin: Volkseigener Verlag.

Nohl, H. (1949), *Die pädagogische Bewegung in Deutschland und ihre Theorie*, 3rd edn, Frankfurt/M.: Schulte-Bulmke.

Ortmeyer, B. (1996), *Schulzeit unterm Hitlerbild*, Frankfurt/M.: Fischer.

Phillips, D. (ed.) (1995), *Education in Germany, Tradition and Reform in Historical Context*, London and New York: Routledge.

Plessner, H. (1959), *Die verspätete Nation, über die politische Verführbarkeit bürgerlichen Geistes*, Stuttgart: Kohlhammer.

Reble, A. (1992), *Geschichte der Pädagogik Dokumentationsband*, 2nd edn, Stuttgart: Cotta.

Ringer, F. K. (1969), *The Decline of the German Mandarins, the German Academic Community 1890–1933*, Cambridge, Mass.: Harvard University Press.

Samuel, R.H. and Hinton Thomas, R. (1949), *Education and Society in Modern Germany*, London: Routledge and Kegan Paul.

Schelsky, H. (1960), *Die skeptische Generation. Eine Soziologie der deutschen Jugend*, 4th edn, Düsseldorf and Cologne: Ullstein.

——, (1963), *Anpassung oder Widerstand? Soziologische Bedenken zur Schulreform*, Heidelberg: Quelle and Meyer.

Schlicht, U. (1980), *Vom Burschenschaftler bis zum Sponti. Studentische Opposition gestern und heute*, Berlin: Colloquium.

Schmid, J. R. (1973), *Freiheitspädagogik. Schulreform und Schulrevolution in Deutschland 1919–1933*, Reinbek b. Hamburg: Rowohlt.

Sieferle, R. P. (1995), *Die Konservative Revolution*, Frankfurt/M.: Fischer.

Sontheimer, K. (1971), *Deutschland zwischen Demokratie und Antidemokratie*, Munich: Nymphenburger Verlagshandlung.

——, (1976), *Das Elend unserer Intellektuellen*, Hamburg: Hoffmann and Campe.

——, (1990), *Deutschlands politische Kultur*, Munich: Piper.

Speck, J. (ed.) (1978), *Geschichte der Pädagogik des 20. Jahrhunderts*, 2 vols, Stuttgart: Kohlhammer.

Spranger, E. (1965), *Wilhelm von Humboldt und die Reform des Bildungswesens*, 3rd edn, Tübingen: Niemeyer.

Stachura, P.D. (1981), *The German Youth Movement 1900–1945, an Interpretative and Documentary History*, London: MacMillan.

Steffen, H. (ed.) (1972), *Bildung und Gesellschaft*, Göttingen: Vandenhoeck and Ruprecht.

Stirk, S. D. (1946), *German Universities – through English Eyes*, London: Victor Gollanz.

Tent, J. F. (1988), *Freie Universität Berlin, 1948–1988. Eine deutsche Hochschule im Zeitgeschehen*, Berlin: Colloquium Verlag.

Treue, W. (1961), *Quellen zur deutschen Schulgeschichte seit 1800*, Göttingen: Musterschmidt Verlag.

Waterkamp, D. (1987), *Handbuch zum Bildungswesen der DDR*, Berlin: Berlin Verlag.

Index

(Referring to persons and concepts. First names appearing in full refer to persons of historical importance; first names with initials only refer to critics. Most headwords are given in English, except in cases where German technical terms are used.)

Index

Index

Dutschke, Rudi, 125
Duve, F. et al., 132n63

East Germany, 91, 98f, 137–58, 173
  contacts with FRG, 113, 116–19, 121
  demise of GDR, 159–66, 168, 179–81
Ecole Polytechnique, 37
economic miracle, 119f
Edding, Friedrich, 118, 130n18, 131n20
education system, 18, 50, 55
  criticism of, 66, 104, 133, 163
  federal, 113ff, 159ff
  socialist, 97, 137f, 144
Eilers, R., 86n55
Einführung in die sozialistische Produktion, 143, 146
Einheitsschule, 55
Einjährige, see Mittlere Reife
Einklassenschule, 103
elementary education (*Volksschule/ Grundschule*)
  changes to, 30f, 32, 55, 66f, 80f, 95f, 143, 172
  crisis of, 56f, 101, 166
  for girls, 33, 62
  system of, 17, 25, 98, 165, 169
Elias, N., 42n6
elitism/elite, 26f, 51, 91f, 95, 139, 142
  academic, 16, 54, 102, 159
  in school, 114, 128f
Elternbeirat, 56
Elternrecht, 102, 115
emancipation, 15, 83, 121, 127f, 159
  ideal of, 2, 4, 6, 9, 71f, 74
  of women, 34, 62
  of youth, 40f
engineering, 18, 36, 174
English Studies, 149f
Enlightenment, the ix, 18, 37, 76, 83
  German concept of, 1–6 *passim*, 74
  rejection of, 40, 46, 71f, 129, 172
Erhard, H., 108n58
Erhard, Ludwig, 119
Ernst, Paul, 82, 89
Etzold, S., 179n57
eugenics, 75, 95
European Credit Transfer System (ECTS), 171, 174f

Fachbereich, 126
Fachhochschule, 168f, 173f, 175f
Fachoberschule/Fachschule, 37, 123, 169
Fest, J., 84n1
Fichte, Johann Gottlieb, 3–10 *passim*, 18, 23f, 40, 81
Fink, Heinrich, 167, 178
First World War, 28, 41, 51, 73f, 151
Fischer, Aloys, 57
Flex, Walter, 69, 82
Flitner, Wilhelm, 49, 75, 78
'Flottenprofessoren', 28
Formalstufentheorie, 31
Fortbildungsschule, 67
Four Power Kommandatura, 98
Frauenschule, 62
Freie Schulgemeinde Wickersdorf, 41
Freitag, W., 154n42
French, 4, 26, 30, 96f
French Revolution, 1, 9, 11, 29, 46, 151
Frenzel, H. A. and E., 106n10
Freud, Sigmund, 39, 41
Frey, Robert, 77
Frick, W., 85n41
Friedeburg, L. von, 43n34, 64n26, 108n59, 130n9, 132n55
Fröbel, Friedrich, 25
Froese, L., 107n36, 130n12
Fromm, Erich, 39
Fuchs, H. W. and Reuter, L. R., 177n21, 181
Führ, C., 64n22, 130n7, 178n30
Füssel, K. H., 105n1, 107n41

Gadamer, H.-G., 20n20
Gardner, M., 179n62
Garton Ash, T., 177n14
Garve, Christian, 3
Geibel, E. 110
Geisteswissenschaften, 29, 45, 46, 53, 93, 171
Gemeinschaft, 52f, 76, 88, 90, 93, 182
George, Stefan, 52
German 1848 Revolution, 11, 17, 26, 30, 32, 34
German idealism, 4, 91
German Studies
  as academic subject, x, 51, 57, 93
  in school, 33, 36, 81, 95, 123, 148f, 163

Index

Index

Index

Index

Index

Index

Treitschke, Heinrich von, 28
Tucholsky, Kurt, 64
Twain, Mark, ix, 65

Ulbricht, Walter, 149, 154
*Unabhängige Sozialdemokratische Partei
Deutschlands (USPD)*, see Independent
Social Democratic Party (USPD)
unbewältigte Vergangenheit, 105
university, 13, 62, 66f, 109, 135, 169
concept of, 1, 11, 14, 53f, 114
policies, 76, 80f, 93f, 100–4, 124, 141, 160,
173
Unterrichtstag in der Produktion, 142f
US sector, 94, 96, 98f, 100f

venia legendi, 62
Verband akademisch gebildeter Lehrer, 56
Verein deutscher Studenten, 61
Vermeil, E., 106n27
Verordnung zum Schutz von Volk und Staat, 80
Vischer, Friedrich Theodor, 31
vocational education, x, 18, 115, 174
Berufsschule, 97, 123f, 169
changes in, 14, 32f, 99, 119, 164, 176
in the GDR, 142, 144f, 160
Volk/völkisch, 6, 17, 50–3 *passim*, 71–5 *passim*,
78f, 82f, 93
Vorschule (prep school), 56, 80

Waldorfschule, 125, 171
Wander, Friedrich Wilhelm, 24f
Wandervogel, 39, 40, 45, 69
Waterkamp, D., 137, 153n2
Weber, Alfred, 28, 65
Weber, Max, 21n31, 40, 51, 53, 66
Weber, Max Maria von, 37
Wehle, G., 43n30
Wehrgeschichte, 82
Wehrunterricht, 146, 152
Weimar Republic, x, 45, 72, 95, 115f
and education, 50f, 55–63, 81, 97–102

passim, 113
intellectual and social change, 51–5, 87, 104
Weiß, Peter, 120
Weiße Rose, 76
Weissmann, Karlheinz, 171
Weltanschauung, 29, 52f, 72
West Germany (FRG), 139f, 141f, 145, 150f,
159ff, 167f
and education, 113–36 *passim*, 167
intellectual and social change, 104, 159ff
Wilder, Thornton, 92
Wilhelm II, Kaiser, 35, 36, 87, 110
Wilhelmine Empire, x, 32, 78, 93, 98, 116
Wilker, Karl, 40
Willharm, I., 130n17
Winckelmann, Johann Joachim, 6, 11
Wissenschaftsrat, 117, 125, 174
Wolf, Christa, 143, 162, 179f
Wolf, Friedrich August, 23
women's education, 33, 50, 115, 140
in secondary schools, 34, 62f, 83, 121f
working class, 16, 40, 97, 138, 140f, 144,
150–2
access to higher education, 99, 104, 115,
121f, 144, 173
Württemberg, 35
Wyneken, Gustav, 39f, 41

Yom Kippur War, 126
youth culture, 27, 30, 39, 104
Youth Movement (*Jugendbewegung*), 34, 49,
53, 108, 125
and education, 32, 39–41
its anti-intellectual stance, 61, 66, 72, 77f

Zentrum, 41, 55f
Ziegler, K., 64n20, 84n22
Zimmer, M., 178n48
Zinzendorf, L. von, 19n8
Zock Commission, 102
Zweckrationalismus, 52
Zymek, B., 85n29